Here Come the Brides!

Reflections on Lesbian Love and Marriage

Edited by Audrey Bilger & Michele Kort

Here Come the Brides!

REFLECTIONS ON LESBIAN LOVE AND MARRIAGE

Part of the essay "I Don't Want to Be Part of Your [De]volution" by Stephanie Schroeder first appeared on Shewired.com under the title "Gay Marriage=The End of Queer Life," August 18, 2009.

A version of "Four Same-Sex Weddings and A Funeral" by Susan Goldberg first appeared in *Lilith* magazine, Winter 2009-2010. 35-37.

"Contemplation of A Name" by Caridad Moro-McCormick first appeared in *Lavender Review*, Issue 2, 2010.

"Let's Marae!" by Mary Meriam first appeared in *Chiron Review*, 2008.

Published by
Seal Press
A Member of the Perseus Books Group
1700 Fourth Street
Berkeley, California 94710

Library of Congress Cataloging-in-Publication Data

Here come the brides : reflections on lesbian love and marriage / Audrey Bilger and Michele Kort, eds.
p. cm.
ISBN 978-1-58005-392-1
1. Same-sex marriage. 2. Lesbian couples. 3. Lesbianism. 4. Weddings. I. Bilger, Audrey, 1960- II. Kort, Michele.
HQ1033.H47 2012
.306.84'8--dc23

2011045010

9 8 7 6 5 4 3 2 1

Cover design by Domini Dragoone
Interior design by Amber Pirker
Printed in the United States of America
Distributed by Publishers Group West

To Phyllis Lyon and Del Martin
and all of the lesbian couples
who waited thirty, forty, fifty years
to be able, at last, to stop living in "sin"
—and to those who are still waiting.

Contents

∴ Wedding Belles

∴ The Best Laid Plans

∴ Happily Ever After

Introduction

∴

Audrey Bilger and Michele Kort

Here Come the Brides began, as you might expect, with a marriage. In 2008, Audrey legally married her partner of twelve years, with lots of love but no fanfare or party or white dress. She thought marriage wouldn't change much in her life, but as months went on—and in the midst of campaigning against Proposition 8, the ballot initiative to ban same-sex marriage in her home state of California—she began to feel fiercely proud and protective of her marital status.

The opponents of same-sex marriage were saying awful things about gay people: that we menace children and damage the idea of family; that we want to bring about the end of civilization. In the bitter aftermath of Prop 8's passage, Audrey couldn't stay silent: She started writing about what it meant to both have a wife and be one; about what it was like to live in a state that still acknowledged her marriage but denied other lesbian and gay people the right to marry; and about how it felt to be a newlywed who couldn't cross a state line without losing her marital rights.

As a feminist scholar, she also noted the gender issues that were not being publicly discussed in conversations about gay marriage. She thought about lesbians in similar marital straits and those in far worse ones, and she mulled over the idea of a book that would tell the story of these tumultuous times. An anthology would be best, she thought, with reports from the front lines of the marriage equality struggle.

Don't Take My Wife, Please! was the book's first working title, a protest spin on Henny Youngman's famous one-liner and a slogan Audrey and her friends had printed on T-shirts when they were trying to stop Prop 8. She was just beginning to formulate a plan for the book when an email dropped into her inbox in mid-2009 from Michele: A friend of Michele's wanted to visit Audrey's college—would Audrey show her around? After saying yes, Audrey mentioned the book idea and slipped in a parenthetical note that "a co-editor would be really nice . . . just a thought, hopefully not a too-presumptuous one!"

Michele immediately took the not-so-subtle hint. "Hey, it's a great title—sign me up! Glad to be your co-editor!"

Michele had no idea what she was getting into, actually. She and her longtime partner had *not* gotten married during the brief window of opportunity before Prop 8. But she was a stalwart supporter of same-sex marriage, and was looking for an interesting book project as a sideline to her work as an editor for *Ms.* magazine. Plus, Audrey said the magic words: that she'd be willing to do the bulk of the "grunt work" at the outset on the project because she was starting a yearlong sabbatical.

As we researched and began developing our book proposal, the state of same-sex marriage continued to evolve. The year 2010 turned out to be a big one in the history of marriage equality—especially in California, where a lesbian couple and a gay male couple led a federal challenge to the constitutionality of Prop 8. Audrey wrote several opinion pieces in which she discussed gender issues that were central to the Prop 8 trial (and Michele edited some of them for *Ms.* and the Ms. Blog). The timing was perfect for a book, and Seal Press agreed.

In that trial, defenders of the marriage ban didn't talk about lesbians and gays as dangerous figures who molest children and desecrate the institution of marriage (because bigotry, it turns out, doesn't hold legal water); rather, they brought up the state's interest in regulating *procreation*. Yes, they argued that the state needed to make sure that all children were born within wedlock, and that only opposite-sex couples could adequately raise children. The plaintiffs' expert witnesses shredded these claims with peer-reviewed studies, the consensus of scholars and professionals being that same-sex marriage was actually *good* for children because it helped alleviate the stigmas LGBT couples and their families face.

On August 4, 2010, Judge Vaughn Walker declared, in no uncertain terms, that Proposition 8 is unconstitutional because it discriminates against lesbians and gays and deprives them of a fundamental right. In response to the idea that only opposite-sex couples deserve that right, he stated emphatically, "Gender no longer forms an essential part of marriage; marriage under the law is a union of equals." The state, he made clear, doesn't need to know what married couples do in the bedroom or how they organize their personal lives. Marriage is a public affirmation of two people's private commitment to one another, and it's a right that should be available to all. The Prop 8 decision was a major triumph.

Around this time, our idea for the book shifted. We changed the title to reflect a new optimism about the direction the United States was heading. We moved out of a defensive crouch and began viewing lesbian marriage more proactively in the context of this dramatic and unfolding historical moment. We formed a plan to bring in a diverse array of voices to the anthology—not just married lesbians, but those who wanted to marry and couldn't, those who married and then sought divorces, those who fretted about assimilation. We wanted to do justice to the complex meanings of marriage in these times, even as we celebrated the victories for marriage equality.

With all due respect to gay men—we love gay men!—marriage has been an especially vexing issue for women. Take the traditional vocabulary for spouses and its cultural meanings: Husbands wield power; wives are supporting cast members. The very idea of patriarchy is classically centered in the home, with the father (that's *pater* in Latin) as the head of the house and representative of the state, while the mother remains in a subordinate position ("the little woman"), often characterized as a drain on the man's freedom ("the old ball and chain").

Other male-dominant phrases echo in the corridors of American households: "the man of the house"; Father knows best"; "Wait 'til your dad gets home." When two men marry, there may be some social confusion over who gets to be top dog, but two wives do more than raise eyebrows: To those who still believe in the hierarchy of men over women, lesbian marriage means the end of the world as they know it.

Given the secondary status of women, bonds between them, particularly intimate ones, redefine the political landscape as well as the domestic realm. Viewed this way, lesbian marriage can perhaps be seen as a source of growing power for women. But we're mindful, too, of the dangers of women involving themselves in an institution that has been so deeply rooted in a male-dominated system of authority.

Our work on this book has been filled with surprises, serendipitous discoveries, amusement, and tears. At first, we were looking primarily for nonfiction essays, but when, shortly after we posted a call for contributors, Lydia Stryk submitted her poignant and bittersweet play, "The End of Civilization As We Know It," we knew we were going to find room for it. The same held true when we read Colleen Michael's charming poem, "An Arbor on Arbella Street." We found another wonderful play, by Wendy MacLeod, when we attended the L.A. production of *Standing on Ceremony*, a collection of one-acts about lesbian and gay marriage, and we actively sought out additional poems to include as well.

In her academic work, Audrey has particularly explored humor in a feminist context, so it was natural that she would seek out cartoons for the anthology. We even matched one of our favorite political cartoonists, Jen Sorensen, with a writer/actor friend of ours, Judy Scheer, and we think their collaboration is a delight. Comedians Monica Palacios and Gloria Bigelow gave us even more to laugh and think about, as did writer/performers Holly Hughes and Sara Felder.

As submissions poured in, we discovered that many brides had stories to share about the unexpectedly heavy baggage they carried into their new married lives. Although most of our contributors revel over their marriages, several ponder whether marriage will damage the outsider status that they see as an essence of queerness. Another common theme, even among those who chose to wed, turned out to be feminist anxiety over embracing an institution they had long defined as fundamentally oppressive.

Then there were the legal issues. Because of the patchwork of laws and prohibitions that exist from country to country and state to state, a lesbian couple that marries in one place and then moves elsewhere may find themselves in legal limbo. Several of our contributors wrote about how the road to same-sex *divorce* may be even rockier than the path to marriage.

Every bride frets over what to wear, but lesbian brides have some special concerns that are reflected within these pages. Even those who like classic butch/femme sartorial choices might nonetheless offer a queer revision of the white gown/tuxedo pairing, while some resist friends' desires to put them in neat gender boxes, asking why one of them has to be the "boy." As the bridal photo portraits we include illustrate, lesbian couples can inhabit traditional poses in daring new ways.

Many of our writers were surprised by what marriage ended up meaning to them when it became legal in their state, whether or not they decided to take the plunge. Some who thought their relatives would be indifferent or even hostile were amazed when their weddings became true family affairs. One of contributor Susan Goldberg's sons told her that he's glad she's married but couldn't say exactly why. "It's just good," he said, voicing what those studies brought up in the Prop 8 trial showed—that children may gain a sense of security when their lesbian or gay parents are married. Writer Helen Zia loved when her wife's father identified her as his "favorite daughter-in-law."

We hear from a number of women who helped make marriage equality a reality—as activists, expert witnesses, researchers, and protesters. Their efforts have paid off in the United States and Canada, and we include essays from both sides of the border. In addition, U.S. expatriate Chella Quint tells us what it was like to wed her bride in the U.K., where civil unions are recognized, while Heather Purser reports on her successful efforts to legalize same-sex marriage within the sovereign nation of her Suquamish tribe in Washington State. Since more and more countries have now legalized same-sex marriage, we would like to have heard from lesbian brides from around the globe—but that will need to wait for our next anthology.

Our favorite research excursion was a trip to the San Francisco Bay area to meet with activists Kate Kendell and the legendary Phyllis Lyon. We spent a magical afternoon with them, hearing from Phyllis about the mid-twentieth century, when lesbians feared being seen dancing together because it might jeopardize their jobs, and about the incredible story of how Phyllis and her longtime partner and fellow activist, the late Del Martin, helped bring marriage equality to California.

We organized the book around certain stages that anyone considering lesbian marriage might go through, from a practical or philosophical standpoint: from wedding planning to marriage doubts; from protesting in the streets to marching down the aisle; from breakups to makeups to ever-after (hopefully happily). We present a wedding banquet that includes not just sugary-sweet multitiered cakes, but some sour pickles and a dash of hot sauce, too. A few grumpy relatives skulk around the margins, disapproving of lesbian couples in general, but none of our essayists let them ruin their Big Day.

As *Here Come the Brides* shows, even though there are a few thorns in lesbians' bridal bouquets, there's plenty of champagne and roses to go around. If you've ever cried at a wedding or as the credits rolled at the end of a rom-com, you know that marriage matters. We *need* to hear the stories of women who love women, who find their happy ending and who claim their right to dream.

"Women's history gets erased all the time," notes contributor Patricia Cronin in her essay about the remarkable sculpture she created, "Memorial to a Marriage." "And lesbian history is often not written at all."

In these pages, that history *is* written, and we were fortunate to be able to bear witness. Now please, everyone take your seats as the brides and bridesmaids begin their procession.

Let's Marae!

∴

Mary Meriam

My nearest, my queerest,
my conjugal dearest,
my closest, my mostest,
what shall I call you?

My lavender gayspeak,
queerspeak and queenspeak,
lost lambda pipsqueak,
your name preference, please?

My love, my dove,
my heaven above,
my who I want more of,
what, what, what?

Mon amour, mi amigo,
spouse in my house,
muse who I choose,
q'est-ce que c'est le bon mot?

My Rae of hope,
my missing mishpochah,
my saving grace,
a bissel hint-hint?

Significant other,
this one, not another,
my own homo lover,
onomastically who?

Woman plus woman,
man plus man,
an accepted plan,
I pronounce you, nu?

Will you marae me?
Darling, what did you say?

The word is marae.
Will you be my rae?

rae [RAY]
-noun - the affectionate, legal, and religious term for the spouse or partner of a gay or lesbian person.

marae [ma-RAY]
-verb - to join as spouses or to take as a spouse, in the marriage of a gay or lesbian person.

The neologisms *rae* and *marae* are derived from "My Rae," the name Lillian Faderman gave to her courageous and devoted aunt. As a new term for gay and lesbian partners, "my rae" honors Faderman's tremendous courage and devotion to gays and lesbians. *Marae* means "sacred place" in Polynesia. At the marae, culture is celebrated, customs are explored and debated, and weddings and birthdays are held.

Wedding Planners

On the previous page:

Shannon Goulet (right) and Khrista Messinger were broke and homeless when they met on August 3, 2006 at a drug rehabilitation halfway house in Rock Hill, S.C. They began to build a life together: maintaining their sobriety, finding a place to live, getting jobs, and eventually applying to adopt a child. Five years to the day after they met, they got married in Washington, D.C., and arrived home from their wedding to learn that they had been matched to adopt a pair of sisters. "Well," Shannon remarked, "you are supposed to be married before you have children. Life is great!" *Photos by Maggie Winters, Maggie Winters Photography, maggiewinters.com.*

A Tale of Two Cakes

∴

Candace Walsh

Right around the time that I began fretting over whether I'd end up an old maid cat lady in my Lower East Side walk-up, my fascination with wedding cakes began. My primer was Rose Levy Beranbaum's *The Cake Bible.*

It was a cinder block of a book—so much girth that its binding began to tear within a few months, due to my avid paging and how frequently I pressed it into use on my teeny kitchen counter.

I learned how to make surgically even layers for layer cakes by using a handheld lathe that looked like a repurposed coat hanger. I learned that when piping borders and writing in script in frosting, a pedestrian plastic bag, snipped at the corner and combined with a good-quality metal tip, gets the job done just fine.

I learned how to create roses on the head of a nail. And that to make the world's best ganache, all you need are bars of bittersweet chocolate and sour cream. There tends to be some left over, and, spooned from a jar, it tastes much better than Nutella.

I fell in love with Beranbaum's judicious apportioning of sugar. The bakeries of my youth had superb cookies (Italian sprinkle–studded, German almond–floured), but the cakes were so terrible as to be almost more suitable as elements of decor. The brisk women behind the glass display cases described the frosting as butter cream, but they should have put air quotes around the words *butter* and *cream*, since the frosting contained neither. It was made up of Crisco, gritty sugar, and food coloring. It piped beautifully but tasted vulgar. That said, my grandmother was always pleased when my father brought over a seven-layer cake from the bakery, in a wonderful satiny white cardboard box tied up with red-and-white floss that I tasted once, to see if it was candy-cane flavored (it wasn't).

I volunteered to make my friend Nina's wedding cake, a chocolate cake with vanilla *crème anglaise* frosting, adorned with pale purple rosebuds. It started off okay but soon spiraled into chaos. I had to run out to the bodega mid-cake-bake to obtain more butter, and they only had the salted kind. Then I tasted the batter and got raging raw-egg food poisoning. So I constructed, iced, and decorated the cake in between violent attacks of nausea; letting down the bride was not an option.

As the sun peeked over a smoggy horizon, I finished the cake, called the bride, told her of my condition, and she arranged for her friend Amber to pick it up on her way out to New Jersey. After I passed it off, I went straight to the ER. That took the bloom off my event-baking rose. But I still made cakes.

When I met my husband-to-be, I wooed him by sending him a gossamer-textured poppy seed cake injected delicately with lemon syrup. He proposed less than a year later.

When it came time to decide on a wedding cake, I wanted to make it myself. "Oh no!" everyone said, as if I had proposed serving it to guests off my naked body. "You can't! You'll be too busy!" So I conceded. Making a cake for Nina hadn't gone so well. My mother knew a guy. He made beautiful wedding cakes. We should order it from him.

I emailed back and forth with this baker and sent him a photograph I found in *Martha Stewart Weddings* of a three-tier silver-fondant-covered cake, each tier encircled with pearls of white frosting. "We can't do the silver," he said. "It's been outlawed."

I was undaunted, did Internet research, and found food-grade, approved silver powder.

"What about the cake itself?" he asked.

"I read about a cookie layer. Could you do vanilla cake with a cookie layer?"

"Sure, whatever you want, I can do it. We can talk more, closer to the date."

"Okay. I just really can't emphasize enough that I don't want it to be too sweet. Can I give you a recipe from *The Cake Bible*?"

"I have thousands of recipes," he said snippily. "No need to give me yours."

"Closer to the date" ended up being seven days before my wedding. My little sister blew in from Antioch College, smelling of patchouli. She encountered a stress case of the highest order. I had seven days to accomplish a month's worth of stuff.

"I have the perfect thing for you: some really kind bud," she told me. "And we can smoke it out of my pink glass fairy bowl!"

It would be nice to take my anxiety down a notch. I took a toke, and then another. Within a few seconds, I was plunged into a torpid, malevolent, panic-attack aquarium.

"Ooh . . . maybe this was laced with something," she noted.

I felt like I'd had a bottle of Robitussin with a whap of evil LSD's speedy underbelly. Words . . . couldn't . . . really . . . be strung . . . together. *And it was seven days to my wedding and I had so much to do!* But I was at the bottom of a well, looking up at the circle of light that signified a place where I could indeed be productive. It was that remote.

The phone rang. It was the cake guy.

"So we need to decide on cake layers and flavors of your syrups and creams," he said. "Your wedding is *only a week away*."

"I know!" I said, hyperventilating slightly, hanging onto the phone as if it were a car door handle and I were being dragged down a gravel road.

I just needed to act normal.

Apparently acting normal meant saying yes. To everything he suggested. Lemon, raspberry, pistachio, white chocolate, cookie layer, and possibly even gingerbread. He kept on offering options. I kept saying yes, while sweating through my bra. "But not too sweet."

My "wedding cake picture" shows me taking a bite and unsuccessfully masking a grimace.

It was far too sweet. Tongue-stinging, teeth-grating sweet.

But I also had an awareness that, as the bride, I had to act like it was delicious. Or at least palatable. The cake, inside its creepy gray carapace, was made up of sedimentary-looking layers of strange bedfellow flavors.

And because I cared so much about cakes, especially wedding cakes—*unlike everyone else who served Long Island bakery crap, I was going to have a wedding cake that tasted notably good*—this was a bitter moment. My new husband, not a fan of sweets no matter how dulcet, supported me in my pique. We went up to the roof of the catering facility and flipped our pieces off the china plates and into the New York sky.

We rejected what wasn't good enough for us, and it felt redemptive.

At some point about seven years later, we did the same thing with our marriage. We hit the ground along with it, as you do during a divorce. But on that wedding day, we felt light and jaunty, and ran downstairs to dance.

When Laura asked me to marry her, we were sitting on my small back patio in a well-designed but oppressively dense Santa Fe subdivision neighborhood. I was a divorcée in my thirties. I had two small children, who were with their dad that night. It was July, and we had come outside to cool off in the night breezes.

I decided to date women after my marriage ended. I had always felt a romantic interest in women that I had decided was, in no particular order, undergraduate experimentation, fear of men, daddy issues, stepfather issues, being drunkenly libertine, wanting to subvert the dominant paradigm, and feeling disappointed in my boyfriends. Dating women wasn't easy, logistics-wise, but it was the simplest and most appealing next step after the divorce.

And making love to a woman blew my entire heterosexual romantic past (which was varied and robust, mind you) to kingdom come. I was no longer fantasizing about Sapphic porn-y sex scenes in order to come. I came from the sheer excitement of the present moment: all of the gloriously slippery, undulating, yielding, and pungent elements of getting it on with a woman. This was it.

And Laura was the it of my it. We were doing the thing that everyone else does but I had only scrabbled after the idea of as I partnered with men: We were loving each other, already, 'til death do us part.

I didn't know if she would ever want to marry me. We were two women, and we couldn't get married in New Mexico. She hadn't ever considered getting married to her previous partner of twelve years. Why would she want to marry me?

My divorce had been finalized for five days when we found ourselves out on that patio, well into a bottle of chewy red wine, with stray lissome pasta strands on plates that had moments before held caramelized squash, onions, and wilted greens from the farmer's market. We were staring at each other dreamily, grinning until our faces hurt.

"I could marry you," she said, with a smile both soulful and cheeky.

My body replied. It vaulted me into her lap, my chair flying across the porch sideways from the force of my launch. For what seemed like an hour, I just held her, hot tears streaking down my face, which was buried in her neck. I couldn't say anything. I just held her. And she held me.

"I'm so moved," I said. "And I do want to. I do."

"I know," she said. "I took that as a yes."

We stayed there in our melting bath of exquisite nuptial intention, sweating and kissing for some time. And then, like two brides, we began to plan, unlocking our limbs from the proposal chair and heading toward the kitchen.

"I've always wanted to get married at the Wayfarer's Chapel in Palos Verdes, California," she said. "It's made of glass and was designed by Frank Lloyd Wright's son. They have same-sex ceremonies."

We peered at the website's photographs, which looked enticing. And at the time, California, Laura's home state, was performing same-sex marriages.

"Let's go to the supermarket and buy lots of different pieces of cake," I said. It was midnight. Bakeries wouldn't be open. "We can buy champagne and have a cake tasting!"

We drove the few blocks to a big, fluorescent-aglow supermarket, which had that middle-of-the-night zombie-occupied feeling. Not that we noticed. Usually shy about PDA, we held hands as we picked out a bottle of Gruet sparkling wine (which we had sipped on our first date), a piece of red velvet cake, a piece of German chocolate cake, and a piece of carrot cake, each in its own small plastic clamshell. I knew we wouldn't buy our wedding cake at Smith's, but it was a fun gesture, and the humble squares tasted better than my first wedding cake by a mile.

And then, a few months later, California did the do-si-do that reversed same-sex marriage, and reinstated it, and clamped down on it, and brought us both to a place of impotent frustration. There was a chance that California would make it legal again, enough of a chance that kept us from tying the knot in, say, Iowa. Bless those Iowans, mind you, but I don't have a warm fuzzy for Iowa or any of the other gay-marrying states. But then it was demoralizing to wait on California like orphans asking plaintively for more porridge.

We were engaged, and I had a wedding dress hanging in my closet for just shy of three years when New York began to seem like a strong maybe.

I immediately started flogging my Facebook wall with every kind of call to action I could find. I emailed and called Mark Grisanti—who was not only an undecided swing voter, but the state senator of my off-campus neighborhood in Buffalo—and asked my college classmates to do the same. I called the undecided senators on Long Island, which felt pointless but necessary. I hoped, I prayed, I dreamed, I signed petitions, I held space and visualized and did every woo-woo thing you can imagine. It was like being on a turbulent airplane. I got very spiritual very quickly.

I didn't know if it would make a difference, but I did know that if I didn't give it my all, I would feel deep regret.

Laura swung from guardedly optimistic to resignedly pessimistic. Our hearts lurched every time the vote was seemingly delayed or passed over for discussion by the New York Senate. Thousands of people poured into Albany, and I ached to be there. The approval of my home state felt almost as good as getting the imprimatur of my entire family of origin. I had given up on both, and so the majority thumbs-up of both was all the more sweet.

We watched the vote on the eve of Gay Pride. And same-sex marriage beautifully, circuitously passed.

So we're getting married in New York. Unlike my first marriage experience, my family has not rushed forward to hustle us through the preparations, planning, and execution, throwing money our way at every turn. But my sister, brother, mother, and cousin are excited for me, and will be there. Others are either too "uncomfortable" to attend or have ignored the announcement—as if I had told them that I want to rent out Carnegie Hall to give a zither concert, and would they like to come? They're hoping that I'll come to my senses before the zither concert date arrives, but they just can't bring themselves to countenance the spectacle.

Thus apprised, we have pruned the guest list back so that only people who are absolutely jubilant for us will receive a thick, creamy invitation envelope.

Laura and I will get married outside Hudson, New York, in her high school friend Peter's 1786 home. She'll wear a pale gray bespoke suit, which nestles against her shape as intimately as I like to. Like the first draft of our wedding plans, my initial dress has gone by the wayside. In the last three years I've gone down three sizes and am wearing a backless ivory silk dress with a skirt that flares out at the knee.

We rented a townhouse on the main street of Hudson for the week, for lots of practical reasons. But to be sure, the most important factor for me is the squat Viking oven nestled into the house's fully stocked kitchen.

I have promised Laura that one tier will be chocolate, but I have yet to decide what the other flavor will be. I'm looking forward to cracking open and poring over the pages of *The Cake Bible.* If there has to be a bible on our wedding day, let it be one that gives the recipe for the one true butter cream—not the one "right" way to love and live.

I claim this silver lining (but please hold the silver fondant): We have the privilege of inventing our marriage edifice with impunity, and designing every right-sized detail. And within the plans will be this cupola: I will make my wedding cake . . . sanely and methodically . . . myself.

Ten Days of a Lesbian Engagement

∴

Leslie Lange

DAY ONE:

I'm sitting on a concrete bench in a small outdoor lot at the mall on Palm Canyon Drive, thawing myself in the bone-roasting heat of a July afternoon in Palm Springs. All around me, the toys of retired gay men—convertible BMWs and the like—glint and wink as if in on a secret. Five minutes ago, I'd been shivering with a cheap paperback and an iced coffee inside a subarctic air-conditioned meat locker of a café when my girlfriend, Elliott, called to let me know her interview for a volunteer position at the local thrift shop was done. She'd be by in a few minutes.

When her silver Prius silently pulls up, my heart leaps to its feet. I climb in.

"So," I say, "that took awhile—did it go well?"

"Great!" she says, adding, "Of course." She's wearing a cute black outfit that I can't stop staring at. "Something did come up though . . . hope you don't get mad."

"Uh-oh. What?"

"Well, I had this great interview with Gloria, and when I happened to mention I was an artist, she was . . . well, oddly enough, she was just really intrigued. She wants to go out for drinks with us."

"Right now?"

"Is it okay?"

"I'm dressed like a slob."

"You look gorgeous."

What can I say about Elliott? In addition to all her other amazing qualities, she always knows the perfect thing to say.

Turns out we're meeting Gloria at the trendy Viceroy Hotel. My ripped T-shirt and cargo shorts stand out like sore thumbs next to Elliott's sleek black ensemble as we saunter into the lobby holding hands, yet the staff greets us with unusual vigor.

"Good afternoon!"

"How are we doing today, ladies?"

"Welcome to the Viceroy!"

Each staffer offers a radiant smile and makes prolonged eye contact, kind of making me feel like royalty and kind of making me feel like I'm trapped in a really creepy dream sequence. Of course I'm clueless about the real reason for these smiles. The smiles are because they're *in on it.*

"Hi, ladies, how can I help you?" This comes from the bartender, a stocky guy in a tuxedo. He's friendly, but not quite comfortable; there's a certain lack of eye contact, a shiftiness. The truth is, he's also *in on it.*

Gloria isn't here yet.

Elliott says, "Let's not order till she gets here, okay?"

As we peruse drink menus, Elliott looks around. "I love this place!"

"Me, too," I say. "We should come here more."

"Do you know what I want to do? I want to ask to see a room!" she says. "Because we might want to stay here some time . . . like, for an anniversary."

"Of course," the bartender cuts in. "People ask to see rooms all the time."

Elliott gets up and goes over to the desk. Still drinkless, I follow her.

"You'll love the rooms," the bartender calls out after me. "They're in that . . . old style."

Okay, Elliott and I are both in our late forties, but still.

Note to self: Do not overtip the bartender.

When I catch up with Elliott at the desk, the clerk is just finishing her computer search. We're in luck! They have a great room for us to check out. The clerk holds out a white plastic key card, gives careful directions to Elliott, then lifts a yellow pencil to draw a circle on a map.

Elliott thanks her and walks off *sans map*. Whoa! I grab the map, nod at the clerk as if to say, "Sorry, my friend here's just a little bit airheady today." She gives me a kind smile. *In on it!*

Elliott strides through the hotel courtyard, alongside the beautiful outdoor pool.

"Are you sure you know where you're going?"

"Yes."

"Don't you wanna see the map?"

"No, I got it."

"Isn't that a great pool?"

"It is."

She tolerates my questions, then, "Yup . . . it's here."

The door is red.

I watch her hand, the shape of which I love, dip the white key card into the slot.

She cracks the door, holds it for me, and I go in. The room is lovely. And it's full of floating yellow balloons. Each balloon is tied to a piece of furniture with a single curled white ribbon, and written on every one with a black felt-tip marker are the words I WANT IT. One balloon, floating in the middle of the room, is white, and inked on it are the words: SO I'M GONNA PUT A RING ON IT.

Tied to that balloon's white ribbon is an engagement ring.

Elliott has tears in her eyes. "I had a whole speech prepared, but now I've forgotten it. Anyway, I remember one thing, which is that I'm the happiest I've ever been."

DAY TWO:

Elliott and I walk around all glowy. Did you know Beyoncé rhymes with fiancée?

"Hey, fiancée," one of us says.

"Hey, fiancée," says the other.

I post my engagement on Facebook, and a mere fifteen seconds later . . . up pops a bridal gown ad!

"$112 China factory direct."

Ugh! I'm okay with Facebook knowing about my engagement, but it hurts that they would think me so cheap.

DAY THREE:

Since Elliott proposed, I've been afraid I'll do something stupid to make her change her mind.

This morning, I ask a very incriminating question and become terrified she will finally see me as the unworthy partner I am. After having lived together for sixteen months, the question is: "Honey, do we own a toilet brush?"

DAY FOUR:

We decide we are both wearing gowns. Black gowns, with the elaborate headgear known as *fascinators*. We absolutely must have them.

It is considered that Dr. Swami, our Rottweiler—"lab mix" to the insurance carrier—though an excellent bearer of small birds and chipmunks, would not make a very good ring bearer. However cute he might be.

DAY FIVE:

Elliott spends the day looking at wedding accessories on the Internet. I spend the day packing. I've taken a physical therapy travel position in Northern California and will be living there—without my fiancée!—for the next three months. What was I thinking?

DAY SIX:

While driving up north, I decide to make a list of some of my favorite things about Elliott.

Favorite Thing #1: She knows how to apologize. #2: She's a brilliant comic improviser. #3: She helped me rescue a feral kitten with its head stuck inside a can. #4: Our sex life. (No, I am not going to talk about it.) #5: She's vulnerable. #6: She's strong. #7: She can speak in tongues.

And so on.

I also daydream about when we first met. Then about the second time we met. Then about the third time we met, because it was the third time when things really started to take off.

We ran into each other at this lame dance party—the L-Party, or something like that—at a swank Palm Springs hotel. Hobbled by a torn Achilles tendon, I was determined to have a good time and failing—until Elliott showed up. The hotel cranked the air up (another subarctic meat locker), and since I couldn't dance or move around much, I was freezing. Elliott saw an empty cocktail table near the bar and asked, "What if I go over and get that tablecloth? Would you let me wrap it around your shoulders?" I said yes. She got the tablecloth and wrapped it around my shoulders. And I wasn't cold any more.

A year later, that tablecloth reappeared, wrapped as an anniversary present.

I'm thinking it'd be great to use that tablecloth at our wedding.

Just before midnight, I have a mini-crisis. I'm dozing in bed in my little rented room when my mind starts doing something I've told it a thousand times not to, especially not when I'm trying to sleep: It thinks negative thoughts. *Does our plan to get somewhat tradition-*

ally lesbian-married really signify we've succumbed? Are we now active participants in the oppressive regime of compulsive capitalistic patriarchal society? Are we just two more non-heterosexuals sucked into the rubric of heteronormativity?

Deep breath.

Sigh.

DAY SEVEN:

Thanks to my Facebook announcement, and because I've traveled here before, my straight Pittsburg, California, coworkers are ready for me when I show up this Monday. They want to see my ring. No, I correct myself, they want to see my *bling*.

"Hey, congratulations! Sooo, where's the bling?"

Bling?

There's no bling, people. No diamond. Just a silver band with the silver insignia of a tiny honey-gathering insect, otherwise known as *apis mellifera,* whose non-scientific name I sometimes use as a substitute for Elliott. Not a pet name, not at all—just a *substitute*.

This just feels way too personal to me. I don't want to be vulnerable to these people, no matter how accepting they are. Being a lesbian has always meant having extra access to privacy. I don't want to share the little bee. Yes, the little bee, okay? I don't want them—or anyone, including anyone who might be reading this—to know I'm corny.

"Don't worry," Elliott reassures me. "Everyone knows you're a big mushball."

To the best of my knowledge, she now has a second full-time job, which is to stare for hours at her laptop screen mulling over various bridal gowns. From the thousands she surveys, she will email me ten to twenty as attachments. Tonight, I spend about forty-five smart-phone minutes perusing designer knockoffs from China, then another fifteen or so on a used bridal gown site called "Recycled Bride." After the gowns, we cover various fascinators, then gloves, engagement rings, wedding rings, and cakes. To say I might be having some attention-span issues, well, that is the most colossal understatement of all time.

"Leslie? Leslie? Are you listening to me?"

God, I am such a dude.

DAY EIGHT:

I send Elliott my list of "wedding gowns for lesbians" (factory direct from China!), complete with my own terrible cartoon illustrations.

There's the Joined-at-the-Hip (gowns are literally joined at the hip); the Natural (made of hemp, cotton, and found antlers); the Portia de Rossi (self-explanatory in that it looks just like Portia de Rossi's wedding gown); the Gown-Tux; the Tux-Gown. We laugh, mainly at the cartoons, which are extremely bad. We discuss the nature of the "Wedding-Industrial Complex" and decide to be more careful of it, to treat it with respect—like when you work in a factory, and there's this really cool piece of machinery that, if you get too close to it and aren't careful, a little snag on your sleeve could get sucked into the gears, and then it's, well, you know . . . *curtains.*

We don't need to lose our heads in a whirring grind of society-mandated spending.

But an arm might be okay.

If we can just unplug the machine fast enough. . . .

DAY NINE:

Elliott and I decide on a budget. I decide to start working weekends to pay for all the things that will surely take us above that budget.

Oh, and there's a change of plans: white gowns. White gowns and opera gloves, we absolutely must have.

DAY TEN:

That's the day I call my mother.

No, she does not have a Facebook account. In fact, she recently wrote up her income tax form by hand on a yellow legal pad. The IRS didn't like that much. When I came out in 1984, she wept herself to sleep every night for two weeks. Mom's come a long way since then, but I'm not sure how far. She still thinks Tea Partiers are "marvelous people."

"I'm getting married," I tell her, surprised at the huge dopey grin on my face.

"To Elliott?"

"Yes."

"Congratulations! Well, let me know the date, so I can ask for the time off."

She and Aunt Romita will drive all the way from Texas.

I think about the balloons again. When I walked into that hotel room and saw all those balloons, I knew exactly why they were there, but still the first thing out of my mouth was, "Are you sure this is the right room?" The spectacle of it all, the romance of it, was impossible for me to believe.

Elliott tells me yes, and, as she walks into the midst of the balloons and turns to make her proposal, my mind short-circuits.

Wha . . .? Is this a propo . . .? Did someone forget to clean this room?

Then it finally sinks in.

Elliott has tears in her eyes. "I had a whole speech prepared, but now I've forgotten it. Anyway, I remember one thing, which is that I'm the happiest I've ever been. I love and I want to love you forever. Leslie Lange, will you marry me?"

I go to her and I fall to my knees. I throw my arms around her waist, look up at her, and say, "Yes, yes, yes!"

She's the Boy

∴

Cate Glass

It was a cool, rainy morning; a Northwest spring has no other kind. I was on my knees in the damp earth, pulling weeds and chatting with my friend Meg about my upcoming wedding—the service, the music, the ongoing antics of my mother and future mother-in-law. I don't remember how we got onto names.

"We haven't decided what we're doing yet." I tugged at a dandelion root the size of my thumb, trying to spare the tulip beside it. "We'll probably combine them somehow."

Meg blinked. "But you should take Annie's name."

Annie's name? I love Annie, and there's nothing wrong with the Basques as a people, but her surname is four syllables long and impossible to spell. Besides, I like my surname. I can trace it all the way back to my Irish great-great-grandparents, who were pig farmers in County Cork. I sat back on my heels. "Why Annie's name?"

"Because she's the boy."

Now it was my turn to blink. Meg is a queer radical bondage fiend who claims allegiance only to something called the "Red-Blooded Society of Earth." The thing is, I'm a bit of a queer radical bondage fiend myself, and compared to Meg I am vanilla in a vanilla cone with delicate Republican sprinkles on top. I'd heard sentiments like this from other friends; I had even come to expect them. But not from her.

A few hours later, I peeled off my mud-encrusted clothes and poked my head in on Annie, who was scoring her sixth-graders' fraction quizzes in the bathtub.

"Hey. Meg told me I should take your last name when we get married."

She reached for a new felt-tip pen. "Whatever. Seriously, how difficult is it to reduce two-fourths to its simplest form?"

I retreated to the bedroom to puzzle things out. Thinking back on other moments like this, I realized there was a pattern after all. Our straight friends have no trouble understanding us as two women in a relationship; they never try to convince us that we're anything else. Only our queer friends—especially since we announced our engagement—feel compelled to cast us hetero-style. It's always other lesbians who tell me I should be the one to get pregnant, change my name, or drop my career to make room for Annie's. I'm the woman; she's the man.

I'm far from the first person to discover that weddings can open up a Pandora's box of gender questions. Here are a few more that have surfaced for Annie and me:

—When members of a couple are two brides, but each has the personality and (let's face it) aesthetic sense more commonly ascribed to grooms, who gets stuck with the niceties of choosing flowers and table linens?

—How do we refer to the members of our wedding party, especially when our chief attendants are my best friend from kindergarten, who's transgender (and whom my entire extended family still calls by his former, female name), and Annie's best friend—a married straight woman who told us she'd like to be called "best person"?

—Are they both simply bridesmaids, since we are simply brides? How about Annie's "little" brother Bobby, who stands six-three in socks and once told me in apologetic tones, "Dude, I know you weigh like a hundred pounds less than me, but if you ever hurt my sister I'm gonna have to beat you up"? Does he have to be a bridesmaid, too?

—And how do we dress all these people in matching outfits?

When you're planning a wedding, of course, you don't have to make these decisions on your own, or even rely on your weak and fallible friends. Being engaged is a bit like being pregnant: Everyone you meet, even strangers in stairwells, feels entitled to give you advice about it. Suddenly your life becomes public domain.

You should take Annie's name. She's the boy.

Who's the man in our relationship? Annie wears men's jeans; it's a rare day if you catch her without a baseball cap. Her weekends are devoted to televised sports. But she also loves scented candles, has a crush on Brad Pitt, and wants to bear our babies. Every few days she gets mad or sad or worried about something, and she won't tell me what. She likes sex well enough, but secretly prefers back rubs.

Who's the woman in our relationship? I own my share of short skirts and tall boots, and there's black lace in our communal underwear drawer that you won't find on Annie anytime soon. (I tell everyone that we "share" all our clothes, while Annie's perspective is that I "take" all of hers.) I like being told I look pretty. While I'm stomping around in my lingerie and mascara, though, if there's a heavy thing to be lifted, I lift it; if there's a door to be opened, I hold it; and if we're going somewhere together, there is no question that I will drive. I am repelled by the notion of pregnancy. I have three basic emotions—happiness, sadness, and hunger—and there is never any doubt about which one I'm feeling. I don't care much about back rubs and I hate scented candles. I am always, always in the mood for sex.

She cooks; I clean. I iron our shirts because she can't. She goes grocery shopping because I won't. We share a work wardrobe and bicker every morning over who last got to wear the gray sweater. (We really should break down and buy a second gray sweater.)

Parts of the butch/femme dichotomy work for us, and parts of it don't. Parts of our lives are just like those of straight couples; parts of them aren't. We may be two ordinary people, but we are like nobody else.

And our fellow queers should know this best. Right?

But somehow they don't. Maybe it's because our straight friends already know what it's like to be straight, and they can see that whatever we're doing, it isn't quite that. Having no real decoder to work with, they let us do our own thing. Our queer friends, meanwhile, aren't measuring us against straight couples; they're comparing us to the lesbian archetypes in their heads and settling for the ones that seem to make sense—this one in Carhartts, that one in heels.

And after a few months of wedding planning, I can see where they're coming from. Our world demands that couples fit into neat boy/girl compartments, and nowhere is this more pronounced than in the grandiose halls of the wedding-industrial complex. Queer writer/performer S. Bear Bergman put it best, calling the bridal registry phenomenon "a glorious bulwark of heteronormativity against the rising queer tides." Now let's not discount the enlightenment of the modern department store; you don't have to *be* straight—you only have to *act* straight. It's fine to bring your co-bride to the registry station as long as one of you plans on wearing a tux.

The boy and the girl, the bride and the groom: these roles work for plenty of people, but not for this life I'm living. If those are the caricatures we have to draw of ourselves, if I have to stop moving furniture and Annie has to give up her scented candles, then we might as well put Bobby in a taffeta dress.

So what, you may be asking, does all this gender panic have to do with the wedding? Right! The wedding! The short answer is: We're negotiating each step with patience, good humor, and plenty of compromise. Not such bad practice for marriage, I guess.

Take the question of the bridesfolks and their outfits. We settled on a dress option and a pants option and told everybody to pick one or the other. Rather than mucking around with brideswhatevers, we're calling them all "attendants." Our respective best friends will be the chief attendants (I couldn't bring myself to say "best people" with a straight face).

Then there's all that father-daughter stuff. Annie and I are immensely blessed with families who love us and support our marriage, and we're both close with our fathers. That being said, I'm not too jazzed about the symbolic value of the father escorting the bride down the aisle and handing her off to her new owner. So I'll be walking with both my parents. Annie and her family are traditionalists to the bone, so her dad will be handing her off to me. He's a good guy, her dad. While he doesn't seem to mind that I'm not quite the Prince Charming he once envisioned for his only daughter, he doesn't want to be cheated out of a single page of the storybook. (The day after we announced our engagement, he called me to say indignantly: "You never asked me for her hand!")

Of course after the father-daughter aisle march comes the father-daughter dance. I don't especially relish the idea of dancing with my father in front of a hundred guests, but I'm taking one for the team here, since the other father and daughter are on board. Nobody seemed keen on my suggestion that we add a mother-daughter dance to level things out.

And the brides' outfits?

Ah. Yes.

The truth is, with the ceremony four months away, we still have no idea what we're wearing. Part of this is due to Annie's gender panic. She doesn't really want to wear a dress; she'd feel more comfortable in a suit. But she's not quite ready to stand before her extended family in suit and tie. And she most *definitely* does not want to dance with her father in suit and tie. So she'll probably wear a dress. But she doesn't really want to wear a dress. . . .

It should be an afterthought in this celebration of our lives together, but every wedding has some ridiculous sticking point—and for us it's been the clothing question that has developed a tremendous, exaggerated importance. Our friends assume volumes about our relationship even from our everyday dress—my skirts, Annie's baseball caps. We know that whatever picture we present at the altar will form our families' lasting impression of who we are and how we relate to the world. We also know that the picture will never quite reflect reality, but we're taking our time to think about what we want it to be.

So it goes: The wedding's this summer. We didn't invite Meg. We still like each other. My chief attendant might have a beard by June. Wish us luck.

Postscript: We celebrated our marriage on July 2, 2011, in the company of 120 friends and family members, including twenty-five first cousins. Annie looked stunning; nobody asked any questions about our matching white dresses. Our grandparents danced the night away, Annie's evangelical step-aunt flirted shamelessly with the tranny chief attendant, and a good time was had by all. We've promised to stay together forever so that we never *ever* have to plan another wedding. That being said, it's worth doing once.

Getting Civilized

∴

Chella Quint

I have always been a big fan of weddings. I'm convinced I actually remember tripping up the aisle as an eighteen-month-old flower girl, for which my mom prepared me by letting me stay up to watch the wedding scene in *The Sound of Music.*

After that, I loved watching any film or sitcom episode with a wedding in it, joining in and pretending the curtain was my wedding veil. Over the years, I dressed every one of my dolls in Crystal Barbie's white gown with iridescent ruffles so they could each have a turn marrying Ken (that anatomically incorrect polygamist).

Later on, I serendipitously worked at a movie theater the summer *Four Weddings and a Funeral* came out. I saw it nine times. I learned about meringue-shaped dresses, wedding lists, and what to do if you forget the ring.

By this time I had discovered my three related loves—soccer, the Beatles, and Shakespeare—and thus became a full-on Anglophile. So it was no surprise to anyone that I moved to England for postgraduate work in theater. It was a bit surprising to everyone that I came out as a lesbian once I got there. But I figured I could handle or ignore any familial reprisals from 3,000 miles away.

I met Sarah Thomasin, a performance poet from Yorkshire, at the National Gathering of Lesbian and Gay Youth. We ended up directing a skit together for the final session, parodying the trials and tribulations of attending the conference. In one scene we had to dance badly, on purpose.

I suspect if either of us had realized that this was how we each actually danced, it would have ended there. Happily, we instead discovered other, better things in common. We both loved '50s music, wordplay, and romantic comedies (we watched *Truly Madly Deeply* on our first date). When we found ourselves studying English and drama at nearby universities, we began dating properly.

We moved in together in Sheffield the following year, and started performing together when one of my comedy writing projects—a zine and sketch show called "Adventures in Menstruating"—became popular on the college and festival circuits. We didn't go out of our way to get married, but we assumed it was something we'd eventually do.

Incidentally, in the U.K., only civil partnerships are legal for same-sex couples; legislation was voted in by a Labor government in 2004. Sarah and I jokingly refer to it as "getting civilized." When we'd been together for a few years, we discussed this sensibly over cups of tea one day, and then announced our engagement. Our friends and family were delighted.

Other than setting the date, we didn't quite know where to go from there. To get some ideas, we visited a "Wedding and Civil Partnership Fayre," which sounded like it would be more inclusive than an ordinary wedding expo and might involve a trip to a historic village. It was actually just held in a local hotel's conference room, which was full of tables and displays of local businesses offering free samples and discount coupons. But we discovered something unexpected: If two women go to a wedding expo in a small, northern England city, the last thing people will think is that you are a lesbian couple.

A lot of our conversations went like this:

"Which of you is the bride?"

"We're both brides."

"Oh, so when's your wedding date?"

"The twenty-first of June."

"And when's *yours*?"

"The twenty-first of June."

"Oh . . . what a coincidence!"

"No . . ."

"Oh, a double wedding?"

"No . . ."

"Oh . . . okay. . . ."

After their initial shock wore off, the wedding-services purveyors could hear cash registers ringing, because they realized they could sell us two of everything—which we were happy to let them believe while we stuffed ourselves full of free canapés. Prosciutto and melon is very nice. Just saying.

We managed to wade through the product-hawking without getting hooked into preserving our framed and mummified bouquets for eternity, or creating a "Hollywood-style" DVD with a team of three videographers, a lighting crew, and a voice-over by Morgan Freeman. We did, however, end up in a standoff between two department stores offering wedding registry services.

The first store had no civil partnership option—just "bride" and "groom." Well, *that* didn't bode well for detail-oriented customer service, or a twenty-first-century attitude to marriage, and I told them so. We chose the other registry, whose form read "Partner One" and "Partner Two." A few weeks later, we walked around that department store with price guns, scanning things such as plates you could replace individually and a nearly indestructible toaster—items that could solve Sarah's and my respective high-probability kitchen debacles.

In our post-canapé comedown, we decided that all of those wedding services weren't that important. A potluck dinner would be fine. We'd have the ceremony at the registry office and the reception at the local community center, serve a cupcake cake with Lego people on top, snap a few pictures, and call it a day.

We chose our guests by drawing doodles of everyone on a big sheet of paper. If we couldn't picture them celebrating with us, we didn't need to invite them. We included our families, our friends from university and from our neighborhood, and Sarah's ex and her ex's parents. Is the latter a lesbian stereotype? Of course. But there was no bad blood with them, and in fact they're always the life of the party.

At this point, we discovered that since our straight siblings were happy cohabiting without the benefit of marriage, the mothers of the brides weren't going to let this, possibly their only opportunity to have an impact on one of their children's weddings, pass them by.

It started with Sarah's mother, whose traditional contribution to weddings has always been a professional-style cake. Her cakes are gorgeous, but we felt the choice we had already made reflected our personalities. I had ordered Lego minifigs on eBay—a little face with a ponytail, cute nerd glasses, and freckles for me; a long-brown-haired smiling one for Sarah; Lego wedding outfits; even a Lego chuppah.

But about six months before the wedding, Sarah and I were in bed one Sunday morning when we got The Call. Sarah listened for a few minutes, raised her eyebrows, then passed the phone to me. Nothing could have prepared me for the woman who had given birth to my bride-to-be hissing into the phone, "My girl's going to have a *proper* wedding cake." I was terrified. I said yes. I very nearly said, "Yes, ma'am." She said, "Thank you. I'll start baking today." Sarah's mouthed apology didn't help.

A week later, *my* mom called and hit me up with:

"We *have* to have it catered."

This from the mother who put two slices of store-brand beef salami on whole-wheat bread, showed it to some mustard, and called it school lunch throughout my childhood?

"Oh, and you need to have the wedding and the accommodations in the same place for all the people coming from out of town," she added. "You can't make people sleep on everyone's sofas. Book some hotel rooms."

We almost began to wish they had disapproved.

It was pretty tricky juggling everyone's expectations. We were totally bowled over by our mothers' interest and offers of financial support, and mistook their generosity as acceptance. In fact, they'd accepted us years ago; this was just double-whammy mother-of-the-bride control-freakery.

So now we were looking for a venue, accommodations, and catering. Again.

Eventually we settled on the town hall reception rooms, located in the same building as the registry office. Booking the reception rooms, we discovered on a walk-through with the events manager, had given us exclusive access to the whole building.

Before we knew it, our idea of a potluck at the community center turned into a plan for getting married in a Victorian banquet hall with a stone balcony, velvet curtains, wood paneling, and crystal chandeliers, using the city's collection of traditional Sheffield silver. My mother told me to pay the deposit and she'd deal with the rest.

Our more punk-rock friends were shocked at how traditional the whole thing was starting to look. We began overcompensating. Whenever we could do business with a small, local company, or buy something recycled, fair-trade, organic, or free-range, we did. This was the first time we'd ever had the power to make these kinds of choices on a grand scale, and we wanted every decision to count.

Maybe we were empowered; maybe our power was corrupting absolutely. Our decisions became very specific, very purposeful, and entirely unnecessary, but they added an extra depth that I don't think we would have had otherwise.

In our meeting with the head chef, for example, we requested that he cater to everyone's allergies, dietary preferences, and food intolerances, even though all of those decisions should have cancelled each other out like so much hors d'oeuvres anti-matter. In a departure from the general practice among our peers, we decreed that kids and babies would be welcome at the wedding ceremony, with high chairs provided for those who stayed to dinner and a feeding/changing space made available for anyone who didn't fancy adding breast milk or diapers to the overall ambiance of the main room. Centerpieces and favors would be local, organic herb and plant pots; plant-dyed, monogrammed, recycled gift bags filled with fair-trade chocolates and soaps; and one-inch buttons made by an Etsy-maven pal.

The gorgeous hotel next to the town hall gave us a good rate for group bookings, and we were set.

So far so good, and only mildly terrifying.

I'm not a fan of marriage's historic roots as a religious or legal contract, but I feel that reclaiming and reconstructing meaning is a valuable tool for social change and personal amusement. Justification? Maybe. But there's no denying I like a good frock.

Work colleagues repeatedly asked me one question that I'm sure straight brides don't often hear:

"Are you both going to wear dresses?"

How the heck do you answer that?

—No, I was gonna wear tasselled pasties and a tutu.

—Inflatable sumo suits. Matching.

—It's a nudist wedding, didn't you know? Shall I send you a save-the-date?

I felt a simple "yes" was not going to acknowledge all the things they *really* wanted to say. Like,

—Which one of you is secretly butch?

—Is one of you going to pretend to be the man?

—Someone has to be the GROOM, damn it!

It's not like they hadn't seen us in dresses or skirts before. We were surprised by the number of people who suggested matching tuxedos.

We did feel the need to coordinate, so friends suggested we ask for a two-for-one special at a bridal boutique. It appealed financially, but we didn't want to look like two matching bridesmaids at a wedding where the bride had gotten cold feet and run off. On a whim, after a Dublin comedy show we were invited to perform at, Sarah tried on the first dress she grabbed at Oxfam Occasions, a thrift store that sold ex-display designer wedding dresses for charity. It was in brand-new condition, with a cream, raw silk, bias-cut skirt and gold embroidered raw silk bodice with cap sleeves. It fit perfectly, looked amazing, and was only fifty euro.

Back in Sheffield, a local dressmaker was willing to help me design something that echoed Sarah's dress but was adamantly not identical. I preferred a '50s-style tailored look, but I had to be able to move my arms over my head while dancing to "Jump Around," "Baby Got Back," and "Walk Like an Egyptian."

I also remembered a line from comedian Elvira Kurt's stand-up set that Sarah and I had been quoting to each other for nearly a decade—an inside joke about when you first realize you're a lesbian: *Mom! I need a dress for the prom! Something with pockets!*

Pockets meant I could secretly stash my smartphone, tissues, and emergency lipstick. It was an outstanding piece of accidental advice—thank you, Elvira Kurt! Once my wedding dress had pockets, we realized anything was possible.

We decided our mothers would give us away. We asked the venue to ensure that the aisle was wide enough for us to march in four-abreast. Our best men (and, conveniently, our best friends), Matt and Graeme, waited down front. We had a ring bearer and a flower boy (unintentional—just a lack of girl babies in the family), and their mothers were our matrons of honor. Rounding out the party were my younger sister and best college friend as maids of honor. We got a kick out of using the classic definitions for all of these roles.

I'd studied enough feminist theory about media representation and body image to know it would alienate our nearest and dearest to force them into matching ruffled ball gowns in mint green or hot pink that suited no one and frightened everyone and had different bits of each bridesmaid bulging out in different directions. So I told them to wear chocolate brown cocktail-length dresses, left any further coordinating to them (which they did beautifully, actually), and slapped a small, Tiffany-blue silk clutch bag on each one.

Matt wore a brown suit. Sarah's best man, Graeme, wore a kilt because he's Scottish. That really was the only reason he gave, and we accepted that, no questions asked.

⁂

In the U.K., while wedding ceremonies legally have to include certain language in order to form a binding contract, civil partnerships are different: The registrar can say pretty much anything. As long as we signed the paper, we would be civilized.

I was, as they say here, gobsmacked. The difference between weddings and civil partnerships had been virtually nil in my mind before that point. The registrar put a positive spin on it, but I was upset that there was no formal wording.

I often use humor to deflect homophobia and educate others about taboo subjects, so it was my go-to response. First, in drafting a ceremony, I decided to stick to the stuff people expect to hear. So there was a bit of *we are gathered here today* and *now the rings* going on. But then the freedom of choice made me delirious. Suddenly all of the wedding film fantasies I'd absorbed as a kid came back to haunt me.

I included "Bride or groom?" from *Four Weddings and Funeral.*

And "The Short, Short Version" of the wedding from *Spaceballs*: "Do you? Yes. Do you? Yes. Good, kiss her. You're married."

And I rounded it off with a nod to *The Princess Bride:* "Wuv . . . twoo wuv. That dweam wiffin a dweam . . ."

When Harry Met Sally, *So I Married an Axe Murderer*, and *The Wedding Banquet* also drew mentions.

Luckily, my nearest and dearest from both continents dragged me out of my fugue state and encouraged me to put some "serious" back into the occasion. So I did.

I asked our adopted godfather, Nick, to give what was basically the sermon, about how long he'd known us and what we were like.

I had the registrar say: "If any person present knows of any lawful impediment to the formation of this civil partnership, they must declare it now." This was a setup for me: I turned around and cast one raised eyebrow at those assembled, as if to say *I dare you,* which got quite a laugh. Okay, so it wasn't all serious. But I also asked the registrar to say this:

> *We would also like to acknowledge that civil partnerships are illegal in many countries, including most of the United States, and that in some places, homosexuality itself is punishable by death. Here in Sheffield we are coming to the end of Refugee Week, which seeks to raise awareness around issues of asylum. We would like to ask you now to observe a moment of silence for LGBT asylum seekers.*

Sarah's and my vows were genuine, too, until the final line:

> *I promise to dance—badly—with you, to continue creating annoying in-jokes with you, and most of all, to never let you take yourself too seriously.*

After the ceremony, everyone in the universe made us pose for photos until we thought we would melt and die. I wish we'd booked a professional photographer. At one point, we snuck outside in the rain with massive umbrellas to snap some "Look, we're in England!" photos of us by a red phone box, etc. In one of these, we're all making faces, Matt is choking me, Graeme is making an obscene gesture, and Sarah is attempting the Running Man dance move in tribute to the decade in which we were last cool. That became the official wedding portrait.

At the reception, we felt perfectly within our rights to indulge our interests, having gotten the formal stuff out of the way. The evening was a cavalcade of bad '80s karaoke and comedy video tributes from family and friends who couldn't make it. We had twice the number of awesome best-man speeches—it was practically a roast.

Our first dance (which we knew how to do, yet still managed to clunk heads) was a waltz to "Que Sera Sera." We ended the night with "Stand by Your Man," a choice that most guests thought ironic but was actually a movie reference. I hoped people would leave singing it, *Four Weddings and a Funeral*–style.

Throwing two bouquets? Awesome. My sister caught mine, a close friend caught Sarah's. They were heartily congratulated.

After the wedding, we spent the weekend in the countryside with several of the guests, then came home to receive the gift-registry presents, open cards, and write thank-you notes. Little did we know that the cards we received would reflect a gap in the market, which people tried to cover up with desperate attempts at appropriateness:

—*This card has two women on it, but it's not a wedding card. They look sad and pensive, but we hope you will be happy, so we've written a very cheerful message inside!*

—*This* is *a wedding card, but we chose one with animals instead of people on it. We feel that these anthropomorphic characters on the front are not strictly male or female per se. Happy wedding!*

For our honeymoon, we went to see *Hamlet* at Stratford-upon-Avon, then performed at Ladyfest Berlin (I named the show *Honeymoon Period)*, and capped it off with a trip to New York. My parents hosted a luau for us in their backyard. We wore the wedding dresses again, and *finally* had the cupcake cake with the Lego cake toppers.

∴

Back in the U.K., several more of our friends, of all sexualities, have since gotten civilized or married. Our nephew has been the ring bearer at three more weddings; he's practically a professional. Sarah's ex has gotten engaged; so has my sister. They're both asking us for advice, and suddenly we're the establishment, doling out wise platitudes:

Hold your ground when dealing with pushy parents.

Wedding dresses with pockets are the next big thing.

It's more than okay to bend the rules.

And we've just celebrated our third wedding anniversary. That's traditionally the "leather" anniversary.

I know. I know.

Sarah got me a new leather strap.

For my watch.

My Trojan Dress

∴

Kari Lerum

As a child I was scared of weddings, especially the thought of starring in one. Although I was painfully shy, the kind of shy that physically hurts, my fear of weddings had nothing to do with stage fright. Rather, it was the vision of being ushered into a world away from my parents, forced to live alone with a man I did not yet know. When one day my mom said, cheerfully, "Someday you'll get married and have a house of your own!" I reacted with a horrified, "Do I have to?" To which she replied, "Don't worry, you don't have to think about this for a loonnngg time."

During my childhood, I never actually attended a wedding, never even saw a bride up close. Brides were contained within clusters of family wedding portraits: photos of my mom, aunties, grandmothers, and great-grandmothers, all in their late teens and early twenties, captured on their wedding days. Both of my grandmothers died young, so I knew them mostly through these photos. At Grandpa's house in farmland Wisconsin, my job was to dust the framed pictures. It was a job I liked: Wiping away layers of dust made me feel useful, and cleaning wedding photos seemed especially important. They seemed nothing short of a family pantheon, an exhibition of responsibility, belonging, and a model for future generations.

Dusting also allowed me to gaze closely at those brides. The faces of my Norwegian-Lutheran immigrant grand- and great-grandmothers were solemn, as the style dictated in those days. Photos from my parents' generation hinted at more abundance, full of smiles, wedding attendants, and flower girls. I wondered which of the brides were scared, if the non-smilers were less happy than the smilers, and if any of them wished they could just duck out of the wedding and run back home.

My anxious and dusty relationship to weddings took a giddy turn when Princess Di got married. I was thirteen and living in England—my dad was doing research there—when Diana Spencer took up with Prince Charles. Everyone thought that she was perfect for the job of queen-to-be: pretty, blond, demure, of royal blood, and so, so young. At nineteen, she was just six years older than me—and she was shy, tall, and lanky like me, too. But with her marriage, Diana would instantly and publicly morph into an adult woman.

Marriage might be a circus hoop through which I would eventually need to jump, but Diana's hoop seemed to be lined with opportunity, not dread; glamour, not fire. She seemed ensured to live happily ever after.

By the date of the royal wedding, I was at my other grandfather's house, this one in farmland Minnesota. Rising at 4:00 AM to sit alone in front of Grandpa's TV, I was, like millions of other vicarious princesses, witness to Diana's stunning metamorphosis.

I was most fixated on her dress: mammoth sleeves and skirt on a narrow bodice, twenty-five-foot train, oversized veil. While elegant, its massive girth made it far too bulky for hoop jumping. Perhaps Diana's transformation into princess-hood was not as effortless as I had imagined. Could it be that her dress was more of a Trojan horse? A sly way of storming the ultimate castle of privilege?

And so, as I marveled at her miraculous, enchanted life, a tiny voice inside also worried: *What will she do once the castle doors close behind her?*

When feminism sparked in my late teens and early twenties, the magic of Diana's wedding faded. I reverted to earlier suspicions about weddings, this time seeing their sinister facade. They were part of an industry that was responsible for the subjugation of women and the exploitation of global capitalism. The dazzle of the wedding seduced women to marry men, tricked them into giving men control through ideologies of romance, and exploited dressmakers in China along the way. The wedding dress was not a symbol of glamour, armor, or power as I once thought: It was a source of oppression and servitude. Those heavy layers of silk, taffeta, lace, sequins? Intellectual distraction and suffocation. Besides, white didn't suit me; it clashed with my attitude and my olive skin. Black was my color of choice, and I collected a wardrobe full of it.

I notified my mother that it was unlikely that I would ever marry, but if I did I would sport a black lace dress—what I perceived to be the ultimate dare to my family as well as to the entire wedding industry. I fantasized my mother's response: *If she insists on wearing black to her wedding, then I give up! Let her go off and explore her godless intellectual ways!*

Despite my declaration, or perhaps because of it, my parents invited to dinner a tall, blond, athletic, Norwegian-Lutheran lad, clearly offered as a potential addition to the family pantheon. He was handsome and perfectly nice, but not my type. I was furious and told them to never do this again. What I didn't say was that my type, by that point, was as likely to be a lady as a lad, and that the Norwegian part was incidental.

So I strayed off the path to marriage and found other routes to adulthood. I played college basketball and helped start a feminist club on campus. I entered a PhD program. I settled in with my first real girlfriend, and at age twenty-nine I finally came out to my parents. In an attempt to counteract their dismay, I informed them—in a part-promise, part-threat—"Someday, gay marriage is going to be legal!" They either didn't care, or didn't believe me. I wasn't sure I cared or believed it either.

Transforming from shy to outgoing to feminist-femme, I streaked my dark hair with pink and ruby red and modeled funky clothes in local fashion shows for designer friends. I became a grassroots media activist, joined a pirate radio collective, and made documentary films about sex workers, punk rockers, and heroin addicts. I marched against the World Trade Organization and the Gulf Wars. I earned my PhD.

Then, my partner at the time got pregnant and gave birth to a baby girl. For the first time in my adult life, I was able to slow the pace of my mind and body and just literally sit—with my baby as well as with myself. Though a committed agnostic, through my baby I was given a glimpse into what seemed to be a sublime love force. I began to silently wonder if such transcendent love could ever be fully achievable (and possible to sustain) between two career-driven adults in the context of a romantic relationship.

When my daughter was still in diapers, I landed a tenure-track faculty job and threw myself into teaching courses in "family," "inequality," and "sexuality." My students critically assessed the politics, practices, and race/class/sexuality privileges of marriage and the wedding industry. I bought a house in what was reported to be the most racially diverse census tract in the United States. I worried that I would become too soft, with my mainstream job and middle-class homeowner status, so I pierced my nose and placed a red glass stone in it to remind myself and others of my political edge.

I had created a colorful, meaningful, scrappy lesbian "lifestyle." My parents were not thrilled with me being a lesbian (or raising a child outside of heterosexuality and marriage), but were starting to tolerate my life choices. I had no need, or desire, for marriage.

But then I met Shari. We were at a Sociology of Sexuality party—the sort of party where scholars discuss sex rather than engage in it.

For the occasion, my six-foot-two-inch frame looked taller than ever in a pink cowboy hat, tight hot-pink shirt, tight black skirt, and ruby red pumps. We were introduced by a mutual gay male friend: "You know Shari, right? No? You have so much in common! You simply *must* meet her."

I had to bend slightly to shake her hand—she was petite and muscular, like a lightweight boxer. Unlike me, she was dressed more appropriately for this scholarly occasion: black dress pants, black oxford shirt, and black loafers. I was immediately taken by her handsome beauty and soon recognized her outrageous wit as well. But it took another friend to call my attention to her eyes. "Now those are eyes that you could fall in love with!" she said. When I turned back to take a peek, I saw the most startling, striking blue I'd ever seen.

This would be the first of many startling moments to come.

Our love affair began as a friendship. But after six months (and after both of us became single again), our connection pierced my heart and brought me to my knees. Our desire for each other's company was also terribly inconvenient. She lived 3,000 miles away, in Manhattan, and was embarking on an ambitious career. I lived in Seattle, had a child (as well as an ex-partner, with whom I shared custody), and my own career. I was not moving, and she wasn't either.

So for the next few years we had a bicoastal relationship—visits every four to six weeks punctuated by dozens of daily emails, texts, and phone calls. I relished the daily intensity. Our conversations never ran dry, she made me laugh out loud every day, and she was the most romantic person I had ever known. Despite the distance and the demands of our jobs, I had never before felt such a reciprocal, hilarious, and creative connection with a lover. Though neither of us are religious, when we were together it felt like we existed in a secret, shiny, sacred bubble.

Sometimes one of us would blurt out that we wanted to get married, though I don't know that either of us knew what that meant. Shari steadied her sights on not just the stabilizing idea of "marriage" but on The Wedding. She sent me photos of wedding dresses and rings. She already knew what music she wanted to play at The Wedding, and sent me romantic notes about living "happily ever after."

I was both titillated and shocked by these feelings, words, and images. Then came my questions: *What, if anything, did our daily engagement have to do with the institution of marriage? How would we get married, living 3,000 miles apart? Would we invite our parents to the wedding? Would they even attend if invited?*

Shari began developing a friendly, lighthearted relationship with my daughter. We met each other's friends and colleagues. Then we met each other's families. Hers is Jewish, from New Jersey via Lithuania and Russia. Mine is, of course, Norwegian-Midwestern farmers. Her parents liked me. My parents liked, respected, and approved of her as well. As a result, they seemed to respect me more, too.

Three years after we first locked eyes, Shari asked me to join her for a summer trip to France, where she was speaking at a conference. Our first night in Paris, on the eve of the city's Gay Pride parade, Shari asked me to marry her, this time "for real." I said yes. For real.

She gave me a princess-cut diamond ring with a band of ruby stones. It was extravagant—and confusing for me. My confusion had nothing to do with our relationship, but about who I would be wearing the ring. I couldn't stop staring at it, as if it were a crystal ball that would reveal its own meaning. I loved glamour and sparkles, but along with other politically conscious white progressives, I wore "bling" as an ironic statement, imagining that vintage hand-me-downs could somehow negate my class and race privilege. This diamond ring left no room for irony; it just called me out of the closet as a middle-class, professional, engaged woman.

I had a long time to furrow my brow over this, since we still had the bicoastal commute, which meant an extended engagement. Over the next two years, though, our time zones aligned: Shari landed a faculty job in San Francisco (a "mere" eight hundred miles away), we bought a home-base house in Seattle, and we were able to settle into a rhythm of seeing each other nearly every weekend and all summer. Shari cultivated a penchant for cooking; I savored her culinary treats and maintained my fondness for dusting. We adopted a cat and published our first academic journal article together. My daughter began to introduce Shari to her friends as her "almost mom." Shari asked: "When will I be just 'mom'?" My daughter replied: "Only after you marry my mom."

Another year passed. I had made it this far before in previous relationships; I knew that after the initial breathlessness of new love wears off, so, too, do romantic wedding fantasies. What's the point after already sharing home, friends, and family?

But six years after we had met, we were still madly in love. And both of us also wanted—for political, social, and family reasons—to step onto a new public platform as a "married" unit. We set a wedding date for the following year: September 3, 2010.

By that time, my ring had become a friend. It hadn't interfered with my political commitments; if anything, it helped me clarify them in light of increased consciousness of my own social privileges. But even with that awakened awareness, I still found myself swept up into the beautiful spectacle of wedding planning. Part of my enthusiasm was simply my fondness for high-femme pleasures. A chance to wear a pretty dress and host a fancy party? Twist my arm!

Still, a lesbian wedding was different. Over the years I had witnessed many hetero-feminist women attempt to exorcise from their weddings the misogynistic and anti-gay ghosts of the marriage industry. I empathized with and appreciated their symbolic subterfuge, but this did not change the fact that when their wedding was over, the social and legal privilege gap between them and me was wider. In contrast I felt that my wedding was inherently a slap in the face of heterosexism. In this era when gay marriage is still mostly unrecognized, the wedding is all we have; it is the entire point.

As a way of working through my thoughts about weddings and the wedding industry while I simultaneously planned our wedding, I launched a blog called "Sapphic Bride," which I dedicated to "Sapphic (queer, lesbian, trans, bi, or just cool) grrls who want an excuse to wear an outrageous wedding gown and/or have critical curiosity about the magnificent, awful, glorious spectacle of American Bridedom." One of the blog's key missions was to wage a Sapphic love campaign: "a public quest for my wedding to be featured as a 'real wedding' (not to be confused with a 'real marriage') in *Seattle Bride* magazine."

Weddings are inherently public acts, serving many different audiences and purposes. While I knew that many would disapprove of our wedding (including, potentially, my family), the blog cast a wider net in search of allies and celebrators. I posted occasional photos of pretty dresses and hairdos, but mainly focused on stories related to same-sex relationships and families. I began to see my own story as part of a much larger thread of global human stories, with unique characters searching for meaning and belonging within their cultural and political environments.

As news of our wedding plans spread we received a variety of responses, from euphoria to confusion to outright disdain.

The euphoria came primarily from women friends, straight and lesbian, who offered to do my hair and makeup, arrange flowers, shop for dresses, throw parties, sing, create photo slideshows, and even officiate. These offers surprised and delighted me; I had suddenly tapped into a deep current of cultural scripts around wedding planning, perhaps made more enthusiastic due to the increasing visibility of gay marriage. I also realized how much stronger—perhaps even tyrannical—the cultural current must be for many heterosexual couples.

The confusion came from straight folks who weren't anti-gay but just ambivalent about marriage. Some would ask, "But is it legal?" To which I would reply, "There is no law against having a wedding." Others suggested that we skip the wedding, save the money, and "just elope." *Huh?* My adult life had already felt like a state of forced elopement, driven by other people's discomfort with my love choices. For us, "elopement" would not just be legally meaningless but redundant.

The disdain was expressed, subtly rather than overtly, by LGBTQ friends and acquaintances who wanted to preserve a particular historical understanding of "queer" life and identity in opposition to mainstream culture and institutions. I support critiques of all social institutions, but can't we not just critique but also help lead conversations on how to best re-create and diversify mainstream institutions? In the past few decades, the institution of marriage in the United States has undergone many progressive legal reforms; can't we see same-sex marriage as simply the continuation of such progressive reforms and one of many pragmatic anti-oppression strategies? Or must LGBTQ activists resist opportunities to join all mainstream institutions, closing ranks around anti-marriage queer activism?

I chose the former strategy, and I began devising my Trojan dress.

In contrast to my youthful black-wedding-dress fantasies, I now (as a tenured professor in my early forties) envisioned something long and sleek, like something I could wear to the Oscars. I found Chrissy Wai-Ching, a hip young fabric artist who designs and sews organic silk clothing out of her studio just a mile from our house. Together, Shari, Chrissy, and I designed a floor-length two-toned cream-colored gown for me, with halter straps and kick pleats. It was both funky and elegant, and the most expensive piece of clothing I had ever owned. It had no taffeta, sequins, or lace, and I wasn't wearing a veil, but there was no mistaking this for just another pretty dress: This was a full-on wedding dress. Yet I had no illusion that it would admit me into the castle of heterosexual privilege, even if I had wanted to go there. Instead, this gown would simply escort me into a new kind of public relationship with Shari, with my family, and with the social world.

As our wedding day arrived, I knew I would be facing my entire living pantheon (now in their seventies), many of whom I had not seen in years. While thrilled and surprised that they were attending, I was emotionally overwhelmed by the significance of their presence.

A few hours before the ceremony, Shari and I donned our

wedding gear and hopped in a car with our photographer. It was a sunny afternoon on Labor Day weekend, so thousands of people were out enjoying the last days of summer. We were on another wedding mission: posing for photos in public parks, on the streets, and in Seattle's famous public market. As our photographer clicked away, so did dozens of onlookers. Knowing that others were watching embolded us to widen our smiles. We felt like celebrities.

Our pre-wedding antics succeeded in breaking our anxiety, and I made it through the wedding ceremony without any embarrassing sobs or fainting spells. My friend Gabriella Gutierrez y Muhs officiated; besides being a women's studies professor, she had officiated weddings for undocumented migrant workers, and saw ours as an extension of helping people who otherwise could not get legally married. Our daughter, then age ten, was my "maid of honor." We had three "flower children," including my three-year-old nephew, who wore a traditional Norwegian outfit. To recognize Shari's cultural background, we included a selection of traditional Jewish music and rituals.

After the ceremony, several people gave prepared toasts and others sang, including Shari's brother, who performed "Love Me Tender." Our parents, who had just met each other for the first time, smiled and exchanged stories about being the descendants of immigrant farmers.

So what, if anything, has changed for us as a result of this? Absolutely nothing in terms of financial or legal benefits. As of this writing, gay marriage is still not recognized in either Washington or California. Domestic partnership is available in both states, but because we keep separate finances and insurance policies, we are not registered as partners. I also never bothered to follow through with the *Seattle Bride* campaign. Compared to the euphoria of our wedding, it just didn't matter to me anymore.

But something profound happened that night, and over the entire wedding weekend. A transformation occurred in us, in our families, and in our friends. Several guests told us it was the most meaningful wedding they had ever attended. Straight people said their kids should have come to see it, as it was a historic event demonstrating the power of true love. Our daughter gave a spontaneous and loving toast to her "moms." One of my aunts said, while dancing next to me at the reception, "Now I have to treat you differently, since you are a married lady."

But perhaps the transformation was best expressed two days later, at a party at my parents' home. After dinner, ceremoniously, my father asked Shari and me to sit in chairs facing the party guests. Then, as if we were being initiated into a secret society, my mother solemnly announced that there was a song that she and my three aunties would sing. Even before they began, my tears flowed. And they cried, too, as they sang to Shari: "Welcome to the family, we're glad that you have come to share your life with us."

It was a song that had apparently been sung, unbeknownst to me, to others who had married into the family. The song felt ancient, surreal, haunting; it also felt familiar and comforting.

As gay marriage is publicly debated, perhaps the private resolution of our deepest conflicts around queer life and marriage can be best resolved in small family gatherings like this. One pantheon at a time.

Photo:
Kari Lerum (in dress) kisses her bride Shari at Seattle's Public Market. *Photo by Lawrence Kim, lawrencekim.com.*

Contemplation of a Name

For Stacie

∴

Caridad Moro

Stay,

see

if I don't taste of *guayaba* and *mamey,* sweet *guarapo* thick as my hips swaying sweaty Celia Cruz rhythms in black-seamed stockings and Cuban heels.

Stay,

see

if I don't bring Dutch parrot tulips, orange and red blazes for your table, Belgian *chocolat* pyramid stacked on Virginia's dishes for your buffet, the essence of French lavender in a cobalt decanter for your vanity.

Stay,

see

if I don't pick three *trifectas* in a row, read stray pony hairs strewn like tea leaves across the stable, kiss you at the window, winners.

Stay,

see

if I don't learn that song you love, pouring it in your ear, my voice sediment settling in your heart, silt that sifts through your veins with every beat.

Stay,

see

if I don't warrant the wait of avocados, figs, or kumquats, whatever your fruit—even the pomegranate, so delicious you forgive its seeds.

NOTE

"Contemplation of a Name" was written for my partner, Stacie M. Kiner, during the beginning of our relationship. Things were complicated then: I was married, the mother of a toddler, trapped bitterly in a closet of my own making, utterly terrified to embark upon the steep climb toward integrity. Her name became my mantra, my strength, permeating every space of my being, heady as the sweetest of perfumes—Stacie. Stacie. Stay. See.

And so "Contemplation of a Name" was born, part promise, part plea, part prediction, part prayer. She stayed. She saw. Now, five and a half years later, the poem hangs framed on a wall and serves as testimony to how far we've come—her ring on my finger, our hearts betrothed, our life together constructed brick by brick as we wait for the day when Florida legally sanctions our union, a union that encompasses a marriage in every sense of the word.

I Do's and I Don'ts

On the previous page:

Sandi Lyman (in gown) and Jessica Hennessy at their Colorado wedding.
Photos by Jeff Ambrose.

Six Reasons Lesbians Should Not Get Married

∴

Jennifer Camper

CAMPER
Six Reasons Lesbians Should Not Get Married
©92
OH! GEE... THANKS...
IT'S JUST WHAT WE NEEDED...
TAROT
1 YOU REALLY DON'T NEED FIVE DECKS OF TOFU-GODDESS TAROT CARDS.
BUT WE REALLY NEED A POWER DRILL!
YEAH—BUT THINK OF ALL THOSE SEXY LEATHER OUTFITS!
2 YOU'LL HAVE TERRIBLE ARGUMENTS OVER WHETHER TO REGISTER AT THE HARDWARE STORE OR THE SEX-TOY EMPORIUM.
NO! I WILL NOT HONOR THAT UNHOLY UNION!!
3 FAMILY MEMBERS WILL REFUSE TO ATTEND THE WEDDING AND YOU'LL FEEL REJECTED.
HOLD IT! LEMME GET A CLOSE UP!
4 FAMILY MEMBERS WILL ATTEND THE WEDDING AND YOU'LL FEEL EMBARRASSED.
I HEARD THAT KIM AND RITA SPLIT UP...
DAMN! AND I SPENT ALL THAT MONEY ON THOSE FANCY-ASS TAROT CARDS FOR THEIR WEDDING GIFT!
5 IF YOU BREAK UP, YOUR FRIENDS WILL RESENT THE FACT THAT YOU GET TO KEEP THE PRESENTS.
6 THERE WILL NEVER, EVER BE ANOTHER OCCASION WHEN YOU CAN BOTH WEAR THOSE EXPENSIVE MATCHING TUXEDOS.

This Flight Tonight

∴

Wendy MacLeod

ALLIE and HANNAH, two attractive women, sit in a bar at Los Angeles International Airport. Their table is covered with the debris of pretzel bags and ALLIE's several martinis. Their carry-ons are in a pile around them. They hear a boarding announcement for a flight to Des Moines and HANNAH starts to gather her things.

HANNAH

Des Moines. That's us.

ALLIE

I'm not finished with my drink.

HANNAH

Well, down it.

ALLIE

Are you sure it's our flight?

HANNAH

Flight 271 . . .

ALLIE

Why isn't it delayed?

HANNAH

I don't know, sweetheart, but we're boarding.

ALLIE

All the other flights are delayed. There's a big snowstorm on the Great Plains.

HANNAH

Iowa's got nothing to do with the Great Plains.

ALLIE

We have to fly across them. I saw the Doppler.

HANNAH

You are *such* a weather geek.

ALLIE

I mean, is it even safe to fly?

HANNAH

Sweetie, we've been through this . . .

ALLIE

Rock stars die in planes all the time . . .

HANNAH

You're just freaking out because the last time we flew somewhere . . .

ALLIE

The plane was exploding!

HANNAH

There was turbulence.

ALLIE

It was scary.

HANNAH

It lasted like three minutes . . .

ALLIE

It lasted *forever*.

HANNAH

Okay. First of all. Our flight being on time is *good* news.

ALLIE

Is it?

HANNAH

My parents are waiting for us at the airport!

ALLIE

Why does your father keep giving me power tools?

HANNAH

What?

ALLIE

I don't know how to use power tools!

HANNAH

Well, you put in that French door . . .

ALLIE

I was *there* when the guy from Lowe's came!

HANNAH

He's trying.

ALLIE

(*mocking Hannah's father*)

"Those lesbian gals *love* the power tools!"

HANNAH

Some lesbians do like power tools.

ALLIE

You know what lesbians love? Staying home. We're *homebodies*.

HANNAH

They just announced Group Three.

ALLIE

What if your mom got one of those supermarket cakes?

HANNAH

She didn't.

ALLIE

And what if the organist is some old lady with a bad perm?

HANNAH

Does it matter what she looks like?

ALLIE

I wanted to pick everything. In Silver Lake they sell those lilies that totally look like vulvas. And I wanted a *progressive* church. Not some Mormon thing.

HANNAH

Lutheran.

ALLIE

The church in West Hollywood has, like, an entire gay choir.

HANNAH

Everybody has a gay choir!

ALLIE

It's not some Norman Rockwell thing with *corkboards* and *potlucks* and *Bible study* . . .

HANNAH

My family's church happens to be on the historic register . . .

ALLIE

It's about the *vibe.*

HANNAH

Okay, no, we don't have vibe-y churches in Iowa.

ALLIE

I wanted a clambake.

HANNAH

It's March.

ALLIE

I wanted a wedding on the beach.

HANNAH

That's not an option in Des Moines.

ALLIE

I wanted our friends to be at our wedding.

HANNAH

Barney's coming. Carrie's coming.

ALLIE

I wanted *all* of our friends to be there.

HANNAH

If they were really our friends, they'd be coming to Iowa.

ALLIE

I don't want to be friends with people willing to go to Iowa!

HANNAH

My family's there. Your family's coming. That's what matters.

ALLIE

I don't want to get married in *Iowa*.

HANNAH

Well, we can't get married here! Everybody's boarding. We need to find space for the garment bags.

ALLIE

Yeah, I'm sure the flight to *Des Moines* is jammed.

HANNAH

The lounge was pretty full.

ALLIE

Why would *straight* people leave L.A. to go to Iowa?

HANNAH

You know what? This is beneath you. Making fun of Iowa is shooting fish in a barrel.

ALLIE

What does that even *mean*?

HANNAH

It means it's too easy.

ALLIE

Do they really shoot fish in barrels there?

HANNAH

Do you want the rest of these pretzels?

ALLIE

Maybe we should wait.

HANNAH

They're *boarding*.

ALLIE

No I mean . . . maybe we should wait.

HANNAH

Wait till when?

ALLIE

Till it's legal here.

HANNAH

You know, it's a little late for this . . . whatever it is . . .

ALLIE

Emotion?

HANNAH

This . . .

ALLIE

Hissy fit?

HANNAH

I didn't *say* that. I just said it's a little late for you to . . .

ALLIE

I didn't know there was a deadline . . .

HANNAH

What is the *problem*?

ALLIE

Just there's your fantasy wedding and then there's . . .

HANNAH

The *actual* wedding.

ALLIE

There's the actual wedding and then there's the actual . . .

HANNAH

Marriage?

ALLIE

No . . .

HANNAH

This is so like you . . .

ALLIE

Is it?

HANNAH

You've been lovey-dovey for weeks and then you won't even hold my hand!

ALLIE

Not at security!

HANNAH

It's not suspicious behavior!

ALLIE

That woman was looking at us!

HANNAH

Which woman?

ALLIE

The cute one! The woman who patted us down.

HANNAH

Oh my God, it was the uniform . . .

ALLIE

It was not . . .

HANNAH

I know you have a thing for women in uniforms . . .

ALLIE

It wasn't the uniform! It was the goose bumps! I got goose bumps when she touched me! It was the first time I had been touched by another woman in a *really* long time. Not that I *wanted* her, not that I want anybody else, but if I *did* it was always *possible.* But after Saturday it's going to be monogamy, monogamy, monogamy until the day we DIE!

Beat.

HANNAH

Do you honestly think you're the only one that finds all this hard? Remember the woman at the stationery store with the thigh-high boots? She smelled *amazing* and for about six minutes she and I were meant to be. *Everybody* wants other people, but at a certain point you have to choose. The goose bumps go, but what you get in return is . . . *everything*. Trust, companionship, reliably good sex. Knowing each other *so* well. Am I the one? I don't know. But I'm *a* one. And I'm a good one. And I love you more than anyone else could ever love you. And every night I'm willing to rub your feet which, no offense, can get a little whiffy.

Beat.

ALLIE

Really?

HANNAH

Yes.

ALLIE

Why didn't you tell me?

HANNAH

Because I love you.

ALLIE

Don't stop.

HANNAH

Don't *you* stop.

ALLIE

How could I? *Look* at you. You're so wise.

HANNAH

(*disappointed*)

Wise?

ALLIE

And hot. *So* hot.

HANNAH

I must be. That girl with the dog crate is totally checking me out.

ALLIE

(*swiveling to look*)

C'mon, Hawkeye. Gimme that garment bag. Let's do this thing!

HANNAH

(*as they exit*)

I'm taking the window seat.

ALLIE

How come?

HANNAH

Because it makes you nauseous, remember?

ALLIE

Did you remember your iPod?

HANNAH

Dammit.

ALLIE

I got it.

END OF PLAY

Almost

∴

Stephanie Hallett

Same-sex marriage was legalized in my home province of Ontario, Canada, by the time I was sixteen years old. Less than two years after that, the 2005 Civil Marriage Act was signed, granting equal marriage rights from coast-to-coast-to-coast. I had the luxury of never having to wonder what it would be like to be denied the right to marry the person I loved.

But I never considered myself the "marrying kind." And despite my own parents' thirty-six-year-long partnership, they never pressured me to get married or have children. I didn't dream of a perfect mate, plan my special day, or even fantasize about my ideal dress (despite a colorful personal style; I was voted "Most Creative Dresser" in my eighth-grade yearbook—middle school code for "weirdo"). I knew exactly what I wanted from life: a cool job, a beagle named Charlie, and a house with a red front door on one of the Toronto Islands. Marriage? Who needs it.

I knew from the age of thirteen that I liked both boys and girls, and as a high school student and college freshman I dated both. One boyfriend, a sweet and simple guy, was desperately seeking a wife, kids, and a house in the suburbs. Since I swore up and down that I would never get married, we couldn't help but fall apart. Well, that was his problem, I declared, I had a life to lead and it didn't include marriage!

That was, until I met Meredith.

She was a red-bicycle-riding, women's-studies-minoring, vegetarian, dog-loving babe from just north of Toronto, my hometown. But we became acquainted thousands of miles away, while students at the University of British Columbia in Vancouver. I had a crush on her the day after we met. And I was determined to be with her, despite my roommate's kind warning that my love interest didn't fancy the ladies.

One chilly February evening at an on-campus, '80s-themed party, I awkwardly kissed my crush on the dance floor. After I chased her down the hall when she subsequently ran away, and convinced her that I wasn't drunk, Meredith and I became inseparable. Turns out, she did fancy the ladies, but at that point she only kind-of knew it.

We U-Haul'd after two months and shared a "character" apartment, complete with decorative, nonworking brick fireplace and an almost-view of the Coast Mountains from our tiny kitchen window.

We were the cool, property-value-raising, "creative class," new queer couple on the block, and we loved it.

Almost from day one, Meredith and I were serious about our relationship. We took weekend trips around B.C. and planned nice surprises for each other, like the time she made me a picnic on the roof of our school's library. We wanted to make each other happy. And we talked a lot about marriage; sometimes in theory, sometimes not.

It was strange for me, but it felt like a dreamy fantasy when I talked about marriage with her, so I entertained the notion. Very quickly I found myself reveling in it. And once the marriage conversations began, the baby talks were right around the corner. We thought about what it would be like to have a child together, feeling sad that we couldn't merge our DNA like straight people.

One Thursday morning, four months into our relationship, I got out of bed after she had left for work and realized I wanted to marry her, for real. For the first time in my life, I wanted to *get married.* I decided I would propose to her that day.

I set to work immediately: First, I had to find the perfect engagement ring. I biked all over town, from jewelry shop to jewelry shop. Finally, in a boutique on West Broadway, I found it: two sterling silver leaves with a mother-of-pearl inlay that wrapped around the finger. It was perfect.

Then I rushed home to make dinner: *spanakopita*, my favorite Greek dish. It was the same meal I'd made on our first Valentine's Day together; Meredith had been horrified by the amount of olive oil the recipe required, but ate a second helping anyway.

Finally, I lit the giant pillar candles in our decorative, nonworking brick fireplace, stuck the ring in the pocket of my oversized zip-up hoodie, and waited anxiously for her to arrive home at six o'clock.

When she walked in the door, Meredith was happily overwhelmed. I think she almost cried twice before I even proposed. After dinner, she said that she loved the surprise, the dim lighting, the candles, the meal, everything. As I listened to her wax poetic while washing the dishes, I casually leaned against the kitchen doorjamb and pulled the ring out of my pocket.

"Will you marry me?"

The words fell out of my mouth more easily than when I asked her out on our first date.

A stunned silence ensued. Then, "Are you serious? *Of course I'll marry you!*" she practically screamed.

And just like that, we were engaged. I was elated. I couldn't stop smiling at her for days; I wanted to show her off like a prize. To seal the deal, we spent the weekend searching for *my* engagement ring—we were both spoken for and wanted the world to know.

In the next few weeks, as we began to plan our wedding, we had some awkward moments in formal bridal shops. The sales girls couldn't understand who exactly was marrying whom, or why we both needed bridal gowns. We got a lot of: "Isn't one of you the maid of honor?" Sure, gay marriage may be legal in Canada, but that doesn't mean everyone has adjusted—especially those working in conventional bridal shops, which tend to be traditional and heteronormative.

Later that summer, we spent a blissful weekend celebrating with family and friends back home in Toronto. My dad was so excited about the engagement that he insisted on taking me all over town to find a dress (I found it eventually, at a very loud shop on Queen St. West: a pinkish, cocktail-length, be-sequined number that screamed diva bride). Meredith found her (much more appropriate) white strapless dress a few months later, at a shop not far from our apartment.

The whole relationship had happened very, very quickly. And perhaps just as quickly, things began to change. First I withdrew, spending more time in the dance studio creating choreography than at home with my bride-to-be. The more I withdrew, the more Meredith tried to pull me back. In turn, I slunk away somewhere dark inside myself.

The biggest fracture in our relationship had to do with our future plans. Meredith was accepted to grad school in Toronto, and I was accepted in Vancouver; neither of us could or would defer. We fought about it. We were both disappointed. Eventually, our mutual resentment drove a wedge between us.

But we carried on with the wedding plans. We didn't know what else to do.

We had decided on a caterer, a DJ, and a photographer. We had an ever-expanding guest list. And we had a vision: green gingham tablecloths, local wine and beer, jazz music from the '20s.

One Saturday morning, there was an ominous sign of where things were headed. I was in the dance studio, teaching ballet to three- and four-year-old girls, when Meredith called, sounding shaken. She confessed that she had a habit of wearing her wedding dress around the apartment when she was home alone, and that she had been doing just that when she exhaled too sharply and burst the zipper.

I wanted to laugh; it was a cute image. But I withheld my chuckles and tried to sound reassuring. We could easily get the zipper fixed before the wedding. What I didn't realize quite yet was that my girl and I were kind of like that zipper: holding together something beautiful, but ready to burst apart at any moment.

It was April 2009 when we finally split, less than four months before our wedding was to take place. The End amounted to a long night of crying, then silence, then fitful ten-minute intervals of sleep, screaming, and still more crying. It didn't start out as a breakup talk, but the more we said to each other, the more our relationship fell apart.

After spending one final day together, we said good-bye and promised to get back together. I said I just needed a break, and maybe the wedding was too much pressure. We both wanted it to work out. I also think we both wanted to believe it was one thing in particular that broke us, and that we could be fixed like the zipper. But it wasn't, and we couldn't. There were a lot of bruises on the relationship: sex, trust, anxiety, expectations. They were things we just couldn't stand to work on anymore.

She moved in with some friends on the other side of town; I stayed in our bed for a few days. I cried whenever I saw one of her socks, or sat in her big yellow chair. Then we had to divide things up: Whose book is this? Whose piece of furniture? What do we do with all the photos of us together when we were happy?

Meredith eventually returned to Toronto and I stayed in Vancouver. The few times we saw each other before she left were hard, each meeting proving that the breakup was the best decision. One night, about six months later, she drunk-dialed me from a hip downtown party. She wanted to say she had finally realized we weren't good for each other, and that she wasn't sad anymore. She wished me the best.

∴

Much to the surprise of those around me, a year and a half later I ended up marrying a man I had met soon after I went to California for an internship. He is kind, warm, and loves with his whole heart. I had remained open to a relationship with a woman, but it just so happened that I met this man who brought out in me the same desire for a long-term commitment that I'd felt with Meredith. In fact, I owe my belief in marriage to her; it wasn't until we were together that the part of me that wanted that sort of relationship was revealed.

Ironically—and sadly—I now live in a country where gay marriage isn't legal nationally (nor even in the state of California anymore). That actually made getting married a tough decision for me: I knew that other queer people don't have the same options and privileges that I do as a bisexual. I married a man whom I love, but I did it in a country that doesn't recognize one-half of my own sexual identity. But I decided that *not* getting married wasn't going to speed up the passage of same-sex marriage legislation; only continued pressure by each of us brings us closer to equality for all of us.

At this point, you might be thinking, what was the deal with Meredith and me? College lesbian phase? Well, you'd be wrong. The thing is, I realized I was bisexual at a very young age, and I was certain of my sexuality. Would you tell a lesbian who was once married to a man that she was probably just going through a college hetero phase? Probably not. I know that bisexuality is confusing to a lot of people, but all that I can say about that is this: Get over it.

Here's what I know to be true: The state has no business defining or policing the "right" type of relationship. Everyone should have the choice to marry the person they love. I also know that marriage is really hard work. Anyone who is willing to put in the time, energy, love, conversation, sacrifice, and devotion that it takes to make a happy partnership with another human being for the rest of their lives deserves a medal. At the very least, any couple who is willing to marry—two women, two men, one of each—should have that right.

Always a Bridesmaid

∴

Michele Kort

As a child, weddings embarrassed me.

I didn't like to watch lovers' public displays. It made me uncomfortable to watch my own parents kiss. When our neighbor Gail was married "in the round," I was stuck behind the rabbi, forced to watch the bride's and groom's glowing faces as they read their vows. My mother was melting with delight; I felt mortified.

I never imagined myself as a lacy-white bride. The best I could do was picture a wedding atop a cliff in Big Sur, overlooking the Pacific. That was the most spectacular place on earth to me. But more importantly, it required a torturous car ride to get there, more than forty miles along a winding cliff-edge mountain road. That would certainly narrow the guest list, I figured, because only the hardiest would make the trek. And, because of my embarrassment, I wanted as few guests as possible.

My family never pressured me to marry. Oh, my Grandma Sarah used to say to me, "Dolly"—she called almost everyone Dolly—"I just wish you should find a nice man, get married, and be happy." I never formally came out to her, but at some point in my late twenties she must have figured it out anyway, because she changed the mantra to, "Dolly, I just wish you should . . . be happy."

In my early twenties, I had to get over my wedding embarrassment because I had graduated to the rank of bridesmaid for a couple of friends' nuptials. The major embarrassment then became the dresses that were chosen for me to wear. Flowery organza? Whatever. I was simply fulfilling the rituals set down for girls of my 1950s generation. I may have questioned them for myself, but I dutifully played along.

By the end of my twenties, as my first cousins married in a cluster, I had developed a full-blown resentment to marriage. It wasn't so much the wedding ceremonies that bugged me anymore, but the bridal showers that preceded them. Why did these women get all the presents? What had they done to deserve them?

Actually, I knew what they had done: They had been successful at heterosexuality. And I wasn't. I had come out in my midtwenties, relieved to finally embrace my true self. I was at least successful at love; I had a girlfriend who had moved five hundred miles to live with me—though we pretended to have separate bedrooms. In the mid-1970s, there was little validation for same-sex relationships; at best there was "acceptance." Certainly there were no gifts given to honor our love.

At one cousin's bridal shower, I mentioned to a woman I scarcely knew that both this cousin and another were marrying men named Larry. "What do you think that means for *you*?" smirked the woman. Uh, that I might marry someone named Laurie? "C'mon, lady," I wanted to say, "don't you know that I'm *gay*? I'm not *getting* married, no matter what the person's name is."

Gay marriage? Never crossed my mind. Not until the late '80s or early '90s, at least, when I heard that some gay folks were having "commitment ceremonies." (I didn't attend any myself until the end of the twentieth century, and though they were lovely, they didn't exactly whet my appetite for something similar.) The idea of legal same-sex marriage was a pipe dream. Like women's suffrage, it would probably take more than seventy years to come to fruition.

Anyway, I was the child of divorce; my parents had split when I was fourteen. That's a really hard age to deal with separation, and I dealt with it poorly. My younger sister remembers me saying to my parents, "How can you do this to *me*?" In my mind, I guess, they weren't divorcing each other but somehow abandoning their daughter—or at least upending my sense of stability.

Did this sour me toward marriage? Possibly. I know that I never wanted to merge my possessions with those of a lover. I was always clear on whose albums and books were whose, so there would be no problem dividing them up should we split. On the other hand, I somehow couldn't stop believing in happily-ever-after. I once read a quote from Jodie Foster that went something like, "Of course I believe in true love—

I'm a child of divorce." My first reaction to hearing that was, *Huh?* But then it made perfect sense: The dream of perfect connection doesn't die with your parents' marriage; the longing just intensifies.

Over the course of the relationship I've had with my partner, Miriam, I never really wanted or expected either of us to ask for the other's hand in matrimony. I *did* try to imagine what we'd wear to our wedding—and maybe that's what stopped me. Fancy wedding dresses? No way. (As a bridesmaid at my sister's wedding, I had already fulfilled my odd fantasy—sparked by the costumes in the 1976 lesbian TV drama *The War Widow*, which was set during World War I—of wearing an ivory-colored, somewhat lacy Victorian dress.) Tuxedos? I could imagine tall, slender Mir in one, à la Marlene Dietrich in *Morocco.* But not me. Maybe we could both wear something flowing and loose, maybe white, maybe . . . I gave up.

For Miriam, we already were wed: The formal ceremony took place at a lousy restaurant where we met with our Realtor to sign the offer to buy our house. Suddenly, after living in separate abodes across town from each other for eleven years, we were committing to a thirty-year mortgage and a shared living space. That was marriage to her.

On the day that gay marriage became legal in California, by order of the state's Supreme Court, a strange thing occurred in the office where I work: As the only lesbian there, I became a putative bride-to-be. All day long, people came up to me, goofy-eyed, and asked, "Are you getting married?!?" Our board chair, Peg, went so far as to offer a spectacular venue for a wedding: her Malibu beachfront home. I was floored.

I had long lost any romantic notions of a wedding by this time, but I did think that getting married had significance politically. If the state of California was going to sanction them, lesbians and gay men needed to put on a good showing of same-sex marriages, if for no other reason than to prove we really wanted them! What many of us wanted, though, was the *right*, not necessarily the wedding itself.

I couldn't help but picture what a great party we could throw at Peg's gorgeous house, with the waves crashing just yards from the wide deck, and maybe some celebrities casually walking by (it's in *that* part of Malibu). And I thought that what would make it fun for Miriam, who's a composer, would be to fulfill one of her musical dreams and hire a *tuba* band to play a funky wedding march. Fun! Laughs! A good excuse for a party with family and close friends! That's all I imagined it would be, not some sort of gooey, romantic thing with bouquets and garters and Kleenex and whatnot.

But when I mentioned it casually as a possibility, Miriam quickly shut down the idea. Marriage was never on her agenda. She likes being an "alternative" person. We were already married in her mind because we'd spent seventeen years together and had a house, two dogs, and a California domestic partnership.

Her refusal to even consider the notion—even if it wasn't a real proposal—was hard for me. I wasn't alone: My therapist (a lesbian) told me that, among some of her clients, the legalization of same-sex marriage in California caused confusion, conundrums, even rifts. It called into question couples' dreams and goals and beliefs and fears. It brought some closer together, drove others further apart. I've since met other lesbian couples who have agreed to disagree about marriage, most recently one pair in which the gung-ho-to-wed partner won't get her beloved to walk down the aisle until the *federal government* legalizes same-sex nuptials (it's already legal in their home state). Like that couple, my partner and I remain together, though; it's twenty years for us now. Even without a piece of paper from the City Hall, a longtime commitment—and the intricate tapestry of family, friends, and loving companionship—is not easily untangled or put asunder.

Among coupled LGBT friends of mine, many got married during that California Summer of Love in 2008, but most did it very quietly, with no rigamarole. We were invited to just two big-deal weddings, both given by couples who had been together for several decades and had children. Arthur and Young celebrated their Chinese heritage at a restaurant in L.A.'s Chinatown, complete with a traditional dragon dance and Chinese opera. Sue and Cheri held a large outdoor potluck, with a "this is your life" ceremony filmed on Flip cameras by their teenaged twin daughters.

Even if I wasn't getting married myself, I was elated by the California Supreme Court decision. It was *validation*. Our LGBT relationships were given the same credence as heterosexual ones—something I realize I've always longed for, even as I've enjoyed the "otherness" of being queer. And when that elation ended on election night with the passage of Prop 8, I felt like I was punched in the stomach. One moment I was literally jumping up and down over Obama's election; the next I sat, mouth agape at the bigotry of voters in my state. Coming out of the closet has seemed like a lifelong process, and it's gotten easier and easier over time, but sometimes the closet feels like a safer place to reside.

∴

I'm no longer embarrassed by weddings. In fact, I've reveled at the ones I've attended over the past fifteen years. Particularly memorable were my sister's (with me in my Victorian finery!) among the oaks and grapevines of Sonoma County's Valley of the Moon; the pre-marriage-equality Provincetown seashore commitment ceremony of my friends Barbara and Honey; my friend Margy's intimate back-porch wedding in L.A.; and my coworker Michel's wear-a-costume affair in the California desert (my costume was simply that I wore a dress).

I'm no longer the little kid who squirmed when her parents kissed; I can now watch others' intimacy without flinching. And I can *kvell* over their joy, just as I saw my mother do. Perhaps just coming out, and experiencing love in my own life, made me feel less estranged from others' pleasure.

Working on this book has made me realize that most of us remain cynical about marriage, in one way or another. At the same time, few are immune from its power. Love beckons us to fall into its embrace and surrender—our loneliness, our unfettered freedom, our fear of intimacy, our fear of loss. In return, we're given the daily gifts of comfort, affection, constancy, cheerleading, a shoulder to cry on, a warm body to hold. We can call the unions we form around that love "marriages," whether we get a license for them or not.

I Don't Want to Be Part of Your [De]volution

∴

Stephanie Schroeder

There's nothing equal (or gay) about marriage. It's an outdated concept, an antiquarian vestige, and a ghost of social mores past.

The resistance to marriage as an oppressive institution, particularly for women, has taken many forms. In Victorian times, lesbians (and others) avoided marriage by forging independent careers. Flappers flouted female convention in the 1920s. Abolitionist-era suffragists worked toward the emancipation not just of slaves but of themselves as well. More recently, twentieth-century Second Wave radical feminists sought to eradicate marriage as an inherently oppressive patriarchal institution, along with other sexist relics such as organized religion and mandatory motherhood.

In the United States today, marriage is on the rocks—hanging off a cliff, even. We actually live in a divorce culture. Depending on where you find your statistics, between 11 and 78 percent of marriages end in divorce. In their July 11, 2010, *Newsweek* article, "I Don't," Jessica Bennett and Jesse Ellison addressed the sorry state of matrimony by writing: "[M]ost weddings are . . . a formulaic, overpriced, fraught rite of passage, marking entry into an institution that sociologists describe as 'broken.'" The two young female journalists also pointed out that, "The percentage of married Americans has dropped each decade since the 1950s, and the number of unmarried-but-cohabiting partners has risen 1,000 percent over the last forty years."

Marriage no longer offers the benefits for straight women it used to. In fact, the promises marriage once conjured—financial security, commitment from a baby-daddy, and a thousand or so rights—just don't cut it in this era of financial depression/recession, cohabitating partners, and single women having children. When playwright and author Sandra Tsing Loh's twenty-year heterosexual marriage ended, she suggested in a 2009 *Atlantic* article called "Let's Call the Whole Thing Off" that the American ideal of marriage had lost its utility. That notion was heatedly debated in the mainstream press, with the *Wall Street Journal* publishing an editorial by Kay Hymowitz in December 2010 castigating marriage opponents—claiming that only low-income people and African Americans are rejecting, or failing at, marriage.

Aside from the racism and classism inherent in such an argument, I'd suggest that commentators who so vehemently defend the institution are actually afraid of facing the truth: Marriage is dead, and the timeworn institution no longer serves modern society and its citizens, particularly women.

Feminist blogger Amanda Marcotte's proposal, partially in response to the criticism of Loh's piece, is that society should " . . . start untying all the benefits that lure people into marriage and expanding them to all people—health insurance, hospital visitation rights, tax breaks—so that married people don't get special status over the unmarried." This is the crux of my social-justice argument against marriage: Why should married people have privileges others do not? Some of us don't want/need church or state sanctioning of our most intimate relationships, but we do need healthcare, living-wage jobs, affordable housing, food, and daycare.

Safety-net services should be made available to everyone, everywhere, regardless of marital status. To single out married couples as the only legitimate recipients of benefits that should be readily accessible to all Americans is simply, yes, un-American. Gay marriage will only result in more discrimination, but this time within our own community. Just as keeping marriage for heterosexuals privileges heterosexuality, LGBT folks of the marrying kind will, where and when same-sex marriage is available, be privileged over single people and non-married lovers, both queer and not queer.

Reformists who seek the euphemistic "marriage equality" are just making excuses for wanting a piece of the bogus American Dream pie. They are lying by telling everyone who will listen, read, or drink their Kool-Aid that lesbians are just like everyone else. Except we aren't.

Being like everyone else is not only boring, it's dangerous, unthinking, uninformed, uncaring, and reckless. Acting as if lesbians are "just like" straight women deprives us of our uniqueness, our community, real visibility, and a distinct herstory that has nothing to do with the way straight women live. It's devastating to me personally and politically that so many of my lesbian sisters are willing to proceed under the marriage equality umbrella in both denial and delusion, without questioning either their own motives and commitments or those of the leaders in the marriage equality movement.

I agree with legal theorist, law professor, poet, and author Ruthann Robson, who comes at the marriage issue from a liberatory perspective and anti-assimilationist stance. She asks women (and men) to challenge their own beliefs about everything they do and every action they take. In legalese, the "interrogation" of our belief and value systems is paramount to putting on the brakes before acting on or believing in ideas just because "that's the way it's always been." Marriage is an example of a tradition that overtakes both practicality and reason but goes largely uninterrogated in the mainstream lesbian community.

Robson also explains that, in the LGBT community, if there is something we cannot have, then we want it no matter—sometimes without thinking it through and often without considering the consequences. Marriage is one of these cases. If the approximately 1,100 rights and responsibilities (and, as Robson points out, burdens) that accompany state-sanctioned marriage were given to individuals regardless of marital status, the landscape of marriage would change entirely. Then, what Robson terms "compulsory matrimony" would lose its validity, and individuals might focus on finding ways to have fulfilling relationships in all their permutations.

It ain't marriage that makes a lasting relationship: a loving commitment does. As Emma Goldman wrote in her 1911 essay "Marriage and Love":

> Love, the strongest and deepest element in all life, the harbinger of hope, of joy, of ecstasy; love, the defier of all laws, of all conventions; love, the freest, the most powerful molder of human destiny; how can such an all-compelling force be synonymous with that poor little State and Church-begotten weed, marriage?

"Beyond Marriage," a modern-day statement in the spirit of Goldman published in 2006 by Queers for Economic Justice, states another part of my anti-marriage, pro-equity thesis: "We believe LGBT movement strategies must not only democratize recognition and benefits, but also speak to the widespread hunger for authentic and just community."

"Authentic and just community," can you imagine it?

I believe marriage equality stymies any chance of such a community by ordaining marriage as the single and most righteous issue for lesbians and gays in the twenty-first century. "Gay marriage" dilutes the strength of our community by breaking down the systems of support and accommodation lesbians have built over the decades since "gay liberation" and even prior to that—the kind of support where friends (not just a single partner or "spouse") are family and a great source of strength and support; where ex-lovers might (or might not) remain as close family; where the pooling of resources to help sisters in need is highly valued; where the nursing and attendant care of a sick friend is shared; where, where, where . . . there are infinite possibilities beyond the one-woman-plus-one-woman model.

For anyone in the LGBT-XYZ community who believes in social justice, our energies and monies are better spent fighting for access to quality healthcare, living wages, affordable housing, adequate childcare, and a gamut of issues that are real, pressing, and increasingly necessary in today's financially and socially depressed times. "Marriage equality" is a dangerous red herring in a larger social milieu where the Equal Rights Amendment has not been ratified, nor the United Nation's Convention on the Elimination of All Forms of Discrimination Against Women; where women still earn almost a third less than men for the same work; and where we still face a rape culture.

It's 2012, and the lesbians of the gaystream are begging for marriage rights. This is how far we've come . . . from Seneca, from Selma, from Stonewall, from Solidarnósé, from Soweto . . . ?

How I long for the days when women would sit together to plan courses of action to take down, break down, destroy, and dismantle the woman-oppressive institutions of marriage, the dysfunctional nuclear family, the military, and the corporate/prison-industrial complex. Gaining access to marriage will *not* make us equal. This archaic institution founded by men to own women, children, land, and animals simply cannot be reformed. The term *movement*—as in the gay marriage movement—implies forward, not backward, propulsion. Marriage is taking us backward; marriage equality is devolution, not freedom or evolution, and certainly not revolution.

Even as marriage is a failing institution in the heterosexual community and straight people are rethinking ways to form families and celebrate relationships, the mainstream lesbian and gay community is steadfast and staunch in their belief that state sanctioning of our intimate relationships is the answer to all the wrongs against us. But marriage does nothing to rectify everyday issues and problems for the majority of lesbians. It's an elitist reality, a pretty-looking package filled with false hope.

Let us not forget the words of self-described "black, lesbian, feminist, mother, poet warrior" Audre Lorde: "The master's tools will never dismantle the master's house."

Let *Them* Eat (Wedding) Cake

∴

Linda Villarosa

On June 24, 2011, when gay marriage became legal in New York, my partner and I got swept away by the joyous frenzy. We decided to get married. Right after the announcement, I got down on one knee and "put a ring on it," although the ring was a piece of duct tape since that's all we had.

I love weddings, and I have attended many fantabulous ceremonies—gay and straight. And we'd been together for more than eleven years and are raising two kids. In the moment, it felt like it was time to make her my wifey or be hers.

Plus, our children had been pressuring us to tie the knot. The two of them have attended many weddings but have never been in one. Most of their friends' parents have split up, and I think they yearn for the security and certainty of a ceremony and a piece of paper. Something both public and tangible, wedding photos posted in our house, the license framed. Our fifteen-year-old daughter fantasized about being a flower girl—a very tall one—and described her perfect dress. Our twelve-year-old son, the main man in our lives, imagined himself doing double duty, walking me down the aisle and bearing our rings.

But even during our happy family fantasy about our wedding, something bothered me. For a number of years, same-sex marriage equality has been at the top of the LGBT to-do list, overshadowing most other issues in the national conversation. Over the past few years, nearly all of our political eggs have been placed squarely in the marriage basket.

But is this what we really want? What has marriage done for heterosexuals lately? It isn't working for them. Marriage rates have plummeted in the last half century, and young people are waiting longer and longer—stalling—before tying the knot. Of course they are; they're scared: Nearly 50 percent of all first marriages end in divorce, and rates of infidelity have apparently surged. I want to scream when I hear people (read: right-wing wingnuts) insisting that same-sex unions damage heterosexual marriage. Wake up: You're doing that all by yourself.

Hey, womyn—and men who went to Vassar—don't forget about the women's studies classes we took in college where we learned that something wasn't quite right about marriage. Of course, marriage has evolved, thanks largely to the insistence and persistence of feminists. But for hundreds of years, the institution revolved around property and wealth, not love and support. A wife had few rights; her husband controlled all the family earnings and all of his wife's property; in effect, he owned her and everything she brought with her to the marriage.

So why are we fighting so hard for sloppy seconds, binding ourselves to a tradition that may no longer make sense? Why are so many of us trying to prove that we're just as good as straights, that we're "normal" just like everybody else? That we, too, live in the suburbs, have children, run for local government, belong to the PTA?

Truth be told, we are not just like everybody else. We aren't just as good; we're better. Of course we go to church, coach Little League, and can cook a chicken casserole. But we're also Audre Lorde, Jane Lynch, Martina Navratilova, Cherry Jones, Larry Kramer, Alvin Ailey, Elton John, Harvey Milk, and a whole lot of other daring, creative spirits. We fought back at Stonewall, chained ourselves to buildings to protest AIDS, cared for each other during the plague, and figured out how to have children by being creative with science. We've written poetry, memoirs, plays, novels, and essays to tell our stories, and we've built our own communities, organizations, media, congregations, and schools to fight for our rights and continue our legacies.

We've also created our own events to recognize and celebrate our relationships. Since back in the day—the day of Sappho and Spartacus—we've gotten along fine without marriage and weddings. Better even, with beautiful and inventive commitment ceremonies invoking the language of love, not of possession and property. Without weddings per se, we've raised kids on our own and communally. Indeed, we understand that it does take a village; our friends and family members—with and without children of their own—have provided a network of aunties, uncles, play cousins, guardians, and all-around general support that heterosexuals often envy. We've also managed to skirt some of society's worst and most rigid strictures, as well as modern-day mash-ups like bridezillas, MILFs, or *The Bachelorette*.

Since weddings have turned into expensive consumerist show-boating and marriage isn't really working, let's call the whole thing off. For equality's sake, in an ideal world—granted, one that doesn't exist now in our polarized culture—we would stop using the word *marriage*. Instead, everyone, straight, gay, and in between, should be allowed to have "unions" and be privy to all the rights and benefits they offer. In essence, what we need is a nice, neat, consistent set of rights that works nationwide and would replace the creaky, inconsistent, illogical, and often discriminatory system that's in place now.

Though this isn't a popular idea, and I'll probably be banned from the slew of weddings I've been invited to, instead of planning our ceremonies, we should shift the focus and plan a more just world. We've fought the good fight, but it's time to move on and use our vast talents to fight better fights—the ones that benefit straight, gay, lesbian, bisexual, transgender, and any and everyone else. These include reducing the gap between the rich and poor; battling HIV/AIDS; providing affordable health- and childcare; creating jobs; decreasing guns on the streets; lowering the prison population; and erasing prejudice and discrimination of every kind and against anybody.

So what about my own wedding? I raise a glass to those in New York who are taking advantage of our fantastic new legal right to wed.

Yes, I admit my partner and I got pulled into the excitement of the New York vote. But in the stark light of day, we decided that being domestically partnered was enough for us. Like marriage and politics, though, nothing is set in stone. When same-sex marriage equality becomes a national right, we might get swept away again and actually go through with it. Or maybe, in the meantime, our kids will talk us into walking down the aisle.

We Have to Talk About It, Someday

Emily Douglas

At Harvard in the early 2000s, among those of us who were gay or something like it, *marriage* was a bad, embarrassing word. I say "something like it" because *gay* was embarrassing, too, and *lesbian* was worse. At Harvard, undergraduates didn't take—weren't offered—identity-affirming classes about gay history or lesbian literature or the psychology of sexual identity. We took classes that rejected the notion of coherent, stable sexual identity, of identity in general: We learned about the folly of tracing gay identity through history, the dangers implicit in understanding homosexuality as biologically determined, and the problems of trying to correct historic injustice with a "rights" discourse.

We never spoke from "experience"; we had all read Joan Scott's "The Evidence of Experience" and knew that just because we felt something—solidarity based on shared experience, identification with terms or labels, common alienation from the expectations of a straight majority—that didn't mean we could bring it up in class. We didn't attempt to understand our situation by starting with how we felt; we started with the theory, not only in class, but also in our LGBT and feminist student groups. Besides, it was gauche to tip your hand—gauche to expose too much of yourself, to pin yourself down.

As a consequence, we were all queer, and we did not want to get married.

If marriage was not our priority, it would be a stretch to say that anything beyond our college campus was—or maybe that was just me. I was political, sure, but abstractly so. It may have been a liberal arts college where queer intellectual life was thriving, but actually *being* queer at Harvard was not a terribly easy thing, and attempting to reconcile my emerging sense of self with the academic community consumed me. Many of the students and professors shared a deep strain of conservatism and essentialism (about gender as well as sexuality), few queer couples were visible on campus, and we were all too busy trying to look smart enough in front of each other to get entangled in the irresolvable love triangles I was sure would suffuse college life. Matters of law and policy, and their consequences for people's lives, seemed too boring to spend time studying during college; I had not yet encountered the world in which I had to earn money and secure food and shelter for myself. The urgent world was the one right around me: interior and interpersonal, theoretical and psychic.

But even within the realm of political demands gay people might someday be granted, same-sex marriage barely even occurred to me. The summer before my senior year, I stayed in Cambridge along with most of my friends, and that June went with my then-girlfriend to the common for Pride. Pride in Boston is a singularly lovable event, due probably to the city's high population of bookish, unmaterialistic residents. A hodgepodge of earnest community groups staff tents decorated with homemade banners and fliers, sharing information about their work on queer youth homelessness, recovering local gay history, AIDS prevention, and myriad other worthy causes. We ended up standing at a table talking to a tall, genial man who might have been straight and might have been gay, who told us that his organization had filed suit against the Massachusetts Department of Public Health for refusing to grant marriage licenses to same-sex couples. They were expecting a ruling in a few months.

I thought he was crazy. Gay people getting married? It was startling, but it wasn't just that: Something about it annoyed me. It was hubris, it was asking too much. It was attempting to leap over a dozen hurdles in one ungainly stride. The Department of Public Health must have thought they were nuts, asking for something like that.

The idea that the state could endorse the relationship of two people of the same sex was to me, at that point, literally unfathomable. I don't think I really even knew what marriage meant—what the legal consequences were, or that being barred from them would negatively affect same-sex couples. I had barely devoted any thought to disentangling the religious and civil aspects, and yet I somehow knew that it was and always would be off-limits to gay people. The institution of marriage could no sooner make sense of me and my same-sex partners than my parents could.

Finding my way at Harvard was, after all, less than half the story: What was going on with my parents was crippling me. My parents are immigrants, from South Africa and Germany, and I am the oldest of their four children. Growing up, we were a little island family, speaking German, eating muesli instead of Cheerios, making observations about what Americans do and say. My parents were enthusiastic volunteer soccer coaches, library aides, and next-door neighbors; they gabbed gamely with our classmates' parents on the carpool line, but always at a slight remove. At a remove from others, but so close to us children: They were at the center of our sense of moral correctness. None of us had ever tried to be anything our parents didn't want us to be.

I'd been having a very bad freshman year—isolated and lonely and impervious to my parents' exhortations to think about the positive things and get involved in volunteer work. Relations had deteriorated. When I began dating a woman and became a little happier, I thought they'd be pleased. It didn't occur to me to decide whether I was gay or not before telling them—why would I need to be one thing or another? They'd know how to react: I had never seen them encounter a situation in which they had not been gracious. But as soon as I told my mother that I was dating a woman, her anger was blinding. When I told my father, he was suddenly, casually cruel. I had broken rules that had been totally unspoken. Now they wanted me to say whether

I was gay or not, and I decided I wasn't—not yet, anyway. My halfway coming-out rendered them, and me, unrecognizable.

I made it to the end of freshman year, but I never quite found my footing in the next three years of college. Class was posing such beguiling, disarming questions: What if gay identity was as much a function of capitalism as of love? What did it really mean if gender was nothing more than performance? Why was I attached to the idea of having biological children? Why did I want to be normal? I found a language for the inchoate longings that had shadowed me since childhood—a language far more nuanced than had I bluntly ascribed those feelings to just being "gay." But I couldn't separate life from class, even when I needed to. I hadn't found an identity before I started problematizing it; I couldn't shake the sense that the self I was discovering was, at its heart, a failure. Whenever I fought with my girlfriend, in my mind our arguments blew up huge, projected on a movie screen. They weren't just about our incompatibility, but about the futility of trying to make a life as a gay person. Harvard seemed intended for the students who were confident, undoubting, even-keeled, emotionally neutral—straight.

Gay couples started marrying in Massachusetts during my senior spring, thanks to the lawsuit I'd learned about at Pride more than a year before. The night gay couples could first marry at Cambridge City Hall, they lined up for hours, and weddings started at midnight. I should have been there, but I was in a gracious, black-shuttered colonial four miles up the road in Lexington, attending the rugby team's end-of-season roast. (That was gay politics to me then: I couldn't imagine leaving my teammates when they were gathered, even for a night!) At the time I didn't let myself realize that the weddings were a big deal—or maybe the idea of going to witness (and care about) them was just one more thing I was relieved not to fit into my overstretched schedule.

My understanding of what the legalization of gay marriage meant shifted definitively a few days later, when my friend Betty and I stood outside the library talking about it. Did these first weddings represent assimilation, or a step forward for gay liberation? Abruptly, Betty left behind our studied, tiptoed theory-chatter and cried, "Face it, if gay people can get married, that's huge!"

Yes, it was, I realized. It was a giant thing. It was what my parents had, it was what I couldn't imagine having. It was going to change everything.

After graduation, I moved into the co-op off campus for the summer, where there were always leftovers in the fridge. I cooked my mom's quiche in giant pans for group dinners and started looking for jobs on Idealist.org, the online classifieds for nonprofits. I'd always planned on becoming an academic, but I was burned out on school and wanted to help people, so I applied to be a case manager for homeless families, to be a counselor at a battered women's shelter, to be an editor at a radical press. Then I found a job listing for a position at the legal organization that I'd encountered at Pride the summer before—Gay & Lesbian Advocates & Defenders, or GLAD—doing hotline and outreach work for the group's education department. In the intervening months, I hadn't learned much more about the law, but I liked the sound of the hotline.

Gavi, the man I'd met at Pride, interviewed me first; I met Ben

Klein, a staff attorney, during the second-round interview. He left me bewildered by questions about my connection to the issues GLAD worked on. I had been taught to believe that personal conviction wasn't a justification for any argument, even the argument that you ought to get a certain job. In response to Ben's question about why I cared about GLAD's work, I mumbled something about it "certainly having a personal impact." On the subway ride back to Cambridge, I wondered why that had felt so strange for me to articulate.

I got the job, and quickly found that GLAD was a tremendous place to learn about the law, not just as it pertains to sexual orientation, HIV status, and gender identity—the organization's specific areas of focus—but the way it conditions every aspect of American life. On the hotline, I got better and better at cutting through a caller's convoluted dilemma to isolate the legal issues at play and explain them in terms he or she could understand.

Though it wasn't really my job, I spent a lot of time helping out with event mailings, feeding a parade of envelopes bearing the names of two women (or two men, but I paid less attention to those) through the mail-metering machine. The women were unknown to me, but their names became a sort of sustenance; I couldn't believe that there was a seemingly inexhaustible well of lesbians who had decided to set up house together. With each letter, I started believing a little more in this ridiculous, exhausting, terrible, taxing project that I hadn't quite chosen but that had ended up being mine.

On the GLAD hotline, I also spoke to hundreds of people who wanted to get married. In college, I had read marriage critic Michael Warner's 1999 book *The Trouble with Normal*, in which he writes,

"False consciousness is an undeniable force throughout time," and I had believed him as applied to the desire to marry, and to countless other situations in which self-consciousness is conditioned by societal norms. But it wasn't so easy to dismiss these couples now that they were on the phone with me, telling me it was marriage they wanted, not civil unions or second-parent adoptions or domestic partnerships.

Unlike me, the callers were adults: They'd left straight marriages, they were raising children, they had struggled through demoralizing jobs, they had managed to forge some sort of rapprochement with their families of origin—or they hadn't. I don't mean to argue for marriage rights as a reward for same-sex couples because they're such upstanding citizens, but these callers had encountered and thought about fundamental aspects of adult citizenship, and decided that marriage was the legal and emotional tie they wanted. They were certainly wiser about their own desire to marry than I was.

Listening to the hotline callers changed me. Learning about the legal consequences of marriage changed me. No one right galvanized me as much as learning that you got them all, in one fell swoop, just by marrying, even if you didn't know what they were. (Of course, gay people *don't* get them all, even when they do marry.) The luxury of not needing to anticipate every right you'd ever need became plain.

Meanwhile, my parents knew I was dating women, my siblings knew, but I was never brave enough to push the point, to force them to accept something foreign to them. I tried sending them photocopies of my favorite pieces of queer and feminist theory, complete with explanatory marginalia; they never responded. My gayness was a graft that wasn't taking. When I was with them, I mostly forgot about being gay, anyway, until one of them made it clear they were still expecting me to end up in a straight relationship. I didn't want to do or be anything that would estrange me from them.

But slowly things changed, mostly while I was busy thinking nothing ever would. During the spring of one of my post-college years in Cambridge, my mother visited, and I took her to the Arnold Arboretum in Jamaica Plain. It was a brilliantly cloudless, still day, and we wandered around lilac bushes and sat by the rhododendrons for a picnic. And she said, *Wir müssen es besprechen, ein Tag*—we have to talk about it, someday. She meant not about me being gay but how she and my father had responded to it. Or at least I'm sure that's what she meant. Tears welled in my eyes, and it seemed a better idea to defer the conversation. Perhaps it had been so unimaginable for so long that I wanted to have the pleasure of anticipating it a little longer. Or perhaps I couldn't bear the thought of us admitting all the ways we'd failed each other.

And now we've never had it. But my parents have seen four children move into adulthood, and they seem to realize that their children's happiness, wherever and however it can be found, is hard-won and to be held dear. My mother became soft to me, became my mother again. My father seems proud of me again.

A few years later, I left GLAD and Boston and moved to New York, and a couple of years after that, my straight friends started to marry. That changed my feelings about marriage, too. They showed no compunction about exercising their right even when some of their friends couldn't, and that, too, dimmed what radicalism I had left. Radicalism was no fun when the immediate and apparently long-term effect of it was that straight people married and gay people were still unable to. That was the very same outcome that would result from pursuing no political agenda at all. A part of me was bitter, too: Straight couples could beg off wanting the traditional trappings for themselves, but, thanks to their families pulling it together for them, they still ended up with a wedding that felt like the real thing.

Then again, I came to see familial meddling in a different light. If your mother had strong ideas about your wedding day, it meant she cared enough to want you to do it right.

I wonder, too, whether it is possible to hear a lingering sense of undeservedness—or an instinctive shame that you might even call internalized homophobia—in gay people's criticism of weddings, their own or others'. When the writer Ariel Levy told the story of her lesbian wedding in *New York* magazine in 2007, she admitted that having a wedding was the opposite of what she still felt she *ought* to be doing: alleviating or apologizing for, as she put it, "the horror of my homosexuality."

I had never heard anyone cop to it quite like that. But Levy nailed the feeling that had dogged me now for so long: the feeling of being an embarrassment, a horror. In the case of homosexuality, throwing yourself a wedding was precisely the opposite of mitigating that embarrassment. Levy planned her wedding after legalization in Massachusetts, which wasn't so long ago but still a time when that state felt like an outlier—before Gallup found that a majority of Americans favor same-sex marriage, before the federal government dropped its defense of DOMA, before mainstream blogs derided bridal shop owners and caterers who refused to work with gay clients.

Nevertheless, Levy and her partner decided to throw a party big enough to accommodate "the scale of our glee," and, in a sensation familiar to anyone who has planned a slightly too-ambitious dinner party, the event took on a life of its own. Her friends believed in it even when she didn't quite, and that buoyed her along—as well as buoying her reluctant mother-in-law. "To me, the piece is about how a very expensive dress and a big party helped both Ariel Levy and Mrs. Norquist [the mother-in-law] overcome their discomfort with the idea of two women marrying each other, and instead honor and celebrate it," my friend Maddy wrote.

I still can't win arguments with all of my skeptical queer and progressive friends about marriage, and I'm not sure I want to. There is unmistakable logic to their opposition to gay marriage. Marriage privatizes a host of caregiving functions the state ought to provide; marriage is a poor match for the varied family forms that exist not only among gay families but straight ones; marriage normalizes social relations, which queer people should seek to upset. In the writing and reporting I've done on same-sex marriage, I've found myself agreeing with critics such as the political philosopher Tamara Metz, who writes that because the institution of marriage "draws the state into the most intimate corners of citizens' lives (family and sexual life, religious and cultural value systems) and effectively privileges some views of the good life while punishing others, [it] *threatens* freedoms of conscience, expression, and association." But this suspiciously unerring argument exerts less of a pull on me now than it once did. I have found other ways of arriving at what I think is right.

My current partner does not want to exercise her right to marry. Tara was in graduate school at Harvard while I was finishing undergrad; she took the same Theories of Sexuality class I had taken. (We didn't know each other then, but when we met years later on a bus to canvas for Obama in Pennsylvania, she was familiar to me.) She makes a convincing counterargument: Same-sex relationships are already valid and serious in themselves, and it's not gay people's responsibility to prove that to others by creating an event their friends and family will comprehend. "I can't get away from the idea that people get married because it's 'what adults do,'" she says. "Like golfing." Sometimes, though, she'll admit that she just doesn't want that many people looking at her all at once.

Last Labor Day, Tara and I attended her best friend's wedding at a barn in upstate New York; we were so full of joy that weekend that it felt like our own wedding, but better because the feeling was our secret. The morning before she was due at the wedding rehearsal (she was the groom's best person), we wandered the grounds of Bard College, on the banks of the Hudson River, with her college friends. In the rose garden in front of the Economics Building we agreed that, were we ever to marry, we'd do it on a farm and give our guests a coursebook of readings to complete before attending. We didn't say why, but I know: because then they would understand how complicated our feelings about marriage are, but also how deliberate our choice to marry was.

Well, it's partly that. We also, I suspect, want to know that the people with whom we would share a wedding were thinking about it the same way we were. Maybe that's another thing I should be ready to relinquish control over when I marry: my own attempt—and it has been going on as long as I've been dating women—to control what others think of me, to preempt their discomfort, their confusion, their hateful thoughts.

I have begun to want to be obligated—legally, yes, that, too!—to people I didn't choose, such as in-laws and my partner's friends; I have begun to want lots of people to have ideas about how I ought to get married. I am beginning to understand that lots of people might care. Though my parents, unfailingly discreet, would never tell me to have a wedding or how, I began to want to have a wedding because my parents would want me to or might enjoy it.

How lucky, how blessed I am, that they might.

I'm Not from Here

∴

Holly Hughes

I

November 15, 2008. An online group, "Join the Impact," has called for demos across the country to protest the passage of Proposition 8 in California. I am visiting Chicago, and a group of friends-of-friends invite me to tag along. Everyone's laughing when we meet up in the shadow of an orange Picasso. Their leather jackets are unzipped, their heads hatless. I'm so bundled in layers of down I look like a supersized North Face burrito. My face grows a large red planet called my nose. The wind off the lake knifes through the layers, counts all my bones.

We introduce ourselves, but the names freeze into clouds before reaching my ears. We recognize we're all members of the same tribe, though: the urban queers, lesbo division. There's so much we don't have to say: Dick Cheney is the worst person in the world and Sarah Palin is catching up. We believe in single payer, that black is always the new black. We believe in the two-state solution, coalitions, and fish oil; in Rachel Maddow and Michelle Obama. We tweet. We know what BDSM stands for; some of us have a better idea than others. We shun single-issue and identity politics. We are so beyond gay; we are here, queer, and couldn't care less if you get used to it.

The rally is a big noise in the background no one listens to. It's like car alarms, jackhammers: a part of city life that you stopped hearing years ago. Our conversations are songs, belted out over the beat of "Hey, hey! Ho, ho! Homophobia's got to go!"

A representative sample: "Gay marriage, can you believe it?" A round of snorts. No need to spell it out. It's part of the tribal lore: Gay marriage is for losers, or for well-heeled white men; gay marriage is for gay people, and we are well beyond gay. Plus it's a distraction from other more urgent issues. It's destroying the movement. Domesticating the queerness in us. There are other ways to distribute the legal benefits of marriage.

A week before, a prominent lesbian leader said to me that gay marriage was to the new millennium what AIDS had been to '80s and '90s: a way for white men to take over. It was a waste of time and money. I'm stopped by the way she joins AIDS to the word *waste* in the same breath. In my memory, they also go together, but like this: a waste of lives. The wasting away. The once-common sight of men reduced to literal skin and bones; the bones walking the streets of Lower Manhattan. I can't claim major AIDS activist cred, I'm ashamed to say. And maybe that's why I don't say, "But people were dying." I would be ashamed to be more specific, to say "my people." To claim allegiance. I sink into silence.

I hide behind this silence at the rally. Look, I get it. I'm a feminist, and marriage is fucked up. No argument there. Marriage is to the patriarchy what guitars are to rock: essential, critical, the engine that drives the whole show. Marriage is like death by casserole. Marriage is a hole that swallows you up, shaves off your edges, and spits you back into the world as something you never wanted to be: a wife. The word *wife* is pink, padded; it sounds like a type of sofa, and if you sat down on it, you would be so comfortable you would fall asleep and never wake up.

But it also seems fundamental, a basic part of being a citizen. I can barely hold that word *citizen* in my head as a left-winger, perennially disappointed in our government, politics, and history. Perhaps better to stay outside of it.

Or I could shape my comments into a joke; I could say that I didn't want to get married until someone said I couldn't. And then the "no" was turned into a big rock on which a political movement got built.

Maybe I could spin a grammatical joke: Since gay marriage was already illegal, isn't a law banning gay marriage a kind of double negative? Isn't gay marriage now, in fact, allowed? But these are borrowed jokes, and would yield at best a slender smile, nothing that could hold any weight.

The memory of other friends, of being nine and playing house. The sky above us is big, the light hard. A group of girls, maybe one boy who doesn't fit with the other boys; is he gay now? I want to play something else, I can't say what. I'm offered my choice: Dad, Mom, child, in descending order of power, but I end up playing the dog. I'm happy to get dirty. I'm scratching at the imaginary door; I need to go out.

One minute you're nine and the next you are in the other part of your life. Now you own a house, and in that house, in the middle of the night, the phone rings. A doctor says your partner has to go to the hospital right away; no, you can't wait till morning, now. She could drop dead. Racing dark streets haunted by fears: She could die. And you might not be able to see her. On the way to the hospital you have to come up with a story of who you are to each other that will open the doors, let you step inside. Who you are to each other is not enough or is entirely wrong. The need to rehearse your parts, get your story straight, before you enter the ER.

This, too, is not a way to start. There's nowhere to go from here. Any argument that begins and ends with rights and legal perks forgets what it was like to be in the eighth grade while a teacher droned on about the Bill of Rights. It's impossible to not look out the window, it's impossible to keep your mind inside the room; you drift out of yourself into the wide world. Anyplace is better than this; you are a crumpled piece of paper, tumbling over yourself in the rush to be in the world and away from the room where facts get hammered into your head.

I could ask a question. What are we doing here? I'm ambivalent at best, and they are adamantly opposed. And yet here we are. Why? The question as invitation. The question as a chair pulled out from the table, the invitation to sit down in the kitchen and talk to one another like you do when you know you will eat together. But I can't get the question to form as an invitation; it rings in my head like an accusation. I'm knotted with contradictions myself, hardly one to enforce ideological consistency. I'm with Walt W.: "Do I contradict myself, very well, I contradict myself." It would be rude to ask these temporary friends to answer the questions I can't answer: "Why are we here? What does our presence mean?" There are plenty of scolds on the left, riding herd; I don't need to be one more.

Then we move, suddenly, we're in the streets. I'm part of a flock taking wing, we're together, the pleasure of being in a flock of like-minded bipeds floods me. Big dopey love thoughts bubble up; *please don't cry*, I say to myself. Someone says: "You cold? You can't be cold, it isn't cold yet." They are kind, they are kidding, they are walking beside me, breaking the wind with their lopsided grins, and so I say: "I'm not from here. I'm not ready for this."

II

I'm being unfair to these women in Chicago. In the media, gay marriage is one issue with two sides: yes or no. A coin you toss in the air—heads or tails. But many queer folk would say it's not one issue but several. Here's my image: the tangle at the bottom of my jewelry box, the broken tangled with the precious, the inherited with what I gave myself; they have knotted themselves together, and it would be a day's work in good light, with luck, to separate what was worth keeping from what I should have thrown out long ago. So the various strands of the personal and political are snarled into a queer knot. This is not the knot featured in "tying the knot." That's a knot you make, it's a deliberate action to join two lives into a recognizable shape, but this queer knot is something that happened on its own, the pattern's irregular, there is no order to it. Easier to shut the box than to try to sort it out.

My generous friend Alisa Solomon is not crazy about the fight for marriage equality but could readily imagine showing up to protest a law like Prop 8. Here's how she describes the knot: the difficulty disconnecting "discrimination, which one must always oppose," from "the eagerness for marriage itself."

Ah, the eagerness for marriage itself. It's everywhere: At the newsstands (such as they still exist) there's an avalanche of bridal porn. Plus websites on weddings, self-help books, and of course the emergence of the wedding planner. Maybe there were always wedding planners for the upper crust, but it seems new for the middle class. According to The Wedding Report, an annual compilation of research for the wedding industrial complex, Americans spent about $20,000 on their weddings in 2009, on an average income of around $40,000. All of which suggests that getting married is a major undertaking that requires a year of your life and big piles of cash, and cannot be undertaken without professional help. I think of the friend who almost splits up with her husband-to-be over the wedding plans. Her ordinarily thrifty self is elbowed aside by a stranger who insists on buying a white dress she'll never wear again, a sit-down dinner, an elaborate cake; she silences his fretting about the cost with: "It's my wedding!" A wedding on the cheap is a sign you aren't serious.

I go to a pre-wedding celebration where the bride is toasted by friends from different chapters of her life. All stories arc toward the same conclusion: "We thought you were gay, but you're not! You have short hair and had a couple of abortions, but you're not a dyke! Congratulations!"

I overhear women talking about planning their wedding like they are training for the Ironman, like they are building their own home with their bare hands, and I feel like I'm from Mars. No, a Martian would be mystified, but I feel like I'm in my Prius of queerness, sneering at the gas-guzzling Hummer-sexuals.

Okay, about my sneer, where's that coming from? Conviction or compensation for a wound I don't remember? My way of saying, "You can't reject me, I reject you first"? Was a rejection of marriage with all the trimmings part of what led me to queerness, or is it something I learned on the margins? My anti-consumerist passion is nowhere to be found when I'm browsing stuff I'm interested in, like the recent Patagonia catalog or anything dog-related.

I side with a friend, C, who complains that her live-in boyfriend wants to get married. He's been married before, and obviously that didn't work out. He jokes that he's the marrying kind but she doesn't think it's much of a joke, she's not smiling. C considers herself part of the queer tribe and doesn't want to be part of something that excludes others. And they are practically married, living together, monogamous, raising a baby, what's the big deal? But there's practically married and *married* married. He didn't want to have a baby but went along, so does she owe him? And there's the baby, legal realities, they are well into middle age. She could get married at City Hall, after yoga. They don't have to ever use the dreaded words *husband* and *wife*, but it will have to be a secret. Friends will feel betrayed by her lack of eagerness for marriage.

Then there's the eagerness for *my* marriage. "Gay marriage is THE civil rights issue of our time," a dear friend declares, hitting the word *THE* with a force that makes me squirm. I'd be happier with *a*, a lower-case declaration of support.

The LGBT movement has a spotty record when it comes to figuring out its relationship to other movements: Often we've been too eager to dress ourselves up in the uniforms of other's battles. We've collaborated with the media's tendency to present gayness as deeply blonde and upwardly mobile and young. Hence slogans like "Gay is the new Black." Um, black is still black and racism is very much alive. We can play the gay note so loudly it drowns out the other parts of the chord. Doesn't help when the media creates a food fight on the left by insisting that African Americans cost California's LGBTs the right to marry.

But I also melt. My dear friend wants to say she loves my rainbow tribe; she sees the inequality and wants to resign from the cheerleading squad and make herself useful. She wants to tell me that she sees my relationship as big and important as hers. She wants me to have what she has. But she gets a whiff of the ambivalence, not about the political battle for equality, but about my own life. She is wounded by my lack of eagerness for marriage itself; she's a woman with a serious and successful career, but getting married was still a big deal, an achievement. My ambivalence renders me illegible to her.

Another friend is more direct when I try to explain the queer knot, the desire among some to reframe the marriage issue: Instead of fighting to expand marriage, maybe we should get rid of it entirely. Find another way to distribute the benefits more equitably. His response: Grow up.

My straight ally friends love me, but they think I'm like them, want the same things. And perhaps I do, but I don't want to. I want my civil rights but don't want to shed my queerness, even if it was forged through stigma. Our queer chosen families, the deep bonds that many of us form with our friends and former lovers because so many reject or were rejected by their bio families: Do we lose that when we make our own families? Maybe the reason so many gay people question lifelong monogamy, even as some of us practice it, is because we've been shut out of the protective frame of marriage. But protection can be containment, can be suffocation. My partner and I are monogamous not because we think it's better or more mature but because we're just not multitaskers; we never had a three-way where someone didn't end up crying. So I walk my monogamous path, but I like that it's a big sexual jungle out there. I like that there are sex clubs, and anonymous hookups, and all manner of polyamorous goings-on, the same way I like living in a city full of night clubs, ballet, and opera, even though I never go to any of these events.

But I'm entirely lacking in the eagerness for marriage itself. Yet it flares up in me when I am faced with members of my own queer tribe who put up a solid wall of "no" when marriage is mentioned. The fight for marriage equality is "assimilationist" and "heteronormative." The words slam down like a pair of electronically controlled garage doors, and I'm on the outside, the wrong side—no, way past the gate, because I have what used to be called false consciousness. I'm not sure if it's the eagerness for marriage that overtakes me at that moment so much as the memories of other shunnings. In 1990, an anonymous group of "radical" lesbian-feminists in Washington, D.C., defaced a theater that produced my work with claims that I was "a tool of the heteropatriarchy." A small footnote in the history of the sex wars, but what lingers is the language. Easy to see how a tool of the heteropatriarchy could grow up to be heternormative.

Then there is the brandishing of the word *radical*. While I still think of my politics in those terms, when I hear it out loud, I cringe. When I hear someone introduce herself that way, I automatically think: *bully*. Someone who is going to suck all the air out of the room telling us what to think. Radicals are always talking about building coalitions, getting away from identity and single-issue-driven politics, but given how little they tend to tolerate dissent among members of their own group, it's difficult to see how they might be able to work with groups they have less in common with.

Locked out of a conversation with my tribe, I slide back into being the sullen teenager, with a pocket full of snide remarks. The anti-marriage queers sound like a gaggle of mean girls, lording it over the unhip gays who can't pull a look together. Is it me, or does it seems like this dialect of queer is spoken mostly by those living in large urban areas with big queer communities, or in large research universities, like the one I work at? Places where it's relatively easy to be queer, where you might even be able to get a degree in queerness, or be gay for pay. I loved my twenty-five years in New York City, but I know it was so much easier to be queer there than it is to be merely gay in Michigan, even in the relatively tolerant city of Ann Arbor.

Here's what I don't get about what I will call the "queer position" on gay marriage: the vehemence, the amount of investment in decrying the gay marriage movement. There's a certain irony in the amount of effort put into the attacks, particularly given that one of the charges is that the fight for gay marriage is a distraction from other, more important issues we should be pursuing. Wouldn't it make more sense to ignore gay marriage and work on what you claim to care about?

Not all the queer critics of gay marriage are so unreasonable. They wouldn't stand in the way of someone who wanted to get married, but they would never want it for themselves. The *never* is firm, it's confident, it's their final answer. I think of the bicyclists in San Francisco, dressed in black, no lights, they weave in and out of traffic on a steep hill. Oh, and it's dusk and it's raining. A friend calls them "the immortals." They'll never slip, they'll never misjudge the speed of that Toyota or who's about to open a car door. No drivers will take their eyes off the street as they change lanes, fail to see them. Never. And the person you live with will never develop a chronic medical condition, or just up and die on you, and you will never wonder if you can stay in the house after you pay the taxes a straight couple would be spared. You'll never be bitter about the fact your straight sister gets two Social Security checks because her partnership was legally recognized. You'll never get dumped and find out you have no rights to even see, much less parent, the kids you helped raise.

But what if this has nothing to do with gay marriage at all? What if gay marriage is just a symptom of something that you are trying to hold at bay with a firmly placed *never*? Something that is lurking behind the words I've just made fun of, *heteronormative* and *assimilationist*. The fear of changes to the gay community. Perhaps it's why some of us bristle at depictions of recent LGBT history as all onwards and upwards, one steady stream of progress. We're not only bristling at those excluded, at the reduction of a stream of currents and crosscurrents to a single line moving in one direction.

There's also the fear of a post-queer, post-gay life. We have created cultures and fantastical identities under pressure: Who will we be without them? Discrimination helped create the ghettos of the Village and the Castro; if it's possible to live an out gay life in more places around the country, what will that mean for Silver Lake? LGBT folks are arguably the most integrated in San Francisco of any city in the United States, but the city struggles to support institutions designed to serve us, such as health clinics and community centers. Gay people are still getting sick and facing discrimination, even in San Francisco, but an activist friend who's moved here from New York City feels that while LGBTs have more clout, are more integrated into the city as a whole, there are fewer resources specifically devoted to our needs. Our friendships were a form of family, but if we can make family through marriage, through child-rearing, won't our sense of community diminish? Hasn't it already, as we glare at each other across the stroller parked in the entranceway of the gay community center?

But we don't talk about it. Okay, we do, in private, but not in the big public way of talking that leads to books and articles, or even blogs. We don't talk about it because we are all pro-choice feminists now. Pro-choice across the board, as Katha Pollitt explains: "These days, feminism's motto is 'You go, girl!' Anything is feminist as long as you 'choose' it. In fact, it's unsisterly, patronizing, infantilizing, and sexist to question another woman's decision on any subject, no matter how dangerous or silly or servile or self-destructive it is; she is the capital of her soul and that's all you need to know. There's no social context and no place to stand and resist; there's just a menu of individual options and preferences."

So we might, and do, carp about how all these individual choices change the landscape we're navigating; we might mutter about how our friends from ACT-UP deserted us the moment we had kids, or, conversely, feel that what held us together was a climate of erotic tension now undermined by the gay baby boom. But we do so under our breath.

Or maybe these tensions bubble up to the surface in the discussion on gay marriage. The fears about assimilation, about becoming like, um, *them*. Seen this way, the vehemence makes sense to me. Because I'm worried, too. Marriage is a big hungry ancient beast. Not unchanging as the right would have it, but maybe bigger than we are. Will we be able to "queer" it the way we've queered Shakespeare? If we can get married, will this beast eat us alive and make us all straight?

I'm brought back to the knot by Alisa Solomon, whose call for a radical revisiting of the marriage battles shines with a generous and nonjudgmental spirit. In an email exchange on gay marriage, she suggests we fight for a fairer vision for all rather than what she dubs "'me, too' privileges." Shouldn't we untie some of what's knotted together: marriage as a civil right from marriage as a part of religious experience? Healthcare as a right for all, regardless of marital or employment status?

Sounds good to me. It also seems like you don't have to choose your battles, you can do both. But can all the legal benefits of marriage be distributed through other means? Aren't some, particularly in regard to parenting or inheritance issues, inherently relational? If I were going to bet on what I might live to see, full federal benefits for same-sex partners or a truly universal healthcare plan, I'd first say I doubt I'll see either but give the former a slight edge. No happiness in that bet; universal healthcare would help more, no doubt.

Do we have to wait till we have a just society before advocating for ourselves? Although the marriage equality battle is frequently dismissed as only a concern of white gay men, wouldn't it be poor gay people who would benefit most? Doesn't it make much more sense to fight for expanding marriage rather than fighting dozens of battles for the various rights and benefits, as some advocate? So it's not perfect. Big deal. Isn't the Dream Act worth fighting for, even if it doesn't help all undocumented immigrants? Every year I sign up for my healthcare knowing that so many people go without, but what good would it do them if I didn't take care of this? These are questions, not gotchas.

Alisa and her partner got married many years ago, long before DOMA was even passed. Okay, that's my word for it; she and Marilyn eschew the term and wouldn't have had the celebration at all if the state were involved. I can easily see her at an anti-Prop 8 rally, even if she is not eager for marriage itself. She says, "I wouldn't have wanted to eat the food at Woolworth's, but I sure hope I would have joined the sit-in." I hope I would have been there, too. When she mentions the food, I can smell the grilled cheese. The kind you can only get on a commercial grill, greasy, dipped in ketchup and why not have fries with that, and a Coke while you're at it. I'm not sure what this hunger says about me; perhaps I'm in the habit of being contrary. I don't know if I would have the guts to sit down, but I know I would have had the grilled cheese.

III

We've talked about doing it. Getting married. Or whatever you want to call it. More than once during the past sixteen years we've said, "Let's do it." But we quickly get tripped up by a tangle of competing desires, deeply rooted fears. We can't get past what to wear. That's always the first question that comes up, before what kind of ceremony we'll have, where we'll do it, who will be there. Before we think what the whole thing means there's the question of what to wear. Which does not take the form of a question; it takes the form of a statement by Esther: "I'm not wearing a suit." She say's she's butch, she's not a man, an announcement that feels well rehearsed, like she's said it a thousand times before, and perhaps she has, but not to me. She is drawing a bright line dividing the category butch from that of man, and I am wondering, who in the hell is this person? What happened to the person I met sixteen years ago, the one whose every gesture seemed designed to blur the roles of man and woman, to write her own story called butch on top of, around, over, and beyond the old myths? Why is she going back and redrawing the lines in black ink? Where is the person who ended the first date by telling me, "I have a truck. Next time, maybe you'd like a ride"?

She'd dress up a little, but basically she wants to be comfortable. I think that part of the point is being a bit uncomfortable. Making a public commitment after all this time isn't as risky as it might have been earlier on, but it's still a leap of some sort. It shouldn't look like every other day of your life. It shouldn't look like it happened on the way to the Agway, you shouldn't wear brown corduroy. I don't know what I will wear, but you can bet two things: It won't be white and it won't go with brown corduroy.

I joke that we could have separate but adjacent weddings. I guess it's a joke.

I marry Esther quickly, secretly, when she isn't looking. When she is sitting in her office, in her comfortable clothes. Facebook makes it easy: There are only two choices that come close to fitting: "married" or "it's complicated." I flirt with the latter when I create my account. But then I decide it isn't, not really. It's not that complicated. Not today. We're married.

People notice. My Facebook friends chime in with "When did you get married?" With jokes edged with a bitter shine: You can't get married. But it's a public space, Facebook; we have had a public ceremony of sorts. In other places and times that was enough. You didn't need to have more of a ceremony; all that was required was that some man said: "I'm married." I'm that man.

I don't tell her. She finds out later. Shouldn't we have talked about this? I used her name. I'm Borat, tossing a bag over Pamela Anderson with a muttered "Consent not necessary."

But I say we have talked about it, we agreed. We just haven't done anything about it. I didn't feel like I was making a claim, I was stating a fact. Married happened to us, like the rain, overnight; we woke up and there were puddles everywhere. I'm just reporting on what happened. But I don't look at her when I say this. Marrying someone when they are not looking is not the same as deciding to take the garbage out even though it's her turn. I do not say, "I'm married to you whether you know it or not." But I do say, "You can decide what you want to say on Facebook. You don't have to say you're married. It's complicated."

Gay Marriage, Semantics, and a Fallen Bridge

Rachel Darling

In December of 2005, I married the love of my life in Toronto. Why elope from Minneapolis to someplace even more frigid? Because gay marriage isn't legal at home (and our warmer neighbor, Iowa, wasn't an option yet). After five years of loving commitment, buying a house together, and blending our families, Kimberly and I would finally get recognition somewhere, dammit. So we flew up to the even-colder tundra.

As soon as we landed in Canada, things were different. Customs grilled us with the standard questions—what did you bring, where will you stay, how long must we tolerate you—but the crusty agent saved the best for last: "Why are you here?" We beamed and burst out with, "We're here to get married!"

Our interrogator softened. She rolled her eyes as she said, "I don't know *why* they won't let you do that at home." She didn't smile (no Minnesota-nice here), but she might as well have pulled us into a hug. That validation from a government official—yes, it was just Customs, but she wore a badge so I count it—made Kimberly and me feel like more of a real couple than we felt back at home. And this was just the airport. O Canada, screw Minnesota-nice: I'll take your politics any day.

The Canadian lovefest continued at Toronto's City Hall, where we applied for our marriage license. Filling out the paperwork, we clenched non-writing hands and cried. They were letting us do this.

Next, we had to find someone to marry us. In Canada, same-sex couples can't be refused a license, but they can be refused a ceremony by homophobic officiants. And there were plenty of those on the list of names we got from City Hall. After being turned down by several of the various faiths (secular ones, too), we finally found a nice elderly rabbi who would accommodate two nice shiksas. Aaron Zimmerman said he'd do it the following afternoon at three, and told us where to reserve space for the ceremony. His hearing was poor, and Kimberly asked him several times, "You know we're both women, right?"

The ceremony had its quirks. First there was our chapel room, rented sight-unseen. The space was putrid—dimly lit, dirty beige, no windows. And then there were the odd witnesses we got for an extra forty dollars: the rabbi's tense, fidgety wife and their eccentric niece (friendly, but overly so, and too clingy for a stranger). And worse, Rabbi Aaron ended up being a little homophobic after all. When pronouncing us legally wed, he parenthetically slipped in, "You know, really you're companions." And then, "You won't be having children, will you?"

Did he really just say that? Yes. Kimberly and I locked mortified eyes, nodded along with him mechanically, and silently agreed to forget that part ever happened. But despite everything, the day couldn't have been more perfect. We were married. Legally.

When we got home, life felt different. Very different. With this new recognition, albeit foreign-only, came a sense of peace. Our connection was suddenly more definable, and in turn stronger. "We're married," I could say, and everyone would know who Kimberly is to me: The woman I cherish. The one I've committed my future to.

I had been quietly out as a lesbian for almost twenty years, at gradually increasing degrees: first to friends, then family, then at work, then at school (where I returned in my early thirties). But when I came back from Toronto as a married woman, I morphed into one of those in-your-face and way-out-loud types. "I'm gay, I got married, and you're gonna hear about it!" Homophobia didn't scare me anymore; we were married.

I flexed my moxie nonstop. At get-to-know-you icebreakers when I started a new semester of classes, I frequently and proudly told my wedding story. Even better, I was able to jump into fiery debates on gay marriage in my poli-sci class.

Over time, though, that charge weakened. My just-married shtick didn't come up in conversations with friends anymore. And I'd started qualifying my "I'm married" status with "legally in Canada." The "legally" was meant to add credibility, but the qualification—by its very nature—probably did the opposite.

Another thing: Though we were now married, I kept calling Kimberly my "partner," not my wife. The *W* word, which Kimberly said she'd prefer, didn't feel natural to me. I'm reluctant to mimic straight people—or even appear to be mimicking them—for fear I'm denying my lesbian identity. Or maybe my own lingering homophobia—despite two decades of outness—made me feel unentitled to the privilege of the *W* word. Most likely, both issues got in my way. Baggage aside, *partner* just felt right for us. For me. Kimberly's more than a friend, and we're committed to each other. *Partner* was enough.

Well, it was enough until August 1, 2007. That's when the 35W bridge collapsed and almost killed her.

At 6:10 that evening, I came out of my neighborhood liquor store, got into my car, and listened to a new voice mail she'd just left on my cell: "Raaaachel? The fucking bridge fell. I'm in the river. Call me."

Kimberly and her friend Kelly were crossing the 35W in Kelly's Saturn (later marked as exhibit "B3" by the National Transportation and Safety Board) when they dropped 114 feet along with the center span into the Mississippi River. After the impact, they had to pull themselves out through the driver's-side window. They could easily have been two of the thirteen who were killed.

They suffered back injuries and shock, but walked away with their glass-covered bodies intact. They rode to the ER in a car, not an ambulance. They relived the terror all night long, but in their own beds at home, not in the hospital. Kimberly was so lucky. I was so lucky.

During the first week after the collapse, I hated leaving her side for class or work. The separation anxiety was so acute that even being in a different room of the house, let alone a different part of town, sent me into a panic.

While staggering through the aftermath, two of my casual acquaintances asked, with pointed hesitation, how my "friend" was. I'd come so close to losing Kimberly and she was still in such severe shock that this normally benign word sounded *threatening*. I felt like I was hanging on to her by a thread, and that word knocked the wind out of me. I could barely squeak out, "My *partner*, Kimberly, is doing okay. Thanks." But neither of those acquaintances acknowledged the difference. There was no "Ohhh, *partner*" or "Oh right." There was just "Uh-huh, uh-huh."

Where did my power go? I fantasized about taking these people by the shoulders, staring into their eyes, shaking them, and shrieking that I did not almost lose a *friend*.

We're *married*, dammit!

These people knew who Kimberly was to me, but didn't know how to refer to her. Maybe they were trying to be respectful, thinking that by fully acknowledging our relationship they might invade my privacy. But privacy wasn't what I needed. Recognition was.

We're married, dammit.

It's so blatantly wrong that same-sex couples can't marry in most U.S. states. It's wrong for a lot of reasons, and the bridge collapse taught me a new one: The current state of marriage law creates too much room for ambiguity. People shouldn't have to give a second thought about how to refer to my mate.

We're married, dammit.

I don't want to mimic straight-married couples. Except when it comes to all the rights they get. Oh, and the clear-cut recognition of their relationships—I'll take that, too. Especially after a catastrophe. When I'm fragile. When the last thing I need to worry about is defining who it is I almost lost: The woman I cherish. The one I've committed my future to. My *wife*.

It took awhile for me to get comfortable with that word. It took almost losing Kimberly. But now it feels right. Doesn't *wife* have a nice ring to it? I think so. And here in Minnesota, we're all about nice.

Marching Our Way to the Aisle

On the previous page:

Barn-door brides Hannah Washington (left) and Lizzie Gordon at their Bristol, Vermont, wedding.
Photo by Sara Franco.

Maxine (left) and Joanne Measham-Richards were married at St. Audries Park, a country house in Somerset, U.K., on May 16, 2010, after having been together for ten years. This photograph was taken just before the ceremony. "I was opening a box of pins to put Maxine's flowers on her suit," says Joanne. "We were so happy to see each other after a morning apart getting ready." Of the rest of the day, she reports, "We walked each other down the aisle and gave ourselves away to each other; we jumped the broom; and then we held a surprise drum circle. I always wanted to drum in my wedding dress!"
Photo by Mike Lacey, Platinum Wedding Photos, platinumweddingphotos.co.uk.

As the Girl Turns

∴

Amelia Sauter

As the GIRL turNS...
Globe
by amelia Sauter
She was young. And restless. In need of a guiding light. But even as a small child, she was sure of one thing:
Boys have cooties.
1970
That girl was ME. Later, when I grew up, HORDES* of men asked for my hand in marriage.
Marry Me!!!
No.
*three men, actually.
No way. Not for me. No.
No. No. No. No
NOPE.
Just no.
UNTIL...

1996
I fell for a girl.
Leah →
Hi.
And I fell hard.
My life turned upside down.
Oh! I'm a lesbian!
SOON we shared everything:
a house
a bank account
P-Town
Beer
baseball hats
a car
three cats (of course)
BUT–we couldn't get married. Not legally.

2001
A year after Vermont created civil unions, we decided to register ourselves as partners, or as we liked to say, "lifers."
ROAD TRIP!!
Vermont→
←Massachusetts
We assumed civil unions would be overturned.
Let's be a part of history while we can!
conservative Backlash

CIVIL UNION
form thing
sign here
X
X
16th of july 2001
We also assumed we'd just be signing a piece of paper.
Quill pen
We told ourselves it was no big deal.
Yay! A wedding!
It's no big deal
I called my friend Michelle.
Awesome, Sis! I'm coming!
It's no big deal
Leah called her brother.

We met for lunch at the Blue Benn Diner in Bennington...
...wearing shorts and t-shirts.
veil
Michelle brought a veil. I loved it! (I'm a total romantic.)
Leah put it on and pretended she was making her First communion.
Ha Ha! ha! Ha!
No rings!
Duh.
We didn't think to buy rings, since it was no big deal.

Ends up we said traditional vows on the back porch of a justice of the peace.
'Til death do us part...
Waaah'.
And it was a really
BIG DEAL.
The day raised so many questions:
Are we married or what?
Does it matter to us what other people think?
If gay marriage is legalized, would we do this again?
Should we have invited people?
?
when does it count as real?
I found it all confusing.

A year later, an anniversary card arrived from my mom.
Mum+Pop
But we've been together SIX years!
HAPPY ONE YEAR Anniver-sary
Maybe marriage is stupid.
HOM GAY HOM
NOW I really wanted to get married.
Really, really badly.

2004
A couple years later, after we moved to Ithaca, we joined 25 other couples in suing the State of New York for the right to marry...
other homos
We'd like a marriage license.
city clerk
I'm sorry.
I wish I could.
united straights of america...
...and we LOST.
we appealed and lost again.

2011
After fifteen years, we stopped letting ourselves dream about a wedding.
Go to Canada. Or Massachusetts.
But we should be able to get married here!
Not like that will ever happen.
And then SUDDENLY, gay marriage became LEGAL in New York.
Holy crap.
Um, should we get married?
Uh, I guess so?

STAY TUNED!
Will Amelia get a romantic wedding and a reason to buy a pair of awesome new shoes?
Will Leah's cynicism take center stage?
Wedding planning is a pain in the ass!
What the hell am I going to wear?
Will marriage ever become legal in the entire US of A?
To be continued on As the GIRL TURNS...
amelia sauter 2011

Marriage by the Numbers

∴

M. V. Lee Badgett

Ten: number of countries allowing same-sex couples to marry
Six: number of states allowing same-sex couples to marry, plus the District of Columbia
91,358: number of same-sex couples in those states (2010 Census)

I'm an economist. It's a profession known as the "dismal science," at least partly because of the rather dismal view of human nature common to many of those in it. Economists tend to believe that individuals are mainly out for themselves, with little regard for other people's well-being. Under those circumstances, who would see economists as romantic, or even emotional, about events like weddings?

And yet weddings have played a huge role in my professional life. Much of my research over the past fifteen years has focused on the economic impact of allowing same-sex couples to marry. Here's the idea: The wedding industry reports that the average wedding in the United States cost about $24,000 in 2010. Multiply that figure by the hundreds of thousands of gay couples who would marry if they could. You're looking at billions of dollars tossed up for grabs like a wedding bouquet, caught by whichever states reach to claim them.

That money has made businesses, and even policymakers (who see tax dollars), pay heed to same-sex couples demanding the freedom to marry. So my work has come to the attention of those debating gay marriage, and I've been asked to testify about my research in state legislatures, and in federal court during the Prop 8 trial in California.

During a sabbatical in 2003–2004, I decided to explore how Dutch same-sex couples dealt with being the first in the world to have the option of marriage. Shortly after my partner, Elizabeth, and I arrived in the Netherlands—and much to our surprise—the Supreme Judicial Court of our home state of Massachusetts ruled that same-sex couples must be allowed to marry. At that point, my research became much more politically relevant and personally charged; we had to decide whether *we* would marry when we returned home.

3,180: number of same-sex couples marrying in Massachusetts between May 17 and June 30, 2004

Twelve: number of months it took from the court decision in Massachusetts to our decision to get married

I had begun my interviews with Dutch couples as an economist, looking for clues that might illuminate economic theories about marriage. But most of the couples told me that economic reasons had little or nothing to do with their decisions. Instead, love, commitment, and public support were the main factors guiding their decisions to marry. The stories I heard from the lesbian couples in particular—who grappled with feminist concerns about marriage, disagreements with partners, and interactions with family—resonated with some of my own concerns.

Back at our apartment overlooking an old canal in Amsterdam, Elizabeth and I pondered our marriage options. We talked about what our coupled friends were planning to do (it turned out that almost all married before we even returned home) and what I had heard from the couples I interviewed and from other married same-sex couples we met. We listed the practical reasons to marry. We thought about commitment. We explored what it might mean for our financial lives. Once, we even cried over our inability to decide.

In spite of that intense effort to make a choice one way or the other, the actual moment that we decided to get married remains murky. While finishing my book back in the United States, I had a humbling experience akin to "Economist, analyze thyself": I was making dinner with Elizabeth and told her how my chapter on couples' processing their decision to marry was emerging. She made some good suggestions. Then she looked me in the eye and said, "You don't know why *I* wanted to get married, do you?"

After an awkward pause, I admitted that I didn't. "Well, you always joke to other people that it's to get healthcare benefits," I said. "But I know that's not the real reason, since you didn't need to be covered on my policy."

"I wanted to because *you* wanted to," Elizabeth said. She had never felt particularly strongly about marrying; she didn't see the need for it. But she loved me, and if I wanted to marry she was willing.

I didn't remember trying to persuade her, but then we re-created the actual decision-making conversation: We had been sitting at our kitchen table when I said, "I think we should get married." And Elizabeth had responded, "Okay, let's get married."

That was the last thing we agreed on for a while with respect to our wedding. Elizabeth's vision was a small ceremony in our living room with a close friend or two in attendance—reflecting the personal and practical meaning of marriage to her. I argued that we should at least invite our families (legally recognized kin as well as chosen family). One of the best things about marriage from my perspective is that it creates a new legal family tie, and having our friends and family witness our commitment would help sustain that mutual bond.

Two: number of times I had to paint our downstairs bathroom in the week or so before the wedding (the first go-round was a color disaster)
Two: number of times Elizabeth had to transplant new flowers outside our back door before the wedding
Two: number of pre-wedding meltdowns (one each)

Somehow we ended up with ninety-three people celebrating in our backyard. (*Number of exes in attendance? Let's just say both sides were represented.*) Our remaining parents at that point, her mother and my father, were in attendance along with almost all of the other people important to us. In addition to reciting our vows and intentions, we spoke about our reasons for getting married: to celebrate our love and affirm our commitment to one another in the context of a public recognition of our relationship by those present and by the Commonwealth of Massachusetts. Several friends later told me that they had never heard people say *why* they were getting married in a ceremony until they heard ours. And I'm told there wasn't a dry eye in the backyard; I think that ceremony was the only thing I've ever written that made people cry.

One of my favorite parts was at the conclusion, when we each, in rough accord with Jewish tradition, broke a glass (actually, two well-covered lightbulbs). Our friend Dennis, a justice of the peace who officiated, read our explanation:

> Like any good symbol, this one comes with a variety of interpretations. Some say that it commemorates the destruction of the Second Temple in Jerusalem. Some say it is a reminder that, even in times of great joy, there is still pain and suffering in the world. Some say that it's meant to remind us of the fragility of love. Lee and Elizabeth suggest that, in their case, it represents a healthy shattering of an exclusionary tradition. Whatever the interpretation, once they break the glass, it is the symbolic finish to the wedding, and your job is to shout, '*Mazel tov!*'
>
> A great cheer went up, and the celebration began.

∴

Two: number of my cousins who declined to attend because the idea of two women marrying offended their religious beliefs (Even these reactions weren't totally negative, though: One wanted to meet Elizabeth if we ever had a family reunion, and the other gave Elizabeth a big hug the next time she saw her.)

Three: number of sweet and supportive letters I got from the older generation of my conservative Southern family that made me cry

Elizabeth and I ended up exhausted but happy after our fabulous wedding party. And the ritual marked the beginning of something, not the end.

We just celebrated the sixth anniversary of our wedding, which roughly coincides with the thirteenth anniversary of our first date. Because of my travel for work, we ended up being in different countries on the official anniversary this year, so we observed it a couple of days early. We both agree that we're still happy to be married. Whatever our individual reasons were for deciding, we now think it made a positive difference in how we feel about each other and our relationship.

While the biggest impact of getting married has been an emotional one, I've also learned a lot more about what happens when same-sex couples are allowed to marry. On the economic side, our local florist, liquor store, and party rental shop got some business from us, just as I have predicted will happen in states that open marriage to same-sex couples. But the most interesting lesson for me was more personal and political.

While our family members—including both conservative religious Southerners and liberal secular Northerners—certainly aren't a representative sample of Americans, their nearly unanimous support for our marriage suggests to me that things are changing quickly. People want to be supportive of their family members, although they might still disagree on the political and religious desirability of opening marriage to same-sex couples. Yet they can recognize and understand what weddings mean for same-sex couples and their families, and they see the similarity to their own marriages. It makes me believe that someday soon our painful public debate on this issue will calm down, and the hardest decision for same-sex couples and their wedding guests will then be what to wear . . . and how much to spend.

$7,400: average cost of a wedding for a Massachusetts gay couple
$5,000: our original budget—of course we went over that, but we just had to hire my guitar teacher's gypsy jazz band to play!

Until then, I'll continue to answer policymakers' questions with my predictions about the economic gains to state budgets, local businesses, and same-sex couples from allowing those couples to marry. But I know from my own experience that behind every million dollars are hundreds of happy couples and a thousand smiles of support from friends and family. The true value of marriage—the love and commitment between two people, the support of a community, and the creation of legally recognized families—can't be measured with dollar signs.

The First Brides

A Conversation with
Kate Kendell and Phyllis Lyon

Move over Gertrude Stein and Alice B. Toklas—Phyllis Lyon and Del Martin are *the* legendary lesbians of twentieth-century California history. Together for fifty-six years, until Martin's death at age eighty-seven in 2008, they were among the founders of the first U.S. lesbian organization, Daughters of Bilitis, and edited its newsletter, *The Ladder*. They also cowrote the definitional book *Lesbian/Woman* in 1972, just as the lesbian-feminist liberation movement took off in the United States.

Phyllis and Del were also the first women to legally marry in

California. Twice, actually: first during a brief window of opportunity in San Francisco initiated by the city's then-mayor Gavin Newsom (those marriages were soon invalidated). And then four years later when same-sex marriage became all-too-briefly legal again, thanks to a California Supreme Court decision (this time the marriages remained valid).

We met with Phyllis, now eighty-seven, in the hillside home she shared with Del for more than fifty years in San Francisco. Joining her, in a conversation moderated by *Here Come the Brides* editors Audrey Bilger and Michele Kort, was lawyer Kate Kendell, a key figure in the same-sex marriage movement as executive director of the National Center for Lesbian Rights. Kate, a longtime friend of the couple, sat in Del's old chair in front of the picture window that overlooks San Francisco Bay—the window the couple used to cover with a curtain in the '50s when lesbian friends wanted to dance in their upstairs loft. We won't include *all* the "laughter" notes in the transcript; just know that it ensued frequently while the sharp-witted Phyllis reminisced.

Audrey Bilger: Was marriage even on the horizon in 1945 when you bought this house?

Phyllis Lyon: Oh, heavens no.

AB: So what was it like to have lived through these changes?

PL: It was kind of weird, if you ask me. *[laughter]* We were married twice.

Michele Kort: Which was the ceremony during which you cried like a baby, Kate?

Kate Kendell: The first one. [*Phyllis laughs*] When I started at NCLR in

1994, obviously I knew who Phyllis and Del were; I had met them. And then I started seeing them socially—at events, of course, but I would also come up and bring lunch, and we would talk. I would mostly just ask questions and hear stories, and sometimes ask their advice.

When we got the call from Gavin Newsom's office saying he was planning on issuing marriage licenses to same-sex couples, it was completely out of the blue. We had talked at NCLR about whether we would want to bring a marriage case in California, but it was at least a couple of years off. We just didn't feel like the court was ready; we wanted to do more public education work. We did not expect Gavin to change that plan. I had never met him—had you, Phyllis?

PL: I don't think so. I think we voted for him because he was cuter [than the other candidate].

[Boisterous laughter.]

KK: He is definitely more gorgeous than your average handsome guy. I mean, there are good-looking people, and then there are people about whom even the lesbians say *Whoah!*

PL: But he's also very smart. And he does great things.

KK: He decided that he wanted to do something about discrimination against same-sex couples after George W. Bush, in his State of the Union address, mentioned support of a federal marriage amendment. I think it infuriated the mayor to have the president take time for this from the State of the Union—I mean, we were at war in Iraq! So he came back and said to his staff, as it was later reported to me, "Let's do something about this." We initially tried to talk them out of it because we felt like it was too soon. We felt like it was a provocative thing to do.

PL: That's right, we didn't want to do it. We didn't want it to happen.

KK: I was nervous. But it only took me about twenty-four hours to get on board. We checked with our colleagues in Massachusetts, we talked to some of our other national colleagues, and I had a lot of conversations with my legal director, Shannon Minter. We came to the conclusion that in civil rights struggles there's a moment when you say, "Game on." Where you just . . .

PL: . . . start.

KK: The strategy can't just be dictated by *you* anymore. That's happened many times, where you just have an ally come out of nowhere, really. They decide *they're* going to take it on.

PL: We thought they were crazy.

KK: Newsom's chief of staff made clear to me, "Well, that's really nice, Kate, your input, but I just want to be clear: Next week, the mayor's going to begin issuing marriage licenses to same-sex couples." So by Sunday night—this was a Friday—we were all in. Monday morning, we met with the staff, the mayor. We got it all worked out, gave him a whole bunch of materials so he could get up to speed on marriage cases. And then we pretty much decided that Thursday would be the day.

PL: And they pretty much decided Del and I were going to be the couple . . .

KK: Well, Newsom's office asked, "Who should be . . ."

PL: . . . without asking us.

[Laughter]

AB: This is how Phyllis and Del were asked to be married?

KK: I know, isn't it romantic? Somebody on Newsom's staff said, "Well, who should be the first couple?" And I think Joyce Newstat, the policy director of the mayor's office, and I looked at each other and immediately had the same thought: "It's gotta be Del Martin and Phyllis Lyon." And everybody was like, "Brilliant! Of course that's right." And so then I called—*then* I called. Phyllis answered the phone; do you remember the conversation?

PL: Not really, but I think I must have said, "You've gotta be kidding. What are you talking about?"

[Laughter]

PL: "Nuts. What have you been drinking?"

KK: Well, I began the conversation by saying that you and Del have done so much for the movement. And you know how much I love you and how much I admire the two of you, and I know that, at this point, you should be able to just sit back.

PL: And I said, "What do you want?"

[Laughter.]

KK: I said, "Well, I do have one more thing to ask you. The mayor's going to begin issuing marriage licenses to same-sex couples beginning Thursday morning. And I want to know if you and Del will be the first couple to get married." And what you said to me at that moment . . . I think you just said: "Oh hell."

And then you said, "All right. Well, let me ask Del." And you put down the phone and about two or three minutes later, you came back and said, "Okay, we'll do it."

PL: Yeah, I don't think she was any happier about it than I was.

[Laughter]

KK: So you agreed to do it more out of a sense of duty?

PL: Yeah, well, we thought maybe that could be a good thing for gays and lesbians. All right, so we'll do it! Damn it. We never wanted to get married. Didn't think we would be doing that, never thought it would happen in our lifetime.

MK: But did you ever think when you were younger, "Oh, I wish we could get married"? I mean, was that part of lesbian yearnings back then?

PL: No. You think of those things more as a kind of religious-something.

KK: It felt very, I think, conformist.

PL: One of those straight things.

KK: Because I know you were feminists [Phyllis and Del were very active in the National Organization for Women] every bit as much as you were lesbians. And the feminists weren't very happy about marriage. I mean, it was pretty much an article of faith of feminism that marriage was not good for women as a general matter.

PL: Because they were marrying men!

[Laughter]

KK: To support marriage, particularly for lesbian feminists, was to ape patriarchy. That's certainly what I thought about marriage for a very long time.

PL: It was old and weird.

MK: So when you went off to ask Del, did you say, "Del, will you marry me on Thursday?"

PL: I said something like, "Hey, honey, do you want to get married?" And she said, "Huh?" So I said, "Well, they've got this idiot thing that's going on," and blah blah blah blah blah, "and they want us to do it." And so we decided we would.

KK: So it wasn't very romantic.

PL: No, it wasn't very romantic.

MK: But how did it feel once you did it?

PL: Well, it didn't feel any different.

KK: After fifty-four years, it really wouldn't.

PL: And how long did it last [the first marriage]? Because we got married again.

KK: It was six months before the court invalidated those marriage licenses. And many couples knew that going in—that this was as much for the principle as the actual expression of commitment to each other. But it was a very emotional morning. Even now I think about it and, oh my God, my heart starts racing. Adrenaline was just coursing. We knew it was historic. And when we finally got Phyllis and Del married and the city treasurer said, "I now pronounce you spouses for life" and they kissed and hugged, I totally lost it.

PL: Gavin was going to conduct the ceremony himself, but he got talked out of it.

KK: He decided that it would be better if he didn't marry couples, given that there was going to be litigation and it might play out that he was just grandstanding. It would take away from the real, larger point he was trying to make. He wanted marriage for everyone. He wanted it as a point of equality. It wasn't really a political ploy as much as making a statement that this is the right thing to do.

PL: And the thing that's hysterical, looking back on it, is that Kate picks us up in the morning at some ungodly hour, we put on the best clothes we had—which were suits we had gotten very recently—and galloped off with her. And then she parks across the street from

City Hall and then we go up the stairs. That was a while ago, so Del could still go up the stairs. And then we had to go a block through the city . . .

KK: It was even more!

PL: . . . I mean, through the City Hall to get to the other end of it, which is where the registrar's office was. Then we had to sit down and fill out all this stuff for your license. They wanted to know information about our parents. And Del couldn't remember her Dad's name because he wasn't much in her life.

KK: They gave you *family planning information*! I was like, well, you never know about that, Del.

[Laughter.]

PL: So anyhow, we finally got through all that, and then we got married.

KK: It took a long time, though—a good three hours at least. The registrar had to change the language on the form. They wanted to make sure that everything was correct, because this was not play-acting. Everyone was very serious—they realized it was going to be a challenge, but they wanted to do this, they wanted it to stick.

PL: Everything I put on my form was wrong, but they didn't know.

KK: And there's a fee for your marriage license. I paid your fee, which I loved doing.

PL: That's a good thing, because we thought that we wouldn't need money.

KK: And then we borrowed rings from the *San Francisco Chronicle* photographer. Because it was not as if this had been planned and all the details had been taken care of.

PL: Well, we actually had rings, but I think Del's was broken, or mine was. So we borrowed rings. We were all standing there. We were married. Kate brings us home. We come upstairs. We're all dressed up. We're looking out the window and we said, "Well, what the hell do we do now?"

And Del says, "I'm hungry." And I said, "Well, why don't we go to lunch?" So we went down to Delancey Street Restaurant. I have no idea what we ate, but I remember thinking as we walked in how strange it was that we'd just done this thing and nobody knew it.

KK: Nobody knew it *yet*. The press was just starting to report on it.

PL: And so, anyhow, we had lunch, and then we came home. Took our clothes off. I mean, we got out of those suits and got into jeans or something. [*laughter*]

MK: Did you get married then, too, Kate?

KK: No, no.

PL: She just made everybody else get married.

MK: Why not?

KK: Um, it felt too weird to be . . .

PL: *She* thought it was weird!

KK: . . . to be the lawyer who would be defending these marriages. It felt like almost a conflict of interest if I was also married. I didn't want my own marriage to be part of the lawsuit. I didn't feel that way once we won in court four years later, though. Sandy and I did get married then, even though we knew Prop 8 was going to be on the ballot. By then my job as the lawyer was pretty much done.

MK: How long had you and Sandy been together before 2004?

KK: Twelve years. When we finally got married, we'd been together sixteen years.

MK: Had you thought about getting married?

KK: My feeling about it was very cerebral. As a legal advocate for LGBT rights, I want couples and families to be entitled to the same protection, security, rights, benefits, and responsibilities as anyone else. My family already enjoys many protections, as we are privileged by all sorts of things—I have a law degree, we live in the Bay Area, Sandy's well-educated, and even though we're an interracial couple, racism isn't an issue that we experience daily. So, for me personally, marriage wasn't about rights, benefits, responsibilities—it was more about the commitment, demonstrating that this is the love of your life. I already felt that way, so I didn't feel like I needed to get married. I would say to Sandy, "Look, you know I can't love you any *more*."

But Sandy was more sentimental than I was about it—more in her heart and less in her head—and more interested in getting married. And as I got more and more involved in the advocacy, it became clearer to me how, when people could and did marry, something clearly shifted. Often their families felt differently about them, especially parents, who all of a sudden had a way to describe them—"my daughter-in-law," "my son's husband." Being able to have that common vocabulary made an enormous difference.

But the biggest difference, and the reason I'm glad we did get married in 2008, is our kids. They loved our wedding day every bit as much as we did. I think everybody should get married *after* they have children, when the children are old enough to be part of the experience.

AB: Well, Phyllis, when you got married for a second time, was it different for you than the first time?

PL: I guess we were more into getting married the second time than we had been the first. We had practiced.

[Laughter.]

AB: Were you defiant because your first marriage had been dissolved, and now here was another chance?

PL: No, I don't think it was our idea to get married again. Somebody else came up and said we should get married.

KK: I think I said, "Do you want to get married where it really will be legal? Where no one can take it away?" And you were both interested in doing that.

PL: The first time was like, "Huh?" The next time was, "Oh."

KK: It ended up being a big celebration at City Hall this time, with the mayor performing the marriage.

PL: Bless his heart.

KK: In 2008, we knew that marriages could be stopped for future couples, but they couldn't be taken away from the couples who were getting married. And, you know, I was feeling a little bit more of Del's vulnerability, physically. [She was in a wheelchair.]

PL: Yeah.

KK: If they wanted to get married and have it be legal—which felt like a culmination—I really wanted that to happen, and soon. And it was great—I mean, City Hall . . . it was the biggest bank of cameras I've ever walked out to in my life. They were the first couple married in California.

AB: What's really clear is that because you and Del were the first both times, this was a political action as well as a personal ceremony.

PL: We were very much into political action.

KK: Yeah, it wasn't just a marriage for its own sake. There are still times when I'll be speaking at a college campus or somewhere and somebody will invariably say, "I don't know what the big deal is with same-sex couples getting married, because I remember when that sweet old lesbian couple got married. I remember seeing their pictures and I thought, 'Who would be afraid of *them*?'"

[Phyllis's laugh is the loudest.]

AB and MK: Awwwwww.

MK: So, Kate, what was your wedding like?

KK: It was, uh, it was not that. *[Laughter.]* It was much more of a low-key affair. We were thick into the Prop 8 campaign. So it was on July 9, a Wednesday morning. A couple of my friends said, "Who gets married on a Wednesday morning?" *[Laughter.]* We got married in the mayor's office. Donna Hitchens, who founded NCLR, married us. Our kids were there and about thirty or forty friends, including Phyllis and Del. We had just a little reception at a friend's house, and then we went up overnight to Sonoma. One night. But we figured that after sixteen years together we didn't need a big honeymoon. I still look back on it—Sandy and our kids, too—as a day filled with as much continuous, nonstop joy as any other day in my life.

MK: Phyllis, how did Del feel about *your* marriage ceremony?

PL: I mean, we were both kind of like, let's just do it and get it over with.

KK: Get it over with. *[Laughs]*

PL: Well, we thought, all right, if it can help move things ahead, we'll do it, we'll do it. You can now see the suits we wore [to both weddings] at the gay historical museum in San Francisco. They insisted they had to get them. And I said, "Well, I'm still wearing mine!"

[Laughter.]

MK: Now do you have to call them up and say, "I've got an event tonight, can I come borrow the suit?"

PL: I hadn't thought about doing that, but . . .

MK: How did it feel to become a symbol for gay marriage?

PL: We were used to being out there—we had been involved and been out and open for a long time—so it wasn't like we were suddenly letting people know that we were lesbians, right? *[Laughter.]*

MK: You had long been considered the foremothers of lesbian rights, but now you were the foremothers of lesbian marriage, too.

PL: We figured, well, when we do it then people that really want to can do it, too. It seemed like it might be helpful.

KK: I think history will look back and say, wow, it made so much possible that marriage, the most conventional of issues, became such a huge headline. And so associated with LGBT equality.

MK: Do you think the Defense of Marriage Act will get taken down?

KK: I think all of this is just hanging by a thread. I think DOMA's going down, but I think it's still going to take longer than it should.

MK: What about the criticism some have made that the LGBT movement spent so much energy on gay marriage when there are other things to fight for?

KK: I get asked that question all the time, and I have a couple of answers. First, this isn't a zero-sum game. And what other issues are you talking about? Healthcare? We've been working on that. Immigration? We're working on that. Youth issues? We're working on that.

I feel like we've been able to do *more* in all of those areas because of the attention and the resources that marriage has brought. It turned a lot of unlikely donors and activists into donors and activists. When marriage became a headline issue . . .

PL: . . . they knew how it affected them.

KK: It brought many more people into the movement, and all of our issues, across the board, were lifted by that.

AB: It just seems like that tension for lesbians between conforming and assimilating or remaining different has been around for as long as you've been working in the movement.

PL: Yeah.

KK: I think marriage makes it possible to understand that yes, we have conventional, very traditional families—and then we have people crazy at Mardi Gras. I mean there is a spectrum, and the movement has to be about some notions of liberation so that people feel sexual freedom in addition to the freedom to be more conventional. My own experience has not borne out that working on marriage has been a distraction or diminished our resources and commitment to other issues.

PL: No, I don't think it has either. You've got all these different issues and marriage is one of them. And they all kind of merge together when you think about it.

MK: The movement has come a long way Phyllis, from the things you were fighting for all those years ago—like not being told you were crazy by the psychiatrists.

PL: *[Laughs]* Don't believe the psychiatrists!

MK: Or to be able to dress in men's clothes—you know, non-gender-normative clothes.

PL: The idea, I think, basically was: We're all the same. We just have different desires and different ways of looking at things. But we're all people. Treat us right and we'll treat you right.

Photo:
Kate Kendell (far left) celebrates the 2004 San Francisco wedding of Phyllis Lyon (with dark hair) and Del Martin. Photo by Liz Mangelsdorf, Corbis Images

Diary of a Love Warrior

∴

Davina Kotulski

JUNE 1998

"We're going to be late, come on!"

"Let me just make this sign." Molly takes a piece of construction paper and staples it onto a paint stick from Home Depot.

"Write Support Same-Sex Marriage," I say, always the bossy one. "Okay, let's go already."

We drive quickly to the BART station and march up the steps to the train. She's wearing a white wedding dress and I'm wearing a makeshift tuxedo that I picked up from a secondhand store in the

Haight-Ashbury district—a white shirt, black pants, black tuxedo jacket, red bow tie.

We are hurrying to San Francisco, where Molly parked her motorcycle, so we can ride in Dykes on Bikes at the San Francisco Pride parade. We rush out of the BART station and run to her bike. She starts it up and I jump on. We need to find the helmet truck so that we can ride down the parade route helmet-free. Molly drives up one block and down another.

Finally, I see it—a moving truck with the rear door rolled up and hundreds of helmets in the back. We drive fast to catch up with it, then pitch our helmets to the women in the back of the truck.

"Too late," one says, and a stream of cuss words race through my head.

Molly, a lawyer by trade, negotiates and wins. They agree to hold on to our helmets. We race toward the head of the parade route, barely making the lineup before the engines roar down Market Street.

The smiles and applause from the crowd are addictive.

"Congratulations!"

"What a beautiful couple!"

"Happy Wedding Day!"

I've never been congratulated for loving a woman before. Two months from now we are getting married. We're just getting a taste of wedded bliss, like the sampler you get when picking a wedding cake. And wedded bliss tastes good! When you look at the world with love, it looks back with love.

We end up on the cover of the *San Francisco Examiner*. Yes, our world is hungry for images of loving same-sex couples, and we can make a difference by sharing who we are and advocating for marriage equality.

SEPTEMBER 1998

It's a beautiful September evening. As I drive to our wedding location, the window of my Ford Ranger is rolled down and I sing, along with the radio, the song I am soon going to sing my bride down the aisle with: "It's Your Love," by Faith Hill and Tim McGraw.

I breathe deeply the sweet-smelling air of late summer, anchoring myself in that magical moment. Slowing down to turn a corner, I glimpse two deer grazing at the edge of the road. We have picked Wildwood Acres as our wedding site because it's deep in the oak-covered hills of Lafayette, California. We want to be surrounded by natural beauty when we make our commitment to one another.

I stand at the altar near an arch of sunflowers and red roses, facing 150 of our friends, coworkers, and family members. I smile nervously, then begin to sing. My bride appears arm-in-arm with her father, who looks proud. She walks down the aisle, and when she reaches me, her father releases her arm. I take her hand and she joins me in the chorus.

And if you wonder
About the spell I'm under
oh it's your love

We finish the song and then the officiant—our friend Shefali Tsabarry—welcomes our guests in her beautiful Indian accent:

> Female couples and male couples have always existed, proclaimed their love and dedication to one another for centuries, but their love and relationships have gone un-

acknowledged. They have been denied the legal and social recognition of marriage.

Shefali asks our guests to vow to support Molly and me through the good times and bad, and vow to help change the laws so that same-sex couples can have the recognition we deserve. She asks my family to stand and state that they agree to accept Molly into our family.

"We do," they affirm.

She asks Molly's family to stand and accept me into their family.

"We do," they echo.

Then Molly and I read our vows to one another.

"I now pronounce you wife and husband-wife," our officiant concludes, acknowledging my identification as "two-spirit."

We kiss. Our guests stand and applaud. We waltz down the aisle as two friends sing the "Wedding Day Waltz." What could be more perfect for a couple who found true love in a gay honky-tonk?

We honeymoon in Hawaii, hoping to return there in spring to get legally married, since the Hawaiian Supreme Court had ruled that it's discriminatory to ban same-sex marriages. But a constitutional amendment would take away that hope only months after our wedding.

FEBRUARY 2001–FEBRUARY 2003

On February 12, 2001, I dress in a tuxedo and a pink ruffled shirt while Molly puts on a wedding dress. Then we drive to San Francisco City Hall. Lambda Legal had declared a National Freedom to Marry Day, so we want to affirm our love and render visible the discrimination that same-sex couples experience at marriage-license counters around the world.

Like the different-sex couples everyone sees openly expressing their affection and commitment, we want to show that same-sex love is just as beautiful, committed, and tender. We also want to declare at that license counter that we are worthy of equal treatment under law.

So we ask at City Hall for a marriage license. And we're denied. It hurts; Molly cries. But I vow to come back every year until we are issued a license. And we do, in 2002 and 2003. Then, on February 12, 2004, our dream begins to poke through the veil.

Journal Entry, February 11, 2004

Last night, Mayor Gavin Newsom stated on the news that he believes same-sex couples should have marriage licenses, and he wants to give them out in San Francisco.

Journal Entry, February 12, 2004

Today we will stand before Nancy Alfaro, the San Francisco City Clerk, for the fourth time and ask for a marriage license. I am hopeful that today she will give us a license and we can begin pursuing a lawsuit. If not, we will go to Oakland and Berkeley sometime in the next few months and ask for marriage licenses there. Then we will go to Massachusetts where, God willing, licenses will be given. I'm going to read Martin Luther King Jr.'s letter from a Birmingham jail now: "We know through painful experience that freedom is never voluntarily given by the oppressor, it must be demanded by the oppressed."

Alright, I'm off to go get it.

LATER THAT DAY

I get into my truck around 10 AM and haul WE ALL DESERVE THE FREEDOM TO MARRY signs to San Francisco City Hall. There are already lots of camera crews when I arrive. I see my bride once again in her wedding dress, and we hold hands and cross the street together.

Del Martin and Phyllis Lyon walk out of City Hall waving a piece of paper. As the news breaks, camera crews and reporters descend on Molly and me. "What happened?" they ask. I burst into tears and tell them about Del and Phyl, who had been together for more than fifty years, and how they were finally legally married. It feels overwhelming.

At this point, we begin the rally. California Assembly member Mark Leno steps up to the podium and announces that he has just introduced the first-ever marriage equality bill into the state legislature that morning. Molly takes the stage and sings, "The Times They Are a-Changin'." Then we go inside City Hall, through the metal detector, and walk hand-in-hand toward the clerk's office.

At the end of a long, narrow hallway is a rope barrier. Camera crews encircle us and a city official tells us to wait because they need to "change the form." An official finally comes up with one; it's blue, different from the white form we'd been denied in previous years. It contains a two-paragraph disclaimer: By marrying, we will jeopardize or lose our domestic partner rights. It also says our marriage licenses may not be recognized outside of San Francisco. We fill out the form anyway. They remove the rope and we're in.

The camera crews follow. We're given a number—sixty-nine. We chuckle. It also happens to be the year we were both conceived. We hand in our form, amazed that we haven't been turned away. The clerk helping us is smiling. He verifies the information and then gives us our form, our marriage license, and a family planning brochure that looks like something out of the 1950s.

"So it starts," one man in the crowd says.

I lock arms with Molly and we proceed back to the grand staircase in the rotunda. We ask Mark Leno if he will marry us. He asks if we have rings. I try unsuccessfully to remove mine, but it will not budge. Molly removes hers.

The ceremony is a blur. I do remember putting Molly's ring on the right finger but the wrong hand. The only other thing I remember, besides the flashing lights from the media that surrounds us, is when Mark said, "By the power vested in me from the state of California, I now pronounce you spouses for life."

I kiss Molly, then Mark. We're legally married. We hug our friends standing around us and rejoice. Then it's Brian and Ted's turn to be married, then Peter and Geoff, Shelly and Ellen, Alison and Heidi. Couple after couple show up at City Hall as people hear the reports that San Francisco is marrying same-sex couples. We don't leave until four thirty, when we go to celebrate at a restaurant with all the newlyweds and our exhausted single friends who have been snapping photos, rolling video, and signing as witnesses.

AUGUST 12, 2004

She's wearing a wedding dress and looking like a beautiful princess—a beautiful princess with a bullhorn, that is. We're marching down Market Street. They've just invalidated our marriage license. The California State Supreme Court said that Gavin Newsom overstepped his boundaries by issuing marriage licenses to same-sex couples.

SEPTEMBER 6, 2005

We're sitting in the balcony of the California State Capitol in Sacramento.

"All those wanting to vote, vote now. All those wanting to vote, vote now."

We need forty-one votes to win. The red numbers light up: 37, 38, 40.

"All those wanting to vote, vote now." Forty-one lights up red! The balcony erupts with screams. We're out of our seats, wild with excitement. Mark Leno's marriage equality bill has just passed in the assembly.

"Order, order!" Someone is banging a gavel and threatening to remove us all.

We sit down, try to stifle our joy.

Weeks pass.

Governor Arnold Schwarzenegger vetoes the bill.

So we're marching down Market Street again, rallying at Harvey Milk Plaza, the LGBT Center, City Hall. Another wedding dress, and the bullhorn.

Two years later, another marriage bill will pass, Governor Schwarzenegger will again veto it. We will take to the streets again.

Years pass.

VALENTINE'S DAY, 2007

I just can't do it this year. I want a real Valentine's Day. I want to be married, not fighting for it. I want flowers, romance, not bullhorns. Marriage *quality* this year, not marriage equality.

MAY 2008

The California State Supreme Court *finally* strikes down the law banning same-sex marriage. We have to wait a month to marry, though, and in the meantime, anti-gay forces qualify a constitutional amendment initiative—Proposition 8—that would change the state constitution to read, "Only marriage between one man and one woman is recognized in California."

BLOG POST FROM VENICE, ITALY, JUNE 20, 2008

It's strange timing, but I just happen to be in Italy during the time that we Californians are finally able to get a marriage license regardless of our sexual orientation. Finally, the long-awaited marriage equality that I have spent a decade of my life working for, and I am missing all my friend's weddings. Luckily I was able to watch them all over the Internet from a little café with WiFi.

There were the nuptials of my neighbors, Diane and Ruth, who were married by Oakland Mayor Ron Dellums; the breathtaking "It's-all-I-ever-wanted" romantic vows of Ryan and Moe; Ann and Christine's long overdue "I do's"; John and Stuart's "I do, I do, I do!" (it was their third wedding); and Dave and Jeff's regal wedding at the Solano County Clerk's Office.

At least Del's and Phyl's wedding was televised on the Italian News. And the story of Molly, with her Universal Life Church minister license, marrying same-sex couples in Bakersfield because the Kern County Clerk wouldn't, was in *USA Today*, which I found at the newsstand and online.

Today I discussed marriage equality with the deputy mayor of Venice, the LGBT and Gender Policies Department of the Municipality of Venice, members of the Venetian gay community, and a professor of sociology at the University of Padua. If that's not *la dolce vita*, I don't know what is. And now I dream of Marriage Equality Italia. Everything is possible!

SEPTEMBER 2008

We wear Indian clothes, because the wedding dress and the tuxedo have become like work uniforms. We want a fresh look. So, we went to Roopams, an Indian store in Berkeley, and bought wedding garb. Molly chose a *sari*; I chose a *sherwani* (a men's suit).

The owner was very supportive. He asked us to bring back a wedding photo so that he can display it with others. He also encouraged us to tell other same-sex couples that they would be welcome at his store.

We held our ceremony on the day we had started "going steady" twelve years earlier, and close to the ten-year anniversary of our first wedding. We picked the same location, and invited 150 of our friends, family members, and coworkers. Many of them had been at our previous wedding; others were new friends through Marriage Equality USA. Since we only had three months to plan and it was Labor Day weekend, several of our close friends couldn't come because they had already made vacation plans.

It was not as magical as our first wedding. The new owner of

Wildwood Acres gave us exactly three hours to set up, hold our event and celebration, and clean up. But my bride looked beautiful in her yellow and red sari. Our parents made wonderful toasts about how proud they were of the work that we'd done.

Senator Leno officiated again. He, attorney Therese Stewart (who had argued on behalf of the San Francisco weddings), and our marriage therapist, Michael Graves, signed our wedding certificate.

It was ironic to finally be legally wed after spending twelve years dedicated to Molly and knowing that we were already married in our lives, in our hearts, and, we believed, in the eyes of God. Our marriage came in installments; the license from the State of California was the finishing touch.

NOVEMBER 4, 2008

Words are hard to find. There's a sick, sinking feeling in my stomach. We lost. Yes on Prop 8 won. We've worked so hard, we've given so much, and they voted our rights away. Just like that. I can't hold back the tears. My heart aches.

MAY 2009

After a spiritual ceremony in 1998, a six-month marriage uprising in 2004, and a shotgun legal wedding in 2008—after which we donated all our wedding gifts to defeat Prop 8—Molly and I can finally know that our marriage is safe and "real."

The California Supreme Court has ruled that the 18,000 marriages that took place between June and November or last year are "valid and recognized in the state of California."

VALENTINE'S DAY, 2011

Eighteen of us sit on the floor in the San Francisco County Recorder's Office next to the marriage license counter. We face each other in a circle, clasp hands, and begin singing "What the World Needs Now Is Love."

We are three lesbian couples, two gay male couples, four ministers (some straight, some LGBT), and four single love-warrior activists.

The police officers tell us over a bullhorn that if we don't disperse we will be arrested. We continue to sing. They ask us to leave a second time. We continue to sing.

We are peaceful; we smile at one another. I am calm, if a bit nervous. After all, there are ten cops with plastic riot-gear handcuffs surrounding us.

We sing the truth:

What the world needs now is love, sweet love.

No, not just for some, but for everyone.

The truth is, some people don't love us, and they don't see our love as sweet. But the people who work at San Francisco City Hall do. They've watched us here year after year, rally after rally. They married some of us in 2004 and 2008. They know how we've been harmed by the denial of marriage and marriage benefits.

Someday the world will understand, like they do, that love is love, no matter the gender of those in the couple. Love between two women or two men is as dignified and holy as the love between a man and a woman, and worthy of the same legal, spiritual, and community blessings. Marriage should be not just for some, but for everyone.

Where the Queer Zone Meets the Asian Zone

∴

Helen Zia

I was as surprised as anyone when my significant other and I got married after being together for twelve years, during that historic Valentine's Day weekend of 2004 at San Francisco's golden-domed City Hall, with thousands of other lesbian, gay, bi, and transgender couples.

In choosing to join the same-sex marriage revolution, Lia and I had no illusions; our civil marriage in no way affected our critical view of this patriarchal marriage institution. We wanted to get married to declare our commitment to each other and to express our defiance against the warmongering, fundamentalist regime in Washington.

But, ultimately, we made it to the altar because of the Asian American women we knew at the San Francisco marriage bureau in City Hall.

I am referring to the people who were in charge of the marriage license bureaucracy at San Francisco City Hall. Mabel Teng was elected City Assessor-Recorder after a nasty and close contest for that decidedly unromantic-sounding job. A former San Francisco supervisor and longtime community activist, Teng hired two other women: Donna Kotake, who also had a long history as an activist in San Francisco's Japantown, and Minna Tao, a well-known leader in the Castro for her work on LGBT causes. After Mayor Gavin Newsom took his courageous and historic stand allowing gays and lesbians to apply for marriage licenses, the task fell on these women to make it so.

Teng, Kotake, and Tao were the city officials who, overnight, mobilized an army of unpaid city employees and volunteers to transform an archaic operation that handled only a few dozen marriage licenses a week into a machine that could process several hundred marriages a day—as many marriages as they could before the anticipated court injunction would shut the operation down. Had it not been for the leadership of these three straight Asian American women, the lumbering machine might have cranked out a few hundred marriages in the two-week window before the courts shut them down. Instead, they brought together a rainbow of yellow, black, brown, white, queer, and straight supporters to process some four-thousand-plus same-sex marriages, including my own.

Initially, Lia and I were hesitant to join the other marriage license applicants because we wanted to include my elderly mother in the ceremony, and the long lines that snaked from Polk and Grove Streets around City Hall discouraged us. Then our friends at City Hall called to ask if we could volunteer to help out with the deluge of paperwork on that three-day holiday weekend. As a writer I could type, and Lia, too, had office skills. So we helped process licenses for several hundred other gay and lesbian couples who had traveled from all over for the chance to be married. When the line of couples came to its end, Lia and I seized the moment and were married by Donna Kotake, with several other friends who had volunteered looking on. We went home that night trying to grasp that we were *married*, so unimaginable only a few days earlier.

One thing that Lia and I couldn't have known was the impact our marriage would have on our families. Perhaps most opposite-sex couples expect to be taken in as family by their prospective in-laws, but that is not so for most LGBT couples. Lia and I have always felt lucky to have family members who tolerated, accepted, even welcomed us, but we still could not assume that they would respond to our nuptials with the same enthusiasm had we married partners of the opposite sex. We are among the very fortunate, though. In fact, it was my mother who suggested that we get married after she saw the news about San Francisco's gay weddings on KTSF-TV, the Chinese-language station. She was excited, happy at the prospect. "Helen, gay people can get married in San Francisco now," she said. "Why don't you and Lia go?"

Lia's father had been a state district court judge in Hawaii, one in the first wave of Japanese Americans to seek elective office before statehood. As a retired judge, he is authorized to perform weddings, and when it appeared that a window for same-sex marriages might open in Hawaii in 1993, we asked him gingerly if he would marry us. The first few times we asked, he didn't answer. Then one day, months after our first query, to our surprise he agreed and we all laughed at the imaginary headlines, "Local Judge Marries Daughter to Daughter-in-Law." But that was not to be; the window for same-sex marriage did not open until Mayor Gavin Newsom's revolution in San Francisco.

A few months after our marriage in the rotunda of City Hall, we held a small wedding party at the Silver Dragon restaurant in Oakland's Chinatown. Family and friends came together from all over the country—from Hilo, Hawaii to New York City. It was the first time in fifteen years that my five siblings and I were assembled in the same place. Six of our young nieces and nephews formed a wedding procession as Lia's brother and my mother "gave us away." Lia's father dusted off his retired judicial robe and performed an affirmation ceremony. Our Hawaii friends and relatives brought beautiful leis, and each of our siblings made moving toasts.

In honor of our marriage, friends performed hula, sang romantic standards, shouted "Banzai!" three times, and toasted us. We served the traditional roast pig as well as wedding cake; we laughed and cried. By all accounts, it was a wedding party that far exceeded our wildest imaginations. It served another purpose, too: the melding of our extended family and friends. Our respective families, already so supportive of us, suddenly transformed their relationships to each other to reflect the more intimate "relatives" status: Lia's father and my mother now see each other as related, and my five siblings and Lia's brother have become family. This subtle yet profound shift has opened my eyes to another aspect of making family. Our niece Emily, the sixteen-year-old daughter of my brother Hoyt, cannot remember when Lia and I weren't together, but after our affirmation ceremony she put her arms around Lia and summed it up this way, "Auntie Lia, now you're really my auntie."

Among activist types, an axiom holds that social movements involve moving people and changing minds, one person at a time. Queer folks have long known that homophobic attitudes change when people get to know someone in their circle who is gay. The same is true for knowing Asian Americans and others who dwell in the margins of society, in every corner of this land. We stop being one-dimensional cartoon characters; we get to be fully human. With each individual who comes to realize that there are Asian queers and queer Asians, that space where the gay zone meets the Asian zone opens a little more.

When I was writing a book in 2001 with Wen Ho Lee, the Los Alamos nuclear scientist who was falsely accused of being a spy for China, I wanted him to know that I am a lesbian so that my sexual orientation would not become an issue in our collaboration. During one of our first meetings in his kitchen, I told him that Lia is my spouse, just as Sylvia is his spouse. At first he said nothing, then made himself busy bustling about the kitchen. Finally, he said in matter-of-fact physicist fashion, "That is your domain. It is not my domain." It was my business, not his, and that was the end of it.

More than a year later, on the last day of our book tour for *My Country Versus Me*, Wen Ho called my hotel room in Los Angeles from his own room just down the hall. He had a question he had wanted to ask me. "Helen," he said, "I've met your brother, and he seems 100 percent male. Is there anyone else in your family . . . like you?" I answered no, not that I knew of. He wanted to know how I ended up gay. I explained that sexual orientation isn't a choice or an absolute, 100 percent this or 100 percent that, but it is a spectrum, like light, where people may fall closer to one end or the other, or somewhere in between. "Yes, a spectrum," he said. "That makes sense."

Then I had a question for him: "What is your feeling about gay people?" Wen Ho replied, "Before I knew you, if I met someone who was gay, I would not want to have anything to do with them. But now I think it makes no difference if they are gay."

As the enormity of the San Francisco marriage revolution began to register, it also dawned on me that this was a movement that has had Asian Americans at its center from the beginning, ever since the first lawsuits in Hawaii in 1993. The Japanese American Citizens League was the first (and perhaps only) national civil rights group of people of color to support same-sex marriage; their convention voted to do so after U.S. Representative Norman Mineta flew in for the sole purpose of arguing that support for same-sex marriage is a matter of fairness, equality, and justice. In three of the states where lawsuits by lesbian and gay couples were challenging the marriage bans, Asian Americans were among the chief plaintiffs. Two San Francisco Asian/Pacific American couples rode the Marriage Equality Bus that toured America, bringing lesbian and gay married couples to Walmart parking lots throughout Smalltown, USA.

The sheer out-loudness of the Asian American presence in this round of same-sex marriage stood in contrast to the first same-sex marriage showdown that took place beginning in 1999 in Hawaii, where, in spite of the heavily Asian and Pacific Islander location, the connection between race and sexual orientation was often denied. In spite of the Japanese American Citizens League's valiant attempt to draw parallels between the injustice of the internment of Japanese Americans in World War II with the marriage ban for gays, the mainly Asian and Pacific Islander electorate in Hawaii voted two-to-one to prevent same-sex marriage. Some Asian American leaders asserted, "This is not our issue," as though queer APIs simply don't exist in the Asian American community. At the same time, some white LGBT advocates insisted that the first lawsuits just happened to be in Hawaii—that this battle could have been filed by anybody, anywhere. That it was simply happenstance that the first ruling for the same-sex marriage took place in Hawaii and that so many of the players happened to be Asians or Pacific Islanders.

But, in fact, Hawaii was the first state in the nation to ratify the Equal Rights Amendment, in 1972, through the leadership of U.S. Representative Patsy Mink. When the national ERA effort failed, the people of Hawaii adopted a state Equal Rights Amendment assuring that "equality of rights under the law shall not be denied or abridged on account of sex." The 1990s Hawaii ruling that the denial of same-sex marriage is unconstitutional came out of the lived history of Hawaii's people, who had forged their state constitution out of blood and tears: Native Hawaiians had been colonized, subjected to genocide, while Asian immigrant laborers were brought to Hawaii's plantations as chattel.

The inability of LGBT advocates from the mainland to recognize the lived experience of Hawaii's Pacific Islanders and Asian Americans was a missed opportunity to forge a link in the common quest for equality and justice. This failure also made it easier for the fundamentalist Christian Right to appeal to homophobic beliefs that gays and lesbians are somehow separate from Asian and Pacific Islander communities. After the 2004 Valentine's Day marriages in San Francisco, Korean American churches organized rallies against the "evil of homosexuality" in Southern California, while seven thousand Chinese American Christian churches mobilized against same-sex marriage in San Francisco's Sunset District. From Christian friends, I've learned that ministers of some Chinese language evangelical churches not only preach that gay children are sinners who transgress God and Nature, but that *their parents* are also damned—a special cultural twist of the knife for Asian families, in which parents are revered.

Asian American queer activists do not all agree on what political stand to take toward same-sex marriage. To some, fighting for same-sex marriage is too petty bourgeois, too much about the nuclear family, cocooning, property rights, and all the negative patriarchal things that marriage stands for. It's rather like fighting for equality in the military when you're opposed to war, as I am. There are so many other pressing issues that also inhabit this queer and Asian zone—hate crimes and violence, immigration and asylum, Patriot Act detentions and deportations, government surveillance of "suspicious" people, the disease and stigma of HIV/AIDS, to name just a few. Indeed, a man from Thailand was among the couples whose marriage licenses I processed—and he had to file for an annulment when his change in status exposed him to possible deportation.

But there are no perfect battles. Same-sex marriage might not be the political battleground any of us would have chosen, but this fragile space where queer meets Asian belongs to us and not to those who attempt to use us as a wedge to extend an agenda that is harmful to our diverse and largely immigrant communities. Our lived experiences in this space are an inseparable part of our communities, and that includes the historic roles that gay and straight Asians have played in making same-sex marriage possible.

I am reminded of the adage, "None of us is free unless each of us is free." Each of us, no matter what our particular "orientation" in life, will face choices that offer the possibility of reaching beyond our own selves and self-interest. By choosing to stand up for the humanity of others, we all become more free. As the space where queer meets Asian continues to grow beyond the Castro, so, too, does the space for everyone, even when it happens one person at a time.

I wrote the above for *Love, Castro Street: Reflections of San Francisco* (Alyson Books, 2007), which was itself adapted from a piece that first appeared in *AmerAsia Journal: Asian Americans in the Marriage Equality Debate* in 2006.

But that was then.

Fast-forward.

Not long after Lia and I were married during that Valentine's Day weekend in 2004, our marriage licenses were "invalidated" by the California Supreme Court, on the grounds that Mayor Newsom overstepped his authority. The San Francisco City Attorney's Office and a number of lesbian and gay civil rights organizations then brought an antidiscrimination suit against the state of California. After arguing all the way to the California Supreme Court, they won! The court ruled that same-sex partners were being denied a fundamental human right, and declared that lesbian and gay couples should be granted marriage licenses at every city hall in California.

June 17, 2008 was designated as the first full day that marriage licenses would be issued. We managed to snag an appointment for 8:15 AM, followed by a wedding at City Hall officiated by City Attorney Dennis Herrera and witnessed by Deputy City Attorney Terese Stewart, who had argued the case for marriage equality before the state Supreme Court. This time my mother was going to be at our wedding, as well as several dear friends. A few days before, the city communications office asked if we would mind allowing some reporters to be present at our vows. We said yes, we would allow a few reporters—especially from the ethnic media, because we felt it was important for communities of color to see that they have queer family members.

What we didn't realize was how much of a media mob scene it would be that morning, and since we were one of the first couples to be married, our vows were recorded by a *New York Times* reporter, an AP photographer, several TV crews, and, yes, ethnic Asian community reporters from TV, radio, and print. Photos of the blushing brides popped up everywhere. Even now, there are videos of our marriage on the Internet, showing Lia and me holding hands and singing, "We're going to the chapel and we're gonna get married," as well as of my elderly mom being interviewed in Mandarin and English. It was a beautiful, joyous occasion—to be legally married after sixteen years together, finally!

And yet there were still storm clouds on the horizon, as anti-gay marriage activists, heavily funded by the Catholic and Mormon churches, campaigned for a ballot initiative, Proposition 8, which declared marriage legal only for "one man and one woman."

In California, where communities of color make up more than 50 percent of the state population, we knew that Prop 8 homophobes were conducting heavy disinformation campaigns to get out the "minority" vote. So Lia and I joined the efforts to bring about visibility for Asian and Pacific Islander queers. When we handed out Asian-language flyers in different Asian communities, we couldn't help but notice how many people would take a flyer and laugh, saying, "Gay marriage? No more people, no more human race"—as though our marriage would stop all heterosexuals from breeding. It was painful to see how far this uniform message of ignorance and bigotry had reached into our own communities.

November 3, 2008: a day of mixed feelings. We were delighted that Barack Obama was elected to be our forty-fifth president, but on the marriage equality vote our worst fears came true—Proposition 8, aka Prop Hate, had passed by a slim margin. The state marriage license bureaus once again shut their doors on us. Lia and I cried that day; it was as if we were attending a funeral while everyone else was celebrating at a wedding. It really hurt us to be told, once again, that our loving relationship and our personhood was less than nothing in the eyes of the law and the homophobes. And what of our June 17 wedding? Would that be "invalidated" again, as our 2004 marriage was?

Everything was back to the lawyers to sort through the complex muddle. The Prop 8 proponents claimed that couples like us who had been legally married before the ballot measure should have our marriages stripped away, but fortunately the courts ruled that it could not be retroactive. Therefore, 18,000 couples who were married between June 17 and November 3, 2008 are still legally married.

But there was no rejoicing in that decision. It felt to Lia and me that we were placed in a strange box, something akin to being "emancipated" when others were still enslaved, and that we might lose our "almost equal" status at any moment.

Meanwhile, the courtroom battles have dragged on. In January 2010, the federal lawsuit to overturn Proposition 8 went to trial as *Perry v. Schwarzenegger*. I was asked to be a witness on behalf of the 18,000 still legally married, to talk about the impact of marriage on our families.

The plaintiff attorneys asked me how I came to realize I am a lesbian, what my coming-out process was, and what my marriage to Lia has meant to me. (The full transcript can be found online at the Americans for Equal Rights website, www.afer.org; I testified on Day 5, January 15, 2010. There's even a cool video online of the wonderful blond, blue-eyed actress Patricia Clarkson reenacting my testimony about being a Chinese American lesbian!)

I told Judge Vaughn Walker that Lia and I never imagined, never envisioned how our families would change and grow closer because we had a piece of paper that said we are married. To our extended family members, our marriage meant that *they* were now related, too. So Lia's father in Honolulu, who for more than ten years lived only five minutes from my brother's house yet never stopped by, suddenly visited my brother to drop off some fruit from his trees—because our marriage meant they were related. And I told him how my niece Emily declared that Auntie Lea was now *really* her auntie.

I also told him how, when Lia's dad was very ill and hospitalized in hospice care, Lia and I were at his bedside quite a lot. The nurses and workers would ask Lia's dad, "Who are these visitors? Are these your daughters?" And Lia's dad said, "This is my daughter, and this is my favorite daughter-in-law."

Lia and I were dumbstruck to hear her father's words. When we stepped out of the room, Lia said, "He said 'daughter-in-law!'" And I said, "He said 'favorite!'"

Even when Lia's dad was so ill, our marriage gave him a way to describe who we were. That was a difference our marriage made.

So in those important moments of life when the family comes together—birth, creating one's own family, and death—being married makes it clear to everyone that same-sex spouses are part of the family.

When Lia's father passed away, there was no question that I was Lia's wife and a member of the family, and there was no ambiguity about what to do with the obituary or the memorial hall seating. I wasn't some partner in business or partner in life. I was her spouse. And I was right there in the first row, with family. And I had my responsibilities as a member of the family.

I still believe that the institution of marriage is rooted in patriarchy, with all that implies; being an advocate for marriage equality does not mean that I advocate marriage for everyone. But through my own marriage to Lia, I discovered so many intangible ways that our family relationships changed. It was as though we had always been forced to drink from separate water fountains and that we always had to sit at the back of the bus, and we just accepted that's the way it is. But one day we tasted the water from the other fountain, and it tasted different; it tasted sweet. And when we sat at the front of the bus, we found it was cleaner. If we had never gotten there, we would never have known.

We don't know exactly what life will be like when there is equality for all, but we know that the water will taste sweeter in a world that embraces the full personhood and full humanity of all people.

Standing on Ceremony

∴

J. Keiko Lane

The morning of our wedding we woke to rain. My parents, who had driven with my seventy-four-year-old auntie from Los Angeles to our house in Berkeley the day before, were already dressed and making lattes. Our friend Becky, who planned to meet us at City Hall, called to ask if we had flowers.

"Ummmm . . ." I said, looking out the kitchen window at a dark sky.

"I'll get some," she said.

It was still raining when we arrived at San Francisco's City Hall.

Waiting for a few friends to join us, we watched the activity in the rotunda. Occasional bursts of applause from balconies and landings announced new marriages. With less than two weeks until Election Day 2008, LGBTQ couples were marrying as quickly as they could, just in case Prop 8 passed and our right to wed was taken away.

Becky arrived carrying a bouquet of Japanese lantern flowers—a symbol of fortune and blessings whose bright orange blossoms were the perfect color for this Halloween morning.

Costume-wearing kids on field trips swarmed the halls and balconies of City Hall. A teacher in a Cruella de Vil costume led a procession of children dressed as 101 Dalmatians, with safety-pinned tails and white-and-black spotted T-shirts. Our friends emerged from behind the Dalmatians, and we walked up the stairs to a small, quiet balcony.

In my Bay Area psychotherapy practice, marriage has been a frequent topic since 2004, when Del Martin and Phyllis Lyon were the first same-sex couple to be legally married in California. Couples who had always dreamed of a recognizable signifier to mark their relationship now began to plan weddings. Couples who had never considered getting married because it wasn't a legal possibility now had to make a conscious decision. I even saw a few heterosexual couples who had refused to tie the legal knot out of solidarity with their lesbian and gay friends but were now beginning to reconsider matrimony. Some clients reported that parents who had not previously considered their children's same-sex partners to be family were now speculating about which partner would adopt whose family's name.

Even my partner's mother, who just assumed we'd get married, wondered if I'd be taking her name.

For as long as I have been a psychotherapist, I have noticed that queer clients talk cautiously about the struggles in their partnerships, sometimes fearing that any exposure of problems might work against the cause of marriage equality—and thus, by extension, their civil rights. Some of my politically active heterosexual clients have hesitated to talk to me about their marriages or engagements while their lesbian, gay, and transgender friends are in awkward political limbo; they say they don't feel right celebrating their legal unions while friends are unable to do the same.

Since 2008, when same-sex marriage was legalized (if only briefly) in California, my LGBT clients have reported that friends, family, and strangers ask if they're married, and what Prop 8 means for them and their relationships. That sort of ever-present discussion tends to make their relationships feel more like cultural signifiers than the emotional life-center that they are. Under constant scrutiny, my clients walk through the world with heightened awareness of visibility and vulnerability.

And so do I.

My partner, Lisa, and I have always been ambivalent about the institution of marriage and its misogynistic legal origins as a business arrangement between a father and son-in-law-to-be. Yet we also come from families in which marriage works. Lisa's parents were married for more than fifty years. My parents, still in love, are an interracial couple: My mother's family came to Hawaii and California from Okinawa, working as farmers before and after internment during World War II. My father's family of Russian Jews came from Europe at the turn of the last century. My parents met as social workers for Los Angeles County, marrying just two years after the *Loving v. Virginia* Supreme Court case made interracial marriages legal.

Lisa and I never planned on getting married. Many years before a legal California marriage became an option, we registered as domestic partners. We share bank accounts, are covered on each other's health insurance, and are named on emergency and hospital forms. But because we are both longtime activists and easily pissed off, when the polling numbers for Prop 8 started tipping toward passage in the weeks leading up to the November 2008 elections, we planned our quickie Halloween wedding. Having it at City Hall with just a few close friends would mirror my parents' marriage at a city hall more than forty years earlier.

When my heterosexual clients decide to get married, it usually marks a transition in their relationship, a deepening into a different kind of commitment, a vow to be faithful to whatever promises they make about the shape and structure of their relationship. For heterosexuals who follow the traditional path of dating-engagement-marriage, the wedding is a rite of passage in their relationship, a public invocation and a formalization of new rules and boundaries.

For queer clients, getting married is often a political action. Some queer couples have come to me to work out their feelings about marriage because their children have asked them to get married; the kids want their families to have the same rituals and symbols as their peers in school. For other couples, the ambivalence about having a wedding stems from the sense that they have already been married, sometimes for decades.

And as queer clients begin planning weddings, some are surprised by the things that scare them. The ones who were already deeply committed, with visions of a long life together, discover that they aren't as frightened about the idea of being married as about the wedding itself, and what weddings signify in their families of origin.

Marriage creates a common language in any given family system to talk about relationships and commitment. For some clients, this has meant thinking about the ways in which they are determined to have marriages different from the marriages of their parents and grandparents. One lesbian client, whose parents had fought daily and whose mother had repeatedly told her that marriage was a trap she couldn't escape, feared that, although she had been happily committed to her partner for almost a decade, once they were legally wed she would feel as trapped as her mother did. For other clients—as well as for my partner and me—marriage lets them acknowledge the ways in which parents have successfully modeled loving and committed partnerships.

Even in families where LGBTQ relationships are accepted, family members may be uncomfortable announcing a queer marriage to people outside the family. My partner's mother has no trouble with that: She traveled from Florida to ride on the PFLAG bus with us during a San Francisco Gay Pride March, and announces to everyone she meets that I am her "third daughter." (We had to train her to say "daughter-in-law" because of the odd looks Lisa and I would get when we held hands or kissed.) On the other hand, my partner and I skirted around possible family conflicts with some of my more devoutly religious cousins and aunties by having a City Hall wedding—echoing how my parents married at City Hall partially to avoid my paternal grandmother's displeasure with my father for marrying a non-Jew.

About a week before our wedding, Lisa and I went there to fill out our paperwork. As we walked through the rotunda, I looked up at the curved second-floor balcony where a few weeks earlier we had sat during Del Martin's public memorial (she had died just a couple of months after her second legal marriage to Phyllis). The hall had been filled with generations of politicians, community members, friends, and activists, all acknowledging Del's role with Phyllis as lifetime leaders in the fight for justice and equality.

As we stood in the rotunda thinking about these icons in the fight for civil rights, a woman in jeans and a sweatshirt approached us, out of breath, shy and urgent. She and her partner of eight years had traveled from Alaska with their two young sons to get married. This was the first vacation they had ever taken with their kids, and they were getting married because they wanted to adopt a third child. Though they were already raising their two biological children, an adoption social worker said their chances of having a child placed with them were better if they had a tangible, legal marker of their relationship. They hoped that the adoption agency would consider a marriage certificate as proof of their stability—even though the marriage wouldn't be recognized in their home state.

I watched them, their ease with each other, the ways they calmed each other's fears as they told us their story, the ways they kept watch over their two sons gleefully running up and down the steps of the rotunda. What other proof did they need? Witnesses. So my partner and I stood next to them, our eyes filling with tears as they read their vows while crying, holding hands, and hurrying through the ceremony as their restless boys raced each other up the marble steps.

I'm wary when clients come in with romantic stories of surprise proposals. It isn't that I don't believe that a proposal from one partner to another can't be sweet and romantic, but the idea of marriage—of committing to each other in whatever ways a couple defines marriage—shouldn't be a surprise.

But my engagement, if we can call it that (and never do), had its own romantic twist. After my partner completed a rigorous graduate program in social and cultural anthropology in 2008, we attended a party held by her department. When it was her turn to speak, she thanked the faculty, fellow students, family, and me. In closing, she faced me and said, "So, if you're not doing anything on Tuesday, how's about we go down to City Hall and get married?"

The room erupted in applause and whistles. She and I laughed.

By that time we had lived together for years, had legal documents protecting us, had exchanged rings, and had taken care of each other's families. We had opted not to get married during the brief window of opportunity in 2004 because there were mixed legal opinions about whether marriage would nullify our domestic partnership, which we depended on for our joint healthcare coverage. So I knew that what Lisa was proposing was a political gesture as much as a romantic one. But for the duration of the party I was repeatedly cornered by excited, chatty women—most of them straight—telling me how charming my partner was and asking if I planned on saying yes. The queer men kept asking to be flower girls.

"You will say yes, won't you?" her classmates kept asking.

"Well," I said, "I'll have to consult with our lawyer."

I was serious about that. Since the legalization of same-sex marriage, we had been talking about the pros and cons of marriage. It would change our legal status, but only in some states. And just as a few of our heterosexual friends had not legally wed out of solidarity with their queer friends, we wondered if we should not wed out of solidarity with our bi-national queer friends for whom a state-recognized marriage would still not offer protection from federal deportation.

We were far less concerned whether marriage might shift something about our emotional security and connection to each other. Weren't we already married? Hadn't we already made promises when we knew we were in love and committed to being together? When my partner moved across the country to join me in California because of my work? When we flew to Florida as her father lay dying, and stayed for weeks to take care of her mother? When we set aside our weekend plans as a couple because one of our friends was having a crisis and needed us? When I was wheeled in for surgery and Lisa paced in the waiting room, calling my parents with updates?

Our Halloween-morning marriage ceremony was brief. It was performed by our friend Steven, a San Francisco City Health Commissioner and AIDS educator, who talked as much to our friends and family as he did to us. He asked them to vow to support us as we moved through the day-to-day joys and difficulties of the life we'd been building together for years.

Steven asked if we had rings. Fifteen years earlier, a beloved friend in the AIDS activist community had given me a set of silver stacking rings, placing them gently on my right-hand ring finger as a reminder of my connection to my community in the wake of a terrible season of deaths. Though my partner and I had exchanged rings years earlier over an intimate anniversary dinner at home, we had wanted something to mark the occasion of our legal marriage. Taking apart the set of rings and giving them to each other in our ceremony marked not only our marriage to each other, but located us within a community to which we would continue to be committed. The slim silver bands fit perfectly against the rings we had already exchanged.

After we signed the marriage papers, my mother and Lisa's cousin signing as witnesses, Steven kissed us good-bye and hurried off to catch a plane to Africa, where he was going to help open an AIDS clinic. This detail of our wedding day, too, fit into what we believe about the landscape of our union: that even in celebration, we are nested in a larger sense of political and cultural context and responsibility.

Part of the uneasiness in the LGBTQ activist community about the political emphasis on marriage equality has stemmed from a concern that a movement toward nuclear families would move us away from a commitment to community. During the 1990s, most of my friends from the queer and AIDS activist community died. Those of us still living took care of them and each other, declaring ourselves a chosen extended family while many of the biological families of our dying friends abandoned them in their dying. The question that gets asked now is, "Had gay marriage been legal in the 1980s and 1990s, would the community have knitted together so closely to take care of our friends and chosen family dying of AIDS?"

Some activists, myself included, have also feared that an LGBTQ focus on the family could deter us from fighting for health care, humane immigration policies, and an end to torture, poverty, gendered violence, classism, and racism. But as I've settled into my own marriage, and watched my clients settle into theirs, I am reminded that the fear would only be true if we believed that families exist in a cultural vacuum—outside of our responsibilities and connections to our communities.

After leaving City Hall, my parents took us to lunch. We looked around the table: My auntie, who spent her childhood in the Manzanar internment camp, was helping distribute origami cranes to our friends and family at the table. My father was deep in conversation about California politics with my partner's cousin. My mother was talking with my partner's college friend and my dearest psychotherapy colleague about gardening. Eventually, the meal was served. My father and our friends toasted us, and we them.

The rain fell late into evening, drowning the candle in the pumpkin my mother had carved. My partner and I couldn't stop smiling at each other as we handed out Halloween candy to the neighborhood children, our silver rings catching the glow from the porch light.

Crossing Borders

∴

Katherine Arnup

"Are we too late to get a marriage license today?" we ask the woman at the reception desk at Ottawa's City Hall.

It's 4:23 pm. At 4:30, the office stops taking new applications. "You can't stop love," laughs the receptionist. "You girls have five minutes to fill out the forms. It'll be faster if you fill out your individual sections at the same time. Good luck!"

Hearts pounding, we take a number from the machine and set about filling in the required details of our lives.

Canadian. Born 1949. Toronto, Ont. Single (never married).

American. Born 1955. Boston, Mass. Single (never married).

"Number eighty-nine," a voice calls.

It's 4:30. Now or never.

"Be there in a second," we chorus, racing to complete the forms.

Marriage for same-sex couples has been legal since 2003 in the province of Ontario, where I live, and all across Canada since 2005. I helped make that happen by being an expert witness in court challenges. Yet until now, until this relationship, I never had any intention of getting married. Neither did my partner. We were more likely to scream "Smash the state!" than to invite the law into our bedroom.

I came out as a lesbian in 1976. "Came out" is an exaggeration—I became involved with a woman during Christmas break from Toronto Teacher's College. When I returned to school, I was certain that everyone could see the enormous *L* on my forehead.

Later, when I began to teach first grade, I was terrified that someone would discover my secret. Though I still attended anti-Anita Bryant protests and gay rights demonstrations, I avoided the lenses of photographers. When I sang and played guitar at rallies, I was billed as "Precious Little." In those days, lesbian and teacher spelled danger.

Although I was certain I would never get married, I was equally certain that I would become a mother. That became a little more complicated after I came out. When my application for donor insemination at a fertility clinic was turned down on the grounds that I was not in a "legally recognized relationship of permanence," I opted for self-insemination, using sperm from a gay friend. In July 1982, my daughter Jesse was born. Six years later I gave birth to my second daughter, Katie.

While many of my formerly radical heterosexual friends got married once they decided to start a family—in order to make it "easier" on the children—my partner and I did not have that option. We drew up wills to ensure that she would get custody of the girls in the event of my death, and powers of attorney for one another, but there was little else we could do to protect our family. Second-parent adoption, same-sex partner benefits, and the like had not yet been extended to lesbians and gay men. Each time another heterosexual friend announced her wedding plans, I felt abandoned in our "outlaw" status.

In the 1970s and '80s, most lesbians and gay men did not even dream about marriage. We lacked basic civil rights, such as protection against workplace or housing discrimination or the right to visit a sick partner in the hospital. When my partner accompanied me into the delivery room in 1982 and 1988, we did so as friends, since we were "legal strangers" for all intents and purposes.

I was a socialist feminist and staunch critic of the role of the patriarchal nuclear family in the oppression of women—but I wanted legal protection for my family. I wanted my children to be free from harassment and our family to be welcomed in the broader community. That would have to wait another decade and more.

Much of my time in the 1980s and '90s was taken up with graduate work, my career as a professor, children, and care for ill and dying family members. Although I researched, wrote articles about, and edited a book on lesbian and gay parenting, and joined demonstrations demanding rights for same-sex couples, I had little faith that the right to marry would ever be granted to lesbians or gay men.

In 2000, a young lesbian lawyer working on a challenge to the opposite-sex definition of marriage approached me to serve as an expert witness. As a historian of the family, I had written on the changing composition of the Canadian family over the course of the twentieth century and the multiple ways in which fearmongers had declared the family "dead" because of the legalization of divorce, birth control and abortion, marriage between second cousins, and homosexuality. The lawyers representing the couples challenging the marriage law hoped I could put the hysteria over same-sex marriage into the context of a long history of unfounded fears about the demise of the family.

"I'm prepared to do it," I said. "But you need to know that I have no interest whatsoever in getting married. And I'd have to say that if I ended up in the witness box. That being said, I can't condone preventing those who want to marry from doing so."

"You really don't want to get married?" the lawyer responded with surprise. "I do! I want a white dress with a long train—the whole nine yards!"

I smiled as I reflected on the naïveté of youth, little knowing that in a decade I would be benefiting from the fruits of my own labor.

Luckily, I was never faced with taking the stand, as the expert evidence was accepted in written form. As we waited for the Ontario case (as well as ones in British Columbia and Quebec) to work their way through the courts, young and older activists alike watched with horror the increasingly vitriolic attacks on gay marriage in both the United States and Canada. In a campaign reminiscent of Anita Bryant's North American-wide Save the Children crusade in the late 1970s, opponents of marriage rights accused lesbians and gay men of converting, corrupting, and abusing children. The rhetoric sickened me, as it flew in the face of more than two decades of scholarship on the quality of lesbian and gay parenting and, of course, the evidence of my own very amazing daughters.

The more vicious opponents became, the more clearly I understood how heterosexuals' exclusive access to marriage maintained our status as stigmatized outsiders. Still, I had no intention of marrying. My twenty-two-year lesbian relationship had dissolved in 1998, and I had no desire to expose myself to the possibility of another messy breakup.

In pursuing a new relationship with Nancy, it was commitment, not legal status that I wanted.

Nancy is an American who was living in Vermont. We met in 2006 through a mutual friend and for four years navigated the border between our two countries. Though the long drive quickly became tiresome, we formed a deep and abiding connection. But our frequent border crossings were rarely easy, especially for me. U.S. border patrol officers would question, "How did you two meet? How well do you know each other?" Luckily I managed to keep the caustic rejoinders inside my head. The last thing we needed was for one of us to be turned back.

Although civil unions had been available to same-sex couples in Vermont since 2000, and the right to marry granted in 2009, those legal victories held no value for us: Marriage, immigration, and the right to work in the United States are federal matters, as they are in Canada. No matter how supportive Vermonters might be of our relationship, I still could not make a living, access healthcare, or collect Social Security benefits from the United States should Nancy die before me. In short, we remained without rights to things that really matter, especially to people our ages.

After the death of Nancy's father in 2009, we began to talk seriously about how we were going to find a pathway for our future. We were not twenty-five any longer, and the fantasy of living six months of the year in each country faded with the reality of our lives. At sixty, I was beginning to prepare for early retirement in order to spend more time writing, working in hospice care, and hanging out with my daughters (and hopefully grandchildren). Five years younger, Nancy had another decade of work ahead of her, and, since our relationship couldn't be fully recognized in the United States, the easiest solution was for her to immigrate to Canada.

In March 2010 we visited an immigration lawyer for advice. She explained that, although we had been in a relationship for nearly four years, we didn't technically live together so we couldn't apply as common-law partners (a relationship status that, in Canada, is largely equivalent to marriage for both opposite-sex and same-sex partners). "Conjugal partners" status was reserved for people who were legally prevented from marrying; since we could, in fact, marry in Canada (though not in the United States) that status was not available to us either. Therefore, marriage was, realistically, the only option available to us.

"Besides," the lawyer told us, "marriage is the gold standard. The marriage certificate is evidence of the veracity of the relationship."

She explained that as a result of growing concerns about marriages of convenience, the immigration department had increased the level of scrutiny on Canadians seeking to sponsor a spouse. "If you can convince the civil authorities that your relationship is real and genuine, and they grant you a marriage certificate, the immigration department is much more likely to take the word of another government authority for it. You'll still have to provide documentation to support your relationship, but the immigration officials are much more likely to view your file sympathetically if you're married."

The meeting was a wake-up call for us. We could take our chances in claiming conjugal status (and likely lose), or we could get married.

Marriage had not been on Nancy's radar screen either.

In Vermont in the 1970s and '80s, as in Canada, lesbians were building a new world that didn't necessarily resemble the heterosexual norm. Nancy and her first partner literally built a house together, but their relationship remained under the radar, as her partner was an educator who might have lost her job if school officials had found out.

"Marriage was between a man and a woman and it was about creating the nuclear family," she says. "I knew from my teens onward that I probably wasn't going to be involved with a man. I might have kids, but I wasn't going to do it in the conventional way.

"But it's hard to say what I really believed, because marriage wasn't available and I never imagined that it would be. I think a lot of my resistance was a form of self-protection. Why hope for something if you can't have it?"

Talking with our lawyer about immigration changed everything. As Nancy put it, she learned that in order to immigrate, "you can go through a huge rigmarole and expose every piece of your relationship, or you can simply get married. At this point in my life, it was either make a commitment to this relationship, engage with it one hundred percent, or stop pretending."

Though we had talked vaguely about getting married in the summer, everyone else's plans seemed to conflict with ours, so we put things on hold. And then Nancy was diagnosed with breast cancer.

In the face of cancer, we were more of a "we" than we had ever been. In waiting rooms I sat with other people's partners and family members anxiously awaiting results. When Nancy arrived in the recovery room after surgery, a nurse came to take me to her.

As I stood beside her bed, I remember thinking: *This is what married people do. They are allowed to be together at times like this. The hard times and the joyful ones.*

I couldn't help but also think that in many parts of the United States and around the world, I would be barred from the recovery room. I would have no right to accompany Nancy to the surgeon's consultation or to ask about her condition. Though these policies have changed in Canada, in much of the world lesbian and gay relationships are still not "real" relationships in the eyes of the law. These are the rights we have fought for. These were rights we would never take for granted.

As Nancy recuperated and underwent six-and-a-half weeks of daily radiation, we watched DVDs, ate maple creamies, sipped wine, and feasted on fabulous summer salads. Cancer helped put everything else into perspective. It reminded us of the fragility of life. And it served as the final impetus for getting married.

In the summer, on a brief holiday in Provincetown before radiation began, we picked out rings at a wonderful store called Ruby's Fine Jewelry. After much deliberation, we settled on simple bands of rose and white gold—the white borders symbolizing our separate lives and selves; the rose our life together. We were a couple of old lesbians who had found love and were tying the knot.

When the rings arrived in Vermont, Nancy and I sat on her bed and opened the tiny box together. Without ceremony, we each put a gold band on the other's ring finger. In the days that followed, we often found ourselves staring at our hands in amazement. We were doing this. We were getting married! Later, when one of Nancy's sisters commented that we were doing it backward, wearing our rings before we got married, we asserted that "we get to do this our way, whatever that looks like."

When I was growing up in the 1950s, City Hall was reserved for "shotgun weddings." Respectable people had a church wedding, with a minister and a large crowd of well-wishers. After the ceremony, there would be a reception at a fancy hotel followed by an extravagant honeymoon. But Nancy and I had no interest in a conventional wedding.

At Ottawa City Hall, the marriage officiants are civic staff who rotate through the position at one-week intervals. "It's our favorite part of the job," said Lorraine, who performed our marriage ceremony.

The marriage room only holds ten people, including the officiant, the spouses, and their witnesses. That left five additional spots, which were taken up by my twenty-two- and twenty-eight-year-old daughters and two of our closest friends. I was full of nerves, pacing in the waiting room before we were called upstairs.

I remember us earnestly facing Lorraine and her reminding us that we should face one another instead. "You're not marrying me," she joked. While my memory of that day might otherwise be a blur, in the pictures one can see that we are full of joy and amazement. As Nancy kept saying, "We're doing this!"

As we signed the marriage certificate, Lorraine told us that she especially loves same-sex weddings. "People are generally older and there's so much love there. And with you guys, you'll always have someone to go shopping with! I can't imagine going shopping with my husband."

Nancy and I laughed, since the closest we've come to shopping together is putting in a joint catalog order from Land's End.

On many occasions during our commuting relationship, I commented that Nancy's family treated us as a "faux family." Like Nancy's previous partners, I was welcomed to Thanksgiving and birthday dinners, included in the family photo calendar. But when we announced that we were getting married, the ground shifted in small yet significant ways. I was now a sister-in-law, a daughter-in-law, Nancy's "wife" (though we rarely use the term). Showing Nancy's mother our rings, sharing photographs of the wedding—all served as recognizable milestones in the life of a family.

For the first few weeks after we began wearing our rings, Nancy would often look over at me and say, "You have a ring on!" After we were officially married, she would say, "You're married," reflecting a certain amount of incredulousness. But the meaning of marriage for us extends beyond the symbolic. Once we were legally married, I could apply to sponsor Nancy to immigrate to Canada as a permanent resident.

All summer we had been collecting "supporting documentation" of our relationship required by the Immigration Department: cards, photographs, the dates we met each other's family and friends, ticket stubs, and hotel receipts. Fortunately, I'm a historian and a pack rat, with an obsession for documentation. Nancy drew up a three-page chronology of our relationship, complete with the dates of all the trips across the border we had made to see one another. And shortly after our marriage on October 15, 2010, we completed the forms, paid the $1,150 application fee, and sent off our application.

Nine months later, we are still waiting for officials to open the envelope, since the department is mired in a backlog of people seeking to immigrate to Canada. But with a visitor's record in hand, Nancy is living in Canada, and we are together, building our lives.

Marriage is not, of course, a panacea. Like all couples, we still face the challenges of daily life—earning a living, juggling priorities, caring for family members. But we face those with more commitment and certainty than we did before. Marriage has provided us with the opportunity to build our lives together—as a couple, as part of the Arnup and Wasserman families, and as part of a broader community.

Since same-sex marriages were legalized in Canada, more than ten thousand couples have "tied the knot." Despite opponents' dire predictions, to the best of my knowledge the family has not collapsed, nor have heterosexual couples ceased to marry. Rather, the institutions of marriage and the family have expanded to include thousands of lesbian and gay couples and our children, providing us with essential legal rights and protections, recognition, and affirmation.

"I'm much more out and open in Canada because our relationship is legally recognized here in a way it isn't in the States," Nancy told me.

We have another reason to celebrate together: On April 15, 2011, exactly six months after our wedding, my daughter Jesse gave birth to a beautiful baby girl, Charlotte. Nancy and I are grandmothers. Another miracle in a year of miracles.

Another Word for Marriage

∴

Gloria Bigelow

It's one of those moments when you wish you were not alone.

I was awakened from a disco nap with a text from my girlfriend that read, "They're voting." I rolled over and grabbed my computer to live-stream the vote for marriage equality in New York. I grabbed my trail mix, desperately needing something to chew on while votes for my justness were being counted.

As I ate an almond, I wondered if I would soon be able to legally make the severity of mistakes my heterosexual friends have made. Would I, too, have the opportunity to feel the same joy on the day of my wedding, or the same anger as I sat across from my once-beloved-now-turned-nemesis in our divorce lawyer's office?

As the voting continued, I began to cry, then laugh. Perhaps the laughter came from embarrassment over the tears, or maybe laughter through tears was the perfect reaction to this long-awaited day.

About a month earlier, my lady and I were discussing marriage. It had been taken off the table for us once Proposition H8, as we like to call it, passed in California. She had said that she didn't really want to marry unless it was legal. But with New York's push for fairness at the front of Governor Andrew Cuomo's agenda, marriage was back on our table.

So there we were at Tiffany's, looking at their conflict-free diamonds, being ignored by the people behind the counter while other heterosexual customers came in after us and were eagerly attended to.

As I was admiring, or drooling rather, over a beautiful Lucida cut set in platinum, I turned to my girlfriend and said, "Do you see a ring you would like?"

She smiled. "I get a ring, too?"

"Of course," I said. "Everyone in this relationship gets an engagement ring."

She smiled again. We waited for someone behind the counter to help us. No one offered. We walked out.

It dawned on me that the women behind the counter had no idea that we would be standing there for the same reason as the preppy guy in khakis, or the fifty-something couple who tried on the most beautiful two-karat Tiffany Soleste engagement ring. We were invisible.

∴

I mentioned to my mother that my lady and I were considering premarital couples counseling. She screwed up her face and said, "Marriage? Marriage, Gloria!?! Is there anything else that you could call it?"

Eggplant.

Or foxtrot.

Or . . . a committed relationship in which we decide to live together based on love, common beliefs, and fidelity; in which we share our hopes, dreams, and lives; not much unlike the one you had with Daddy, or my brother has with my sister-in-law, but one that my own mother doesn't think I deserve even if it would give me the same rights and privileges that she shared with Daddy for twenty-eight years. It seems a little wordy, but there may be something to it. Does she not see my relationship for what it is?

Invisible.

Marriage. At different points in my life I have found myself on either side of the issue. As a not-so "straight" women in my twenties, raging feminist that I was, I deplored the idea of marriage. It's a societal construct . . . it's obsolete . . 53 percent end in divorce . . . blah, blah, blah. You know, the patented manifesto that came along with my unshaven armpits and a well-worn copy of *Our Bodies, Ourselves*.

As a lesbian whose love has been discredited by everyone from my mother to the federal government to the women at Tiffany's, I've found many reasons to reject the idea of marriage entirely—in a sour-grapes kind of way. In the "I don't really want to have full protection under the law," or "Full protection, tax breaks, and being able to visit a partner in the hospital is for *suckers* and I don't need it, I'm a postmodern queer bucking the system before it bucks me" kind of way.

But sometimes, when I'm quiet and feeling less like an anarchist, less like a radical, I ask myself: *Why would anyone take the leap?* Let's just say you decide to get married. Never mind that you're single, or it's complicated, or we don't have those rights, or you haven't had sex in nine months, three weeks, and two days—let's just say none of that exists and you decide to get married. Why would anyone do it?

Now I'm not having one of my all-too-common moments of cynicism brought on by a failing relationship, a breakup, or too much wine. I'm just asking—why do people get married? I've been grappling with this issue since I came out of the closet and said good-bye to my mother's approval and the dream of a husband and two-point-five kids.

A few months ago, I attended the most heterosexual, old-fashioned, anti-feminist, heteronormative, patriarchal, bible-thumping, disturbingly scary wedding that I've ever attended, complete with words like "two become one" and "obey." I should have just tuned out when the hefty woman minister, who needed a retouch and a fresh eyebrow arch, started talking about marriages being ordained by God. But I didn't, and this is what followed:

The minister told the groom that his job as a husband could be summed up with the three Ps—Protect, Provide, and Pray.

She then gave the wifely duties to my friend: the three Rs—Respect, Reject, and Rely.

This is when I started scratching and twitching uncontrollably. I might have developed an irreversible tic in my eye. Nonetheless, the wedding continued, and then I heard the fateful, seal-the-deal words: "till death do you part." Those continued to echo in my ears like I was standing at the bottom of the Grand Canyon. Till death do you part . . . part . . . part . . . just relentless! I could throw those Ps and Rs right out the door, but the echo stayed with me.

As my crew and I are getting a little older, and we've all kind of made a collective decision not to be the "old lady at the club," the idea of a "forever" or a "soulmate" or "for life" has been floating around. A *lot.* I can't eat a bowl of hummus without some lesbian interrupting me with marriage chatter. It's been coming up in all kinds of circles, in all kinds of conversations. I've heard:

—"I'm ready to settle down."

—"I hope that she proposes soon."

—"I can't say forever, but I can say for a long time."

—"I do want a forever kind of thing."

—"We just have a kind of connection that seems timeless. We're just connected."

—"I'm looking for wifey!"

The other day, I was looking for some sex-me boots in Soho, and when I tried on a pair and turned to my friend to ask "Whadouyathink?" she responded, "They're great. I'm thinking more about forever."

To which I responded, "Forever? Girl, please, I'm too hard on shoes. I'll be lucky if they make it past next fall! But I think they're a good deal so, I'll wear 'em through spring and bring 'em back around September."

She looked at me blankly.

"-Oh, you not talkin' 'bout the boots? Shit! We're back on this marriage thing again, eh?" Between the wedding I attended and my friend's constant marriage chatter and the impending vote for equality in New York and not to mention being a woman in my thirties, I've been feeling the pressure to revisit the idea of marriage and what that means to me.

In my youth, I could see no other way of living out my life than as prescribed by my family and society. In college, I had a boyfriend whom I was going to marry at twenty-three, download some kids with at twenty-five and twenty-eight, and then live happily ever after. Can you imagine how unhappy that happily-ever-after would have been?

Imagine me and my gay ass waking up in the middle of the night, shaking and sweating after another "bad" lesbian sex dream. Married while secretly planning a lesbian cruise for my straight girlfriends, a picture of my secret hero, Meredith Baxter, in my wallet, and secretly watching downloaded episodes of *The L Word* on my iPhone. A lesbian married to a man, giving extra-long looks to women with short haircuts at the Home Depot while shopping for new fixtures to update that second-floor bathroom, all the while knowing that society dictated what was right, and I had swallowed the bitter pill, hook, line, and sinker.

That forever? Not so much!

I also remember planning a forever with a woman—a silly but somehow *tasteful* Harlem Renaissance–themed wedding, or a weekend wedding at Martha's Vineyard in the fall. Yes, the Vineyard in the fall, jewel tones, 7 PM ceremony, and women in suits! "Yes!" I said!

But then the backlash of a breakup after a short-lived engagement, coupled with my knowledge of the societal construct and other unpleasantries about the institution, would have me suspicious, skeptical, and intentionally avoiding marriage—like a female, not-so-famous George Clooney. Screw marriage. Screw it! I'd say. Marriage smarriage. It's about ownership—women as property. They just wanna keep us women folk in line. Well, I'm not getting in no line! Unless it's a line for some sex-me boots on sale in Soho.

My friend and I walked into a restaurant. Weary shoppers that we were, I hoped that her forever talk was a testament to her hunger and that it would be cured with a latte and dessert. But over the last shared bite of a warmed Mississippi mud pie, against all my better judgment, I found myself discussing marriage again.

My friend said, "Do you think that you can do forever?"

My mind searched for an answer. I thought: *There is no such thing as a forever, get a grip. Are you kidding? I was engaged, for crying out loud, and how'd that work out for me? People die, you know. Where's the forever in that, missy? You'd have better luck trying to give birth to a rabbit than making a forever, Gloria!*

And then—like an emotional, romanticized, runaway freight train—my heart betrayed me. I burst out with, "I do want someone to walk with . . . in life. I want a witness: a day-to-day witness. I want someone to look forward with—not just to, but also with. I believe in a forever. I want to get and stay married."

As soon as I said it, I knew it was who I was at the core. I knew it was my truth, and I could no longer hide it or pretend that I didn't want it because of the fear of not having it, either because I was prevented by society . . . or by myself.

While sitting in Soho with a dear friend, I finally understood what all of the marching and picketing was for.

∴

As the vote passed in New York, I sat stunned, silent.

I thought back to that minister and her "Ps" and "Rs," and I came up with my own three "Cs" of what, beyond love, would make me say "till death do us part":

Cheerleader—because we all can use encouragement. There is something so magical and fantastic about having someone who's always on your team. I love the idea of saying, "It's me and you against the world." I could commit to being that for someone, and I would love to have someone be that for me.

Companionship—because even though I have a dog . . . and a cat . . . we all can use someone to go to the market with, ride a bike with, and sit in a rocking chair with when we're too old or too disinterested in going to the club.

Commitment—because I believe in the intention of doing things, and there is something truly beautiful, idealistic, and highly romantic about having that intention and fighting like the dickens to keep it.

I called my mother.

"Equality passed, Mommy. If I'd like to, I can marry, and the government is behind me. So to your question of marriage and whether there is anything else that we call it? The answer is no: It's Marriage, with a capital *M*. And I want it and deserve it."

Suquamish Family Values

∴

Heather Purser

I stood as soon as they opened the floor to us—members of the community who had something they wanted to say—just as they have on every third weekend in March for as long as I can remember. Only this time, in 2011 at age twenty-eight, I was more nervous than I'd ever been at the annual gathering of the Suquamish tribe.

I walked to the microphone and poured my heart out to a room full of my Suquamish people. I told them I was a lesbian, which many already knew. I admitted that it was at times intimidating to be gay, and that I wanted more than anything for them—the people

I grew up with and knew my whole life—to formally accept me for who I was.

And for me, the mark of that acceptance would be adopting same-sex marriage within our tribal laws.

When I was around seven or eight years old, I saw this movie where a guy tried to kill himself because being gay had ruined his life and cost him everything. I remember thinking over and over, *If I grow up to be gay, I'll kill myself.* From then until perhaps just a couple of years ago, part of me always believed that I should do the same.

I've never wanted to be different from anyone else. As a kid, all I wanted was a "normal" life where people didn't scream and cry all the time and say how much they hated each other. I wanted to be part of a family in which I could feel loved no matter what I did. I had tried to please everyone—my mom, my dad, my aunts and uncles, my cousins, friends, teachers. Everyone. I was so focused on changing or hiding things about myself that I thought would be unacceptable. I stopped knowing what kind of music I liked, what my favorite food was, or where my true boundaries were. I was anything people wanted me to be, so long as they let me feel that I mattered to them.

My dad is one-half Indian, which makes my siblings and me one-quarter. We're enrolled Suquamish, a small tribe located on the western shores of the Puget Sound in Washington State, and we grew up fully immersed in the cultural and traditional practices of our people. Even though I've never heard anything specific about how we viewed gays in the past, I do know that we have always been open to people;

more than anything we are supposed to love each other as a tribe. I mean, we fight, we argue, we disagree, but in Suquamish we love each other. At least that's what I grew up hearing.

My mom, who's not Indian, would go through my journals all the time when I was growing up. So I always made sure to keep a fake one for her to read that I would "hide" in very obvious locations. But one day, when I was sixteen, she found my real ones, along with the book *Annie on my Mind*—the only book in my high school library about gay people. In my real journals I had started writing lesbian fiction, and I had written a sex scene.

My dad picked me up early from work at Taco Time that day. He wouldn't look at me or say anything until about halfway home when he finally said, "Hey, yeah, so your mom found some writing of yours. Are you gay?"

I was embarrassed and didn't know what to do, so I just said, "What?! No. I don't think so. I don't know."

"Well, she's pretty mad at you," he said. "You better just straighten this up with her." We didn't say anything for the rest of the drive. He dropped me off in the driveway of our house and left again.

When I went in, my mom sat us *all* down at the kitchen table—me and my two brothers and two sisters, who ranged in age from two to seventeen.

"Have a seat, Heather. I want you to have a seat," she said. "Why don't we all just have a seat and listen to the wonderful stories you write, shall we?" She began to read aloud the lesbian fiction I had written. She even read the sex scene.

Then she got into my face and asked, "Are you gay?" And I said, defiantly and almost proudly, "Yes, I'm gay." And she knocked me down the stairs.

She continued to beat and taunt me for hours. Sometimes she would stop to cry and apologize, saying that she truly did accept me and love me for who I am, but then she would take it all back and start screaming and calling me names again. It was a confusing hell, the way it always was with my mom.

I didn't come out fully to myself until I was attending Western Washington University in Bellingham. I started to become really comfortable because the people around me were so supportive. I ran into some homophobia, but not much—everyone was pretty accepting, it wasn't a big deal, and I could hold hands with a girl I was dating and not feel weird about it.

I wanted to have that same feeling on the Suquamish when I went home. I wanted to know that I was accepted, to know that nothing bad would happen. I needed to heal those wounds from what happened with my mom.

When I met Becca, my girlfriend, it was at the most unexpected place to find absolute, without-a-doubt true love: at a bar. I had just completed my training to be a diver—I dive between thirty and sixty feet deep in the Puget Sound for geoducks (pronounced *gooey* ducks), those giant clams that look like penises—and was celebrating with a friend by going out to what I once referred to as the "big city" of Seattle (which I now just call home).

Becca turned out to be the person who could bring me back from the dark places and remind me that life can be beautiful.

Before we met, I was doing well on my own, having come far in healing from my family life, but, after we met, everything I'd read about forgiveness and happiness and joy just clicked. Even though I had started the process to get same-sex marriage recognized in Suquamish before I met her, I don't think I would have followed through if it were not for her influence in my life.

I was at my niece's birthday party on a lake four years ago when I started talking to two women who told me they'd recently gotten married. "Wow, I didn't know you could get married in Washington!" I said. "Oh, you can't—it's just symbolic," they replied. At which point, without really giving it much thought, I announced, "I'm going to get gay marriage legalized in the tribe I'm from."

My older sister was listening, and when the women walked away she said to me, "Is that true? You're really going to do that?" And all I could say was, "I guess so."

Seven members of my tribe serve on a council that meets once a month, and in the fall of 2008 I started making appointments to meet with the council members to talk about gay marriage. Any tribal member can put her or his name on a list and say, "I want to meet with the council to discuss this issue." So I did that. I went in at my scheduled time and said, "I want gay marriage to happen on our reservation. I think it's good for us, and it's something that needs to be done. I'd like to see something happen."

There was a lot of back and forth—all the council members seemed to be in agreement about accepting it, but they were sluggish. I started to get the feeling that no one really wanted it to happen, not because they were against it but because it was just so different, so entirely new. And I was the only person bringing it up; the issue seemed to be only affecting *me*, although I know there are at least several other gay members of the tribe.

So they kind of put me off, and one councilman even told me that if it were ever to happen it would take several years. So I shouldn't get my hopes up. And I said, "Well, I'll see if I can get it done in one."

I've attended the big annual tribal meeting every year since I was a kid. There are about a thousand tribal members in all, and three hundred or four hundred show up at the meeting, just to talk about things. I decided to talk about gay marriage at the 2011 meeting.

After I gave my speech, I saw that a lot of women were crying. And everyone was kind of nodding their heads in agreement. A lot of people came up to me afterwards and gave me a hug—people I'd seen all my life but had hardly ever talked to.

But nothing concrete was being done about what I proposed. One of my cousins finally said, "Hey, you need to go up there and make that council *move*, so they don't drag their feet and we can vote on it."

So I went back up and I introduced myself again—that's what you do in my culture. I said, "Hi, my name is Heather Purser. I'm a member of this tribe. I'm a gay member of this tribe. And I demand that we vote on this issue here today and let the people speak."

Then the council had no choice: They had to open up the floor for voting. First we voted if we *should* vote. Everybody said "Aye." Then we voted on the actual issue of gay marriage, and everybody said "Aye" again. I turned around and saw family standing right behind me—my two brothers and a handful of cousins. I was so excited, so happy, so moved by the support.

On August 1, gay marriage was signed into law by the tribe. An official ordinance. Now the Suquamish will offer marriage licenses to gay couples, and just one in the couple has to be a tribal member. These marriages will be like any others in the tribe, recognized by Suquamish, and the spouse of the tribal member will be entitled to all the benefits the tribal member has.

Now, when I get married, I can do it through the tribe. Actually, I really wanted to ask Becca—and we've talked about it—but right now we're just too shy. Marriage just seems like a really big commitment, and I want to be certain that I'm ready for it. I've got a lot of goals, and I want to meet some of those before I share my life with someone I really care about. If we got married now, it would look like we were doing it just because it was legalized. So we want to wait a little longer; we want it to be very special.

No gay couple has yet applied for a Suquamish license to marry, but hopefully one pair will decide to be the first. After that, my girlfriend and I can be next.

Weddings are different in Suquamish than in non-Indian culture. There are a lot of drums and special dances and family songs and special regalia—wool dresses or cedar dresses. I would probably want a few songs and something cedar at my wedding—cedar is very sacred to us—but I don't know if I would actually do much more than that in the tradition. I think my girlfriend and I would both probably wear white dresses because we'd look kind of amazing—and we're both vain!

I live now in the Capitol Hill district of Seattle, where there are a lot of gay folks. (Seattle, by the way, is named after the famous Chief Seattle of the Suquamish.) They're excited about the Suquamish decision and my part in it. People are always trying to buy me drinks or something, and I'm like, "Oh, nonsense."

The media attention, too, has been strange for me: A lot of people in Seattle who didn't used to talk to me are doing so now. Sometimes when we reach the end of the conversation, they'll go, "Hey, way to go on the gay thing."

I don't talk to my mother anymore. But I'm trying to figure out how to forgive her without ever talking to her again. Not only did she beat me, but then she called the people in my family and told them to watch their children around me. The final straw came two years ago, when she told people that she often wondered if I'd sexually abused my brothers. That was it. I don't understand why she does these things. It makes me hurt for her. Even though I'm still angry and don't know how to resolve the mixed feelings I have about that woman, I know I will always love her and hope she finds some kind of peace.

I want my own children not to fear that they won't be accepted for who they are. And I think a lot about teenagers who struggle with their sexuality like I did; I don't want it to be so hard for them. I believe that if my tribe had some kind of teaching that homosexuality is okay . . . or if my mom had heard something like that when she was growing up . . . well, I always wonder if things would have been different.

I felt that getting my tribe to support gay marriage would be one small step in creating a world, a community, of people who are more accepting and won't harbor hatred. I think every tribe, Indian and non-Indian, should do the same.

Wedding Belles

On the previous page:

Victoria Livingston (in black and white) and Jacqueline Renwer marry in Washington, D.C.

Photo by Maggie Winters, Maggie Winters Photography, maggiewinters.com.

An Arbor on Arbella Street

∴

Colleen Michaels

I wrote this for the wedding of my good friends, Chris and Stephanie. While the poem is clearly about love, it's also about place: their garden, their home, and the Unitarian church in Salem, Massachusetts, where they met. They still live on Arbella Street, and if you enter under that arbor at the front gate, you will probably find them doting on their young son.

Enter under an arbor on Arbella Street
and you will find love.

Its forward motion carries a sea breeze through Salem
a momentum building in our broad smiles,
stitched in the seams of two shimmering dresses.
A perfect thing, a wedding day.

But in love there will be imperfections,
like those in the knitting I once saw Chris do in one of these pews.
The stitches not perfect, but none dropped on purpose.
Their result warm and soft and intricate like love,
linked to one another as Stephanie moved a pew
closer each week until they were shoulder to shoulder.
The beginning strand of love.

There will be chores because that's part of love.
And there will be the neglect of chores, for love too.
There will be grand gestures repeating in the pattern
of wallpaper or the purchase of short-seasoned blooms.
There will be slow to mature, but caring, investments
which are costly up front but serve you well over time
like a good roof and a dry basement.

Within this marriage space you create of safety and beauty,
love will give you conversations,
some as tired as your linoleum floor.
Unfinished, unnecessary to finish.
"Did you get the . . . . Yeah I got it."
This is the talk of time. The talk of love.

Then there's the loud laughing talk,
around your piano or out on the patio.
The conversation you invite others into. The proud talk of marriage.
"Tell them the story of our love." "No you tell it better," she will say.
Everyone here will lean in to hear this talk of love. Over and again.

But we know you own a private conversation
alone when only your words to each other can warm
like good heavy socks on cold feet in a house close to the ocean.
A comfort, a splurge, of compassion and joy
that you have promised
to spend and save for each other.

Photo:
Chris Makary (left) and Stephanie Makary on their wedding day in Salem, Massachusetts. *Photo by Heather Bohm-Tallman, hbtphoto.com.*

More Today Than Yesterday

∴

Bette Skandalis

"How long have you two been married?"

This is a question my wife and I are often asked when we meet new people. I suppose they see our rings, or perhaps, being from Massachusetts, we now share a puffed-up pride regarding our matrimonial privilege. I certainly never refer to Jo as my wife, preferring the standard "girlfriend" or more provocative "lover." "Wife" conjures up a woman in a shirtwaist dress wearing yellow rubber gloves and washing dishes.

We must give off the scent of an old married couple, though, telling stories in tandem or wearing the same sturdy outerwear and shoes (lesbians call it "twinning"). Strangers in stores ask if we are sisters, in spite of Jo's pallid complexion and delicate bone structure versus my olive skin and robust Mediterranean profile. It's obvious that we've been together a long time.

But I resent the question of how long we've been married because it's not exactly the one I want to answer.

The simple response is that we were married in 2004, two weeks after the Massachusetts Supreme Court ruled that same-sex couples could legally wed. On May 17, at one minute after midnight, city offices in Cambridge, where we live, were opened for lesbians and gay men to apply for marriage licenses. We went that night to support our marrying friends, but then were swept into the building with throngs of people wanting to be among the first to tie the knot.

We were not eligible for a license that night; we hadn't gotten the required blood test (because, of course, we had no intention to marry). But it was so much fun to spend a couple of congenial hours in the foyer of City Hall learning the stories of other pairs who actually were in line for that purpose. A few looked eligible to apply for Social Security in addition to a marriage license. One male couple carried a faded picture depicting two handsome young men in Greenwich Village, arms around each other's shoulders. On this night they posed for photos holding up the picture and smiling broadly, tears running down their weathered faces.

We left the building about 2 AM. Police in riot gear lined up to clear our path, and behind them thousands of well-wishers clapped and yelled congratulations. Did I imagine the rice? We felt like the

Beatles stepping off the plane in New York prior to their first U.S. tour. Jo and I looked at each other and thought, *Why not?*

A couple of days later, the lab technicians at Mount Auburn Hospital took blood samples and congratulated us on our forthcoming marriage. We hadn't told them our intent, but everyone in Cambridge seemed on high alert to the significance of the court decision. Or maybe our matching hoodies tipped them off.

Romantic love seemed to be everywhere on display during the two weeks before our wedding. Near our home, in a public plaza where I often witnessed spontaneous fights among drunken men, I saw a man and a woman—all of their possessions in a shopping cart nearby—dancing close and staring into each other's eyes while Peter Gabriel's song "In Your Eyes" played on their dented boom box. My own eyes filled with tears.

And on the morning of our wedding, I was walking my dog, Jack, when I saw another dog wandering down our street. He had tags but was clearly lost. Seeming to like Jack, he followed us back to the house. When Christine from Animal Rescue showed up, she observed the dogs in the backyard and remarked that Jack seemed to be in love.

"Christine, I'd like to chat, but I'm going to be late for my wedding."

"Oh. Hey, congratulations!"

She joked that Jack would finally have legitimate parents. And did I need a ride to the subway stop? I spied a shedding, slobbering dog in the cab of her truck and declined with thanks, thinking I should step up my personal grooming standard at least for the day.

We invited five people to the ceremony: my best friend, Mimsi;

her partner, Carolyn; our college friend Miriam (who pleaded for an invitation because she had not yet been to a gay wedding); my nephew John; and Jo's business partner, Kathleen. We found out later that many of our close friends were miffed that they were not able to celebrate with us. Our parents and close relatives had long embraced our union, but since we'd already been together for two decades, it seemed silly to make a big deal about inviting them.

The seven of us met at the Cambridge City Clerk's office at two on a Tuesday afternoon. The place was packed like Noah's ark, with matched sets everywhere, smiling and preparing for their passages. Getting married mid-week, in the middle of the day, gave the proceedings the feel of a shotgun wedding, despite the fact that, of course, neither of us was pregnant.

The city clerk emerged from her private office and invited us into the majestic City Council chambers for the formal ceremony. Jo recited beautiful personal vows to me; I read her an Emily Dickinson love poem that includes the lines:

If certain, when this life was out,
That yours and mine should be,
I'd toss it yonder like a rind,
And taste eternity.

We capped the ceremony by singing "More Today Than Yesterday," a sixties pop tune by a one-hit wonder called The Spiral Starecase:

All I know is that I fell in love with you
And if all my dreams come true
I'll be spending time with you.

Someone recorded the ceremony on videotape, although neither

Jo nor I can find it now. But I can still hear our voices reverberating in the venerable chambers.

Afterward, we strolled across the street to the 1369 Coffee House for champagne and cake. Then Jo and I did a little food shopping before she went back to work, while I returned home to pack for a business trip. It was, in most respects for a long-term lesbian couple, an ordinary day and night.

Since the wedding happened so quickly, we thought it appropriate to send postnuptial announcements to our friends, family, and business associates. Jo, a graphic artist by training, designed a unique card with ribbon and grommets binding it together. The cover quoted Massachusetts Supreme Court Chief Justice Margaret H. Marshall's eloquent majority view: "The right to marry means little if it does not include the right to marry the person of one's choice." Inside, the inscription read: "After twenty years of love and devotion, Jo Seidler and Bette Skandalis were married at Cambridge City Hall, June 1, 2004."

We were unable to resist the irony of radical feminists from the '70s getting married, so we inserted this addendum: "The brides will keep their own names."

We printed five hundred copies, but never sent them out. Jo had noticed that she misspelled the judge's name, so she scrapped the box of announcements. We never got around to redoing them, and many of our acquaintances still don't know we're married.

In retrospect, our wedding ceremony was a hastily built shed in comparison to the solid foundation of our relationship—and compared to the elaborate ceremonial constructions of some people we know. We've seen lesbians wearing matching wedding gowns with long trains, sitting on the backrests of convertible car seats, waving to astonished bystanders. We've been impressed by the foresight of those who submitted announcements to the *New York Times* that required all sorts of proof, a headshot, and six weeks' advance notice. Recently, I read about a gay wedding on the West Coast in which the grooms' tuxedoed pug was the ring bearer.

Where do you even find a tuxedo for a pug?

Our wedding featured no invitation list to agonize over, no bridal registry, no Bridezilla moments, no garters, and no mutual cake feeding. Nothing old or blue. I picked out the first thing I saw in my closet that morning. (Jo probably dressed with more care, and may have even bought something new.)

In truth, Jo and I were ambivalent—not about our commitment, but about marriage. It was the tradition that felt borrowed.

I grew up in the '50s and '60s not wanting to get married or have children. I never watched the activities of my mother and father, or the parents of my friends, and thought—*I want that*. Mostly I saw the bizarre results of some couples' unions.

During junior high school, my best friend's father set the house on fire by igniting his wife's clothing closet. My mother described her own wedding day, at age eighteen, as the worst day of her life. She hated the Greek tradition calling for the bride to celebrate separately with the groom's family, symbolically leaving her mother and father behind. I think she was also angry about having to pass up a rare-for-females college scholarship in order to become a stay-at-home wife.

Married women did their housework in heels and had perfect, if pesky, children. I saw no place for me in the leafy suburbs. *Leave It to Beaver, Ozzie and Harriet,* and *The Donna Reed Show* illustrated marriage models as foreign to me as the plot of my favorite book at the time, Jules Verne's *A Journey to the Center of the Earth*, which featured an alien world lurking beneath the familiar surface. At least Professor Von Hardwigg's expedition to the earth's core, while fraught with danger, resulted in getting recognition for his accomplishment—as well as winning lovely Fraulein Grauben.

I could never fathom being June Cleaver or Harriet Nelson or Donna Stone; I wanted to be Ward, Ozzie, or even Donna's pediatrician husband, Alex. I didn't want to be the boy; I just wanted to have the love and devotion of the girl. The only portrayals of women-loving-women were in films such as *The Children's Hour*, in which Shirley MacLaine plays a private girl's schoolteacher who hangs herself after rumors suggest a lesbian affair with another teacher. I watched this movie when I was a freshman in college living with a festering secret: My three-year affair with a woman had just ended so that she could marry her boyfriend. I believed then that I would never be able to live openly with the one I loved.

But in 1973, soon after my high school lover got married, I enrolled in a course called "Our Bodies, Ourselves," based on the groundbreaking book by the Boston Women's Health Book Collective. The chapter of that book that would change my life—or, more accurately, reveal it—was nestled between feminist perspectives on "Living with Ourselves and Others" and "Nutrition and the Food We Eat." Reading "In Amerika They Call Us Dykes" proved to be my journey to the center of the earth.

I was lucky to come out in the full bloom of the women's and gay liberation movements. My attraction to women, while not condoned by most people, was at least nurtured in the lesbian communities of college towns and metropolitan centers. I had found my core.

In 1976, inspired as an undergraduate by my radical professors, I enrolled in graduate studies and accepted a teaching assignment in the women's studies program at the University of Michigan. I found a home, not to mention lots and lots of sex, in the strong feminist community of Ann Arbor. I spent as much time organizing feminist guerrilla actions as I did working in the stacks of the graduate library. The overriding message of the time, one that still reverberates in me, proclaimed that the patriarchy was all too alive and well, and that marriage—as its cornerstone—was an insidious institution designed to oppress women.

Meanwhile, an attractive undergraduate was flirting with me during my office hours. Jo Seidler charmed me when she showed up with an article by Susin Shapiro from a 1979 issue of the *Village Voice* entitled "Creeps and Assholes: Character Is Destiny." The article began: "Hey you, you've spent the last decade exploring your inner nature . . . psychodrama, t'ai chi, kundalini yoga, bioenergetics, tantra sex therapy, and yarrow sticks. It's time to face the facts and ignore your feelings: You are either a creep or an asshole, and that's that." I speed-read the rest of the article while Jo burned me with her stare. Did she think I was a creep or an asshole? Which did she prefer? I felt faint.

While we didn't get together then—she was my student, after all—we did begin an affair two years later, and after a couple of years of starts and stops, we hooked up for good.

Which leads me back to the question I want people to ask: "How long have you two been *together*?"

I want to answer with this big number: "Thirty-one years."

Of course I argue with my wife/girlfriend/lover over the definition of "together." I like to count it from the day we met, or at least when we first slept together. Jo feels it is properly dated from the time we made a commitment to each other.

"Babe," she says, "you can hardly count the years you were still living with someone else!"

She throws up her hands and looks to our friends for support. I shrug, and we move on to finish other sentences for each other.

To me, sex was a revolutionary act and marriage its domesticator. I ascribed to the Joni Mitchell school of matrimony, when she sings:

We don't need no piece of paper from the city hall

keeping us tied and true.

And yet, there we were, at the city hall, with many pieces of paper, including *Commonwealth of Massachusetts Department of Public Health Registry of Vital Records and Statistics Certificate of Marriage, Information Given to Same-Sex Couples*, our vows, and the results of a blood test ensuring we would not embark upon married life suffering from syphilis.

I remember so many details from that day, June 1, 2004: How the city clerk asked us to stand and face each other. How lovingly Jo recited her vows. How beautifully Carolyn led us in song. I remember the severe faces of the Cambridge Founding Fathers staring down at us from their gilded frames—quite a contrast to our gleeful marriage improvisation.

I am proud that our marriage has contributed to the political conversation—the revolutionary idea that joining with someone is not a right accorded to a privileged, heterosexual few, but for anyone lucky enough to find somebody to share a life with.

After fumbling into our wedding day, we now recognize it as one of the happiest days of our lives. Life seldom happens the way one draws it up. On *his* journey, Dr. Von Hardwigg encountered lightning storms and oversized human skulls—but those obstacles led him to his destiny.

"Six years," I answer to those who ask how long it's been. "We've been married six years. But it feels like we've always been together."

Old, New, Borrowed, Blue

∴

Mary Beth Caschetta

SOMETHING OLD

I am twelve years old when my mother starts dragging me off to the back pews of dark churches to watch perfect strangers get married.

"Someday that'll be you," she whispers, pinching me.

I'm supposed to want to be the bride, but picture myself more the priest, holy and disinterested. I like his crisp white collar, asexual demeanor, his purported closeness with God. I have learned to keep my mouth shut about this, though. I have a typical Italian American mother who is obsessed with marrying me off, a mother for whom weddings are the ultimate sport. There's no room in her agenda for fantasies of priests.

She trains me hard: field trips to St. Anthony's, St. Michael's, St. John's. Each time a new bride stands at the ready, my mother cries into a wadded Kleenex. "So beautiful," she says.

It isn't true: Some brides are scrawny, with beaky noses. Some are heavy, with wire-like curls sprayed into a nest. Other brides are just plain homely in a way that makes me think of specific towns in western New York, as if a particular brand of unattractive Italian women was left behind on the Genesee River while the pretty got to forge onward to Canada.

Still, my mother can detect the beauty in any girl about to be given away to a man. And we both know that it's me she sees in that long white dress with matching veil and shoes. Not a stranger but her daughter. Me, flanked by a lineup of broad-shouldered women clad in taffeta and men wearing rented shoes.

In Italy, as in my corner of Rochester, New York, wedding receptions are a birthright: soggy macaroni and chicken thighs, DJ'd music and an open bar. My mother can't wait to show me off to the crowd of whiskery *gumbas*, my great-aunts, who magically appear at every reception.

"*That's* who knows about marriage," my mother says when the old women from Calabria stand *en masse* to dance the tarantella. This is the *gumbas'* blessing on every bride, their warning for every groom, the promise of what awaits him. Watching from a distance, I can feel the weight of their swollen stomping feet, their arthritic clapping hands.

Long ago, they let me in on the secret of matrimony: that a man (my father, say, or one of my brothers) could be so *stoonad* as to believe he is king, when everyone knows that women rule. Italian women.

The youngest of four, the only girl in our family, I nod and smile, as if I'm interested.

Aunt Peppie points a gnarled finger. "You, too."

I believe her. I have seen her perform magic: She and her sisters, my grandmother included, can make headaches go away by dripping oil into water and saying *mal'occhio*, the evil eye. (*Mumbo jumbo*, my father calls it.) Any one of them can snap a rabbit's neck in half, skin it, and fry it with greens, conjuring up the most delicious dinner imaginable. Probably they are witches—Italian witches, of course, the good kind. Any prediction they make is likely to come true.

Unable to shake off Aunt Peppie's words as I walk the halls of junior high, I find myself agreeing to go out with a boy who's been pursuing me since seventh grade. I do not yet know I'm queer, but I know I am not exactly like the other girls. I've resigned myself to an eerie certainty that nuptials (like train wrecks and cancer) are what await other people—my cousins, my brothers, my friends—not me. At the time, my secret emergency backup plan is to join the nuns. But somehow I end up a lesbian.

Imagine my surprise, twenty-five years later, when Massachusetts, a state in which by utter chance I am living, makes it legal for people like me to marry.

"Are you sure?" I ask my partner, Meryl. We watch the news on New England Cable. "Do you think it's really going to happen?"

I never figured on becoming a twenty-first-century bride.

∴

I come of age in the early '80s, an era of acquiescence and yuppies. Mornings, my mother curls my hair with a hot iron, picks out pastel clothing, and talks *at* me until I have no desire that isn't hers originally. This includes becoming a cheerleader. Forced into lacy anklets and patent-leather shoes long after other kids are wearing jeans, I lurch haltingly out the door each morning, the first of many surrenders toward a long, illustrious career as a heterosexual.

My mother is happy at first, elaborately dressing me up for Friday night dinners with my pimply boyfriend, his doughy parents, and a sister who's as blond as he is. They are Episcopalians from Maine, practiced at eating fish dinners without ever once breaking into a quarrel, unlike the nightly brawling at my house. Their whispery voices alone are like miracles.

Studying my boyfriend's Teutonic family, I learn to speak low and order salad with buttermilk dressing. It feels like a science experiment, gaining access to this strange planet where no one belches at the table. In time my mother will grow to fear them, these un-Italians, and yet I love them. They talk *to* me, never once mentioning marriage, my hair, my odds for landing the title of homecoming queen. They are teachers who know things; they discuss nuclear weapons, the economy, saving the environment. Their sole agenda is their son's happiness.

For adults, they seem remarkably unafraid.

"He's not good enough for you," my mother says when it finally dawns on her that I've been adopted by this kindly Anglo tribe. In her mind I am Jacqueline Kennedy, with princes and presidents en route for my hand.

But she is wrong about Chris.

Nerdy and sweet, he is endlessly patient with my hesitancy about romance. "You don't have to," he tells me, "it doesn't matter." Whenever I'm near him, I listen for the blood pumping through his body, striving to open the clenched fist of my own heart, to feel what other people feel. I spend the summer doing research, lying on the front porch reading *Anna Karenina*, wondering if love has to be that hard. Since boys do not come naturally to me, every night I get on my knees and pray to Jesus: "Please let it happen tomorrow. Amen."

At last Jesus answers. I fall in love.

From the age of thirteen until I am about to turn twenty-two, Chris is my one-and-only, my heartthrob, my sidekick, my entire world.

Even later, when I learn he is sleeping with other girls at college and try to break it off, I somehow only seem to fall more deeply in love. It's as if Jesus has answered my prayers in one direction: forward. I imagine Him looking down on me with a patient face. *Be careful what you pray for.*

"Date someone," my college friends advise. I do. I go to dinner with a couple of nice guys. I even have lackluster sex with one of them, while shoring up my plans for the nunnery. Then, on a lark, I go to see a couple of movies offered by the American Culture Department with my bisexual roommate.

"You only come to the lesbian films," mentions my writing professor and mentor, Paul Russell, who teaches queer studies. "People are going to talk."

I am the straightest, squarest person on campus, but I have a versatile mind and a bold imagination. As I am standing there, laughing at his joke, it hits me who I might really be.

Within weeks, I stop caring if Chris dates other girls; I've fallen in love with a girl of my own. A woman actually, my major advisor, someone who is not technically even gay.

It happens so fast, there isn't time to pray.

SOMETHING NEW

The next time true love makes an appearance in my life it's late one night in 1999, while I'm watching a rerun of the *The Oprah Winfrey Show*. I'm visiting friends in Berkeley after a harrowing yearlong dissolution from a woman who has broken my heart and stolen my money. My adult life has been characterized by a series of bad romantic choices. Perhaps I've just been unlucky, though I sometimes wonder if I am subconsciously punishing myself.

This particular night, I lie sprawled across a strange futon in a spare apartment reserved for married graduate students. It is a few days before Christmas, the last Noel of the twentieth century, and I am thirty-three years old, depressed, and jet-lagged. In an overcrowded world of 5.8 billion people, I feel utterly, hopelessly alone.

Flipping the channels, I happen upon *Oprah*. The topic is etiquette, but I stay tuned anyway, because her theme song cheers me up. *O* is for openness. Optimism! All I really have to do, I realize, is get through the holidays: another hour, this evening, the rest of my life. How hard could it be with Oprah always there to rely upon at 3 AM, ready with her pragmatic advice? I watch commercials for mascara, feminine pads, rejuvenating shampoo.

When the show returns, I find myself suddenly staring into my future.

I sit up, pointing. "Hey!" I tell the scraggly houseplants that are my only company. "There she is!" *She* is Meryl Cohn, a writer I've met on several occasions.

I've sat across from her—Thanksgiving, Fourth of July, New Year's—at tables of fellow writers. Still, I've never actually *looked* at her before. Now, on TV, she exudes sex appeal and confidence. Even Oprah seems won over by her charm: green eyes, auburn hair, the cheekbones of a 1940s movie star.

During a brief Q&A, edited to one Q *(Should straight people ever ask gay people if they are gay?)*, Meryl chats easily, explaining to the studio audience how to know when something is offensive. She offers a quick rundown of the dos and don'ts of queer etiquette. Joking about the age-old question, "What do women like in bed?" Meryl says wryly, "Other women, of course."

Oprah, lovely and velvety, responds with a deep-throated laugh.

Then, in a flash, the moment (and magic) passes. She is just someone I've met, friend of a friend. Only Meryl Cohn, writer of the tongue-in-cheek advice column known widely in the gay and lesbian community as Ms. Behavior. It's just as well. I'm not looking for thunderbolts and romance. I can barely manage a change of clothes.

Closing my eyes, I sink back into my familiar funk. My life is a troubled narrative, but at least I know what to expect: bad choices, difficult women, anxiety, despair. I fall asleep to the sound of the TV, cozy in my misery, unaware that somewhere, not far away, a perfect stranger is taking my life into her hands. Messages are being received, and some of them, it turns out, are about me.

SOMETHING BORROWED

Back in New York in February, I seek out Meryl's advice about a woman I'm casually dating. (Meryl *is* an advice columnist, after all, and it's obvious I could use some help.) It turns out she is in town for a few weeks, so we arrange to meet at a gay bookstore in lower Manhattan. I launch into my problem without prelude.

"Dump her," Meryl says.

She brings up a little story of her own, how her good friend Linda has been receiving messages about her from someone in California. "My friend Psychic Mary wants me to tell you that you've already met your new girlfriend," Linda tells her. "Psychic Mary sees books."

Meryl doesn't know the woman making these predictions about her future. "I *have* a girlfriend, thank you very much." Her relationship is troubled, but she's loyal nonetheless.

Linda claims she is only passing messages. "Psychic Mary hears voices. Are you going to argue with voices?"

We laugh off the prediction over tea.

Linda has also said something else that Meryl won't tell me until months later: a prediction about Meryl getting married, with none other than Linda herself making the wedding cake.

It's the turn of the new century, but, even so, a prediction of marriage seems absurdly far from reality. The world is hardly our oyster. Even if it were, Meryl is not exactly the blushing bride type, which is part of her allure.

That day in February, Meryl strikes me as definitely attractive, but I fancy myself too short for her. I am five-foot-three, a good seven inches shy of matching her height. Even so, after that meeting I invite her to lunch, the movies, dinner. Each time I share my latest adventure: a blind date who is actually blind, a woman who wants to take me camping after one cup of coffee, a trainer who asks me out for kickboxing. I'm trying to renew my childhood faith in love; also, I'm lonely.

My stories make Meryl laugh.

Between us we have two Seven Sisters' degrees, two master's degrees, a couple of literary grants, one very successful advice column, two published books, and four books-in-progress. We're not exactly dumb. It's just that we're unaccustomed to living out someone else's narrative, a psychic's no less. Who believes in voices, anyway—coming from where, the great beyond?

In my life so far, all predictions have turned out wrong. Love has been a disaster. My only good relationship happened in puberty.

With tickets I can't get rid of, I take Meryl to Puccini's *Madame Butterfly*—by chance on Valentine's Day. And despite the fact that there is nothing like Italian opera to spur on romance, we manage to maintain our ignorance.

To reciprocate, she invites me to Eve Ensler's *Vagina Monologues*.

"Are you kidding?" I say, the guise of friendship beginning to wear thin.

We spend the following Sunday together. After the *Monologues*, we walk downtown in the rain, eat Mexican, cruise a bookstore. Sitting in the self-help aisle, we diagram each other's personalities, confess our biggest flaws. At a coffee shop around the corner, I grill her about her talk-show tour. Flashing back to that lonely California night on a borrowed futon, I can't bring myself to mention Oprah.

Walking down the street, I am suddenly aware of not just how tall

Meryl is but how wide the world, how mysterious. For the first time since junior high, I am truly afraid. But here it is: late and chilly on a dark street corner in Chelsea, my future unraveling before me.

Wary, I look into Meryl's eyes and suddenly understand how Anna Karenina ended up under that train.

I go for long stretches without hearing from her, though, because Ms. Behavior practices what she preaches: No hint of a new relationship will be permitted until her current one comes to its natural conclusion.

Not to worry, my shrink reassures me: "There's no cure for love."

House with a swing, Psychic Mary continues her predictions. *A life together, growing old.*

SOMETHING BLUE

May 17, 2004, 8:30 AM, a raw morning in Cape Cod, Massachusetts: Meryl and I stand waiting to fill out some paperwork. It is the first day gays can legally be married, and we have the first appointment. A line is already forming, couples standing shoulder-to-shoulder on the steps of the town hall.

By nine the streets are filled. Hundreds of onlookers watch and wait, cheering. People throw confetti, take photographs. Some carry signs, others hand out roses to every bride, male and female. Volunteers from the Human Rights Campaign cut wedding cake for any two waving a license to marry. The festive atmosphere harkens back to earlier days: the first gay pride parades in New York City, the marches on Washington.

"This one's pretty," my mother has said about Meryl. She liked her at first sight. My mother has come a long way since the days of hysterical crying, breast-beating, throwing herself at me; my mother hasn't cornered me in a kitchen or attacked my short hair in years. We are in easy daily contact, thanks to the computer we gave her for her seventieth birthday, and while she may say a secret novena now and then, petitioning the Virgin on my behalf, she seems okay with my current situation.

Handing over our paperwork, we race up the Cape to Orleans District Court, where we pay for our waiver of the three-day waiting period, an arcane holdover from the days of syphilis and shotgun weddings when a few days of clarity might have made a difference. (Formerly $65, this waiver now costs $195, the special homosexual rate.) Greeting us in chambers is Judge Welch, a small, worn New Englander in formal robes, whose father, like his father before him, was the sitting judge.

His office is dark and smells of cherry tobacco. "I'm pleased to take part in this special day." His eyes twinkle. He presses our hands into his small but binding grip. "You love each other a lot."

We hold our breath. Here we are: among the first gay people to marry in the United States of America, in the first state to go legal, on the fiftieth anniversary of *Brown v. Board of Education*.

"A fine day for civil rights!" the judge says, breaking into a smile.

Returning to Provincetown for our final license, we are greeted by an army of television cameras. Over the past few weeks we've turned down media requests from *Newsday* to TV Japan, politely declining reporters who want to follow us around to document our wedding day. We are camera shy. Nonetheless, the local news catches our happy moment. (The reel later runs in a continuous loop on the *New York Times'* website.)

At 4 PM, we are married in our living room. We have hired a lovely, elderly, gay African American minister who walks with a cane. She speaks solemnly of candles and circles and unions. It feels suddenly meaningful to participate in an institution designed for our exclusion, more meaningful than expected. It's funny how one can be unaware of one's oppression until the instant it is lifted.

Flown in from New York, Meryl's brother is our witness, ring bearer, best man. Her sister calls from Brooklyn a few moments after we've read our vows; my father-in-law and his wife phone that evening from Florida; Meryl's mother sends flowers from Long Island.

From my family, there is only an eerie silence. On May 17 well through the following Sunday, when our marriage is announced in the *New York Times*, I hear nothing. I imagine them opening the paper to our smiling newsprint faces, cringing each time the word *lesbian* appears in the inky text.

When the moment arrives, of course, none of this matters.

"Do you take this woman?" the minister asks.

And I do. Completely and happily, I do.

Juggling Down the Aisle

∴

Sara Felder

It's our wedding day and we are standing under the chuppah. The rabbi says, "Are you ready?" as he places the wineglass on the ground.

But when I raise my foot to break the glass, I suddenly remember the first time my heart *was broken: when my favorite aunt died. And I learned that sometimes people that you love die.*

And then I remembered the second time my heart was broken: when my father walked out. And I learned that sometimes people that you love leave.

And the third time my heart was broken: when my mother took me to my very first play. And I learned that sometimes people that you love take you to see really bad theater.

—All excerpts from Sara Felder's June Bride *(1995)*

I began writing my one-woman play *June Bride* not long after preparing for my own wedding. It's about two women, Sara and Dev, who want to have a Jewish wedding ceremony, and I tell the story with circus moves, visual imagery, and some other tricks up my sleeve. You could call it *Juggler on the Roof.*

I started juggling in college. I loved the rhythm of the objects on my hands, the patterns I created in the air, and the danger of a potential drop at any moment. It was through juggling that I entered the theater. After a few years performing with San Francisco's Pickle Family Circus, I began creating solo shows that weave my talents and shtick through a significant narrative. For example, in *June Bride*, I come out to my father while escaping from a straitjacket, teetering on a balance board, and tangled up in a phone cord, while the audience sings, "You are My Sunshine."

June Bride is not entirely autobiographical, but it does address some essential questions for me: Would the Jewish tradition affirm a lesbian couple? Would our families of origin attend our lesbian wedding? Would we *both* wear wedding dresses?

> *Mom: I had always hoped when you settled down with someone, it would be with a doctor or a lawyer or, I don't know,* a man.
>
> *Sara: I know how you feel, Mom. When I was little I used to*

> *imagine walking down that aisle and meeting a wonderful man there. I had that same expectation, but then, hey,* I adjusted.

I met Dev Noily in the summer of 1989 at KlezKamp, a Yiddish culture camp geared for adults. It was near the beginning of the klezmer revival, and I dusted off my clarinet and brought it with me into the Santa Cruz Mountains.

Dev was wise, funny, beautiful, thoughtful, sexy, compassionate. And did I mention funny? She coaxed a gorgeous tone from her trumpet, and we would sneak off together to the chapel to play duets of the haunting Yiddish melodies.

At that time it wasn't unprecedented for queer couples to have weddings, but it wasn't that common either. It was soon clear that I wanted to spend the rest of my life with Dev, but not so clear that I needed to marry her. On the one hand, I took pride in my status as an outsider who doesn't need "that piece of paper" to confirm my relationship. On the other hand, I was very angry that I was denied the opportunity to marry legally. This tension between loving being an outsider and craving being an insider became my own ambivalent wedding dance. No wonder I'm a juggler.

I was especially confused about how to act when my straight friends got married. I wanted to congratulate them and wish them the best, but I also felt like they didn't acknowledge that they were joining a club that denied me membership. I didn't hold them personally responsible for my oppression, but their marriages didn't exactly help the cause. Plus, they were always encouraging Dev and me to have a ceremony—as if our "marriage" would be the same as their (no-quotes) marriage.

Still, there was a part of me that wanted to do it. I wanted to state publicly how much I loved Dev and how I intended to spend my life with her. I wanted to stand under a *chuppah* with her in front of all our friends and the family members who wanted to be there, just like they did in *Fiddler on the Roof*. And, with our community, I wanted to eat and drink and dance in celebration of that rare and sweet love.

I also wonder, though, how much of my desire for a wedding was socially conditioned. Is it possible that a rebellious kid who disdained mainstream values really just wanted to wear a white dress and walk down the aisle, like I'd been taught to want in all the movies and fairytales? Or, maybe walking down the aisle as a lesbian in 1993 *was* the most subversive thing I could do?

> *Dev and I decided to get married because we wanted our friends to witness our lifelong commitment to each other, we wanted our families to take our relationship more seriously, and we wanted one of those new cordless drills.*

We knew that it would be difficult talking to some family members about our wedding, and we didn't want the emotional angst (as well as the logistical details) to overwhelm the big day, so nine months before our planned formal wedding we made a radical choice: We held a private ceremony, just the two of us. We married ourselves!

First we rode the trolley car to City Hall in San Francisco and registered as domestic partners. Then we drove out to the ocean at Land's End, had a picnic dinner from Yellow Submarine sandwich shop, exchanged rings, and said our vows. Finally, I smashed an empty Coke can with my foot.

> *There are many reasons why you break a glass at your wedding (because this is Judaism, so there are many reasons for* everything*). One reason is that at the moment of your greatest joy, your wedding, you are obliged to remember the greatest tragedy that has ever befallen the Jewish people. Here I'm not referring to Bob Dylan's conversion to Christianity, or his conversion back to Judaism, but rather to the destruction of the Second Temple in Jerusalem. So by smashing this glass, you are invoking and recalling all the sorrow and sadness there is in the world. Because god forbid there is* one *day in your* whole life *when you can just be happy!*

As we planned a public ceremony to follow the private one, we considered our options. We kept asking questions about how we could imbue our ceremony with meaning: How do we sanctify this moment of awe? How do we invite the holy spirit to bless our union? And the answer kept coming back: Do what your ancestors did, and give yourselves over to the powerful ritual process our tradition provides.

And so, in June 1993, we returned to the same chapel where we had played duets four years earlier to get married in a traditional Jewish ceremony. (*Traditional* being a relative term: Our out gay rabbi officiated as we celebrated with our community of clowns, queers, and klezmorim.)

Prayer

(recited while doing "contact juggling"—rolling a clear glass ball around my arms and torso)

You know how you made the world and everything.

And the trees and the rivers and this woman that I'm in love with. Well, I know it probably doesn't mean much coming from me, but I just want you to know that I think you did a very good job. On the woman.

But I was wondering if, when you created her, maybe you got a little mixed up. Like, maybe at first you thought you were making a tree, because she moves so beautifully in the wind. And then maybe you thought you were making the ocean, because she's very deep and also very clear. But then maybe you thought you were making a mountain, because she's very solid and steady and so hard to budge. Did you have to make her that stubborn, God?

I also want to say that you got the balance just right with her, because you gave her such a good heart and such a good mind.

I know that in general you don't give out guarantees, but I was hoping that in my case you would make an exception—and make sure that we don't leave each other.

One more thing, God, as long as you're matchmaking, I just want to ask you if you would bless this match.

As it turned out, it was precisely the fact that our wedding ceremony wasn't legal that made it so meaningful. Much of the traditional ceremony didn't apply to us, and some of it was downright misogynist or homophobic. Because we had to rewrite the traditional Jewish wedding contract, the *ketubah*, to make it consistent with our genders, we pored over the texts, drawing out their intentions and rewriting them to reflect *our* deepest intentions. This is the gift of being an outsider. Writing our *ketubah* turned out to be the most meaningful aspect of the wedding process. We committed to our love for each other and expressed hope that it would fuel our sense of social justice—wanting to make the world a better place than we found it. We vowed to create a home filled with humor and laughter and a reverence for learning, compassion, and human dignity. Our vows ended with, "I will love you all my days and all my nights with passion, respect, and curiosity."

> *Sara:* I *may want a traditional wedding and* you *may want a traditional wedding. But does a traditional wedding want* us*? We have to change the words of the ceremony, of the* ketubah, *of the prayers, so we can make believe that it applies to us. You can't honestly tell me that Moses and Miriam are happy for us. Do you think it's all right with them that there are two women standing under the* chuppah*?*
> *Dev: More importantly, Sara, is it all right with* you*?*
> *Sara: I don't know. I don't know if two women can* fit *under the chuppah, with all our woman bodies and thoughts and feelings. I don't know if the world will explode, will stop turning. I don't know if Judaism, which existed for thousands of years, will end if two women stand under the* chuppah*! Look, don't take it personally—it's not you.*

To delve deeper into this question of how to have a lesbian Jewish wedding, I turned to my bible, *Fiddler on the Roof*, which had always been "the gospel" on Jewish weddings for me. The story deals with Tevye the dairyman negotiating the marriages of his eldest three daughters, who each push him a little further away from his tradition.

In *June Bride*, there is a scene in which the character Sara goes to the theater and imagines one of Tevye's daughters asking his permission to marry another woman, Rivka, the cobbler's daughter. Responding to Tevye's alarm, she suggests that her relationship is holy by quoting a Jewish legend: "What has God been doing since completing the work of Creation? Matchmaking!"

In another nod to *Fiddler*, the character of "The Jewish Tradition" in *June Bride* is portrayed by a violin, held upside-down and used as a puppet. It was almost as if the June bride wanted the blessing not just of Jewish tradition, but of the movie itself.

> (Sara meets the spirit of the Jewish tradition on a subway in New York. He is a violin, smoking a cigarette, wearing an old suit, reading the *New York Times*.)
>
> *Sara: It's funny that I should bump into you now, because I'm getting married soon and I want to invite you to the wedding. We're going to have a traditional Jewish wedding. It's out in San Francisco. I have directions, if you need.*
>
> *Violin: A traditional wedding in California? What does that mean—the sushi will be kosher? All right, I would be honored to come to your wedding. Tell me, when's the big day?*
>
> *Sara: I can't tell you how relieved I am. Everyone has been giving me the hardest time about marrying a woman. I knew you would come to my wedding.*

> *Violin* (horrified): *What wedding? Two girls don't make a wedding! If you want to have a wedding, have your bride-groom call me.*
> *Sara: Okay, fine, don't come to my wedding. Who needs you? Who cares about you? Who do you think you are?*
> *Violin: Me? I am "nobody." I am the broth in the soup. I am the rabbi's old coat. I am the silence between words. I am tradition.*
> *Sara: You're kidding me. You are "tradition"? Sorry, I just thought you'd be taller.* (beat) *Look, you have to come.*
> *Violin: What do you think tradition is? Do you think you can change* me *overnight? Next thing you know, there'll be electric menorahs, women rabbis, drive-thru synagogues. Where will it end?*
> *Sara:* (to audience) *My guess is the drive-thru synagogues.* (to Violin) *The old generation is gone. Don't you see that you need us as much as we need you? Look at you—you smoke too much, you drink too much, you're out of shape, you're out of tune.*
> *Violin: This tradition will never let you stand under the* chuppah.
> *Sara: Oh yeah? Well, I don't need your permission.*
> *Violin: This tradition will never say "mazel tov." The only glass that will break at your wedding will be at the foot of the poor schnook who tries to dance the bottle dance for you!*

Dev and I worked so hard on making ours a Jewish wedding that I started thinking that we didn't include enough of our fabulous campy queer selves. So, on the day of the event, I called my friend Nancy and asked her to bring four small rainbow flags, which we affixed to the top of each chuppah pole—lest our visibility as a queer couple not be visible enough!

I also didn't want anyone to think that by our having a wedding ceremony we could afford to be complacent about legalizing same-sex marriage. Remember, this was 1993. So we included in our wedding invitations a postcard to then-governor Pete Wilson urging him to legalize gay marriage. Our friends and families were happy to take this political action as part of celebrating our union.

Some queer critics question adopting mainstream symbols, like the fabulous white wedding dress. Why, they ask, should we continue to be slaves to social norms whose origins lie in the subjugation and objectification of women? My answer to these critics is Yes/And: Yes, these forms have oppressed us. And we can claim and transform them so they serve and celebrate us.

In *June Bride*, a wedding dress slowly flies down to the stage accompanied by a jazz version of "I Feel Pretty." It is both a beautiful and campy moment. I take the dress off the hanger, revealing, to my surprise, a T-shirt supporting a local sports team or political referendum on the ballot in the locale where I'm performing—a reminder that the mundane world is never too far away from the sacred moment. Then I put on the beautiful sleeveless dress that shows off my hairy armpits.

(In my real wedding, I wore a white dress with high-top sneakers to the reception. It was also sleeveless.)

Like all rituals that mark a transformation in life, our wedding brought up loss along with celebration, sadness along with joy. Members of each of our families stayed away—some because they couldn't bring themselves to participate in our queer ceremony and others because certain relationships were just too broken. We also had some wonderful surprises: Dev's eighty-five-year-old grandmother, the elegant matriarch of her family, showed up ready to party. She gave Dev a ring that she'd been given by Dev's grandfather on their fiftieth anniversary, inscribed with Hebrew words from the Song of Songs: *ani l'dodi v'dodi li.* "I am my beloved's and my beloved is mine."

My divorced parents had not spoken to each other in more than fifteen years, and my father didn't attend my brother's or my sister's wedding. But, wonder of wonders, miracle of miracles, my dad decided to come to my lesbian wedding.

Then Dev came over, and she said, "Sara, did you notice the Rabbi's brother. He has black hair and big eyes, great smile."
Sara: Are you thinking what I'm thinking?"
And together we said, "Sperm donor!!!"

This is one of the many places where *June Bride* diverges from my real life. As I say in another play, "All the stories are made-up; it doesn't mean they're not true." Our path to parenthood did not involve the rabbi or his brother, but Dev and I do have a son, Jesse Lev, now eleven years old. He's an actor, writer, *Calvin & Hobbes* maven, and he proudly marched in this year's San Francisco LGBT Pride parade wearing a homemade T-shirt that reads "Queerspawn is the best spawn."

We have never lived in a state where same-sex marriage was legal. (We were living in Philadelphia when San Francisco flung open the doors of City Hall for same-sex couples to marry in 2004, and still there when the California Supreme Court briefly made gay marriage legal in 2008.) But things are changing, and I know that I will have the opportunity at some point to marry Dev legally. Ironically, after all my anger about not having the opportunity to marry legally, now that it has become a real possibility, I'm somewhat ambivalent. I'm against the notion that married people should have more benefits than other people. Affordable health insurance shouldn't just be a benefit of marriage.

But it's more than that.

Every minority group wants the perks of assimilation, then worries about losing its unique culture in the big melting pot. A strong part of me wants to be just like everyone else and another part wants to proudly sing out my differences. Part of me rails against the system, the other part wants to be quietly accepted. I am both an activist dyke juggler and a nice girl from Brooklyn. Insider, outsider.

I think that if Dev and I were to get married legally, we would still have a Jewish wedding, but we'd camp it up more. It might look like this: I will juggle down the aisle. Dev will play her trumpet. Jesse Lev will hula-hoop in, sprinkling flower petals. And we will exchange not rings but clown noses. Then, together we will smash the glass of intolerance, inhumanity, and hurtful traditions. *Mazel tov!*

> Sara and Dev are standing under the *chuppah*.
>
> *Sara:* (to audience*) And then I feel this link between Dev and me and all the generations of couples who have ever stood under a* chuppah *and broken a glass.*
>
> *And then I notice, over by the buffet table, an old guy in a new suit with the* New York Times *under his arm. (Violin music is heard.) And he is smiling at us. . . .*

First Dance

∴

Kimberly Reed

The first time I wore a wedding dress was on Halloween. Most girls dreaming of having the perfect wedding someday would probably think that would be bad luck, like putting someone else's wedding ring on your left ring finger. Or maybe they'd just find it ridiculous. But I was dying to be seen as a bride in public, and that meant wearing a wedding dress. I was technically still male at the time, and I would have done anything to have that chance. Every girl's dream, right?

That Halloween was pretty early on in my transition from male to female, but even then I created a lot of confusion in San Francisco's Castro district. Celebrants didn't quite know what gender I started out as, what I was trying to end up as, or whether I was mocking anything—as many Castro Halloween costumes do. Their confusion was due, I'm sure, to the exacting authenticity of my costume. For anyone who realized I was male, I'm sure they wondered why I was taking my outfit so seriously.

Around that time I was also asked to be a groomsman in a couple of weddings. Getting dressed up in a suit and tie was what really made me feel like I was in drag. One groom's father expected me to cut my long blond hair before the ceremony, but that was completely out of the question because it would have threatened my burgeoning femininity.

I continued my transition through my early- and midtwenties, and with it came an inevitable deep and thorough examination of what it means to be female or male in our society. At some point after I had transitioned, probably in my late twenties, I remember trying to imagine myself in a "real" wedding dress in the future. If I fabricated even more, I pictured getting married to a man and fulfilling what I thought might be every girl's dream. After all, I assumed at the time that if I was really to be female it might mean transitioning into the most conventional version of femininity, which would of course mean being heterosexual. It took me a while to realize that, as author Jennifer Finney Boylan reminds us, who I was sleeping *with* wasn't nearly as important as who I was sleeping *as* (once again proving, as if it needs any proof, that one's sexual orientation cannot be chosen). I was also learning that the dream of being that beautiful girl in the wedding dress just wasn't for me; I was in for something much less clichéd.

I met my current partner/life-partner/spouse-to-be/love-of-my-life many years later, long after I had transitioned completely. My first date with this woman happened to be on Gay Pride Day in New York City. Claire and I went to what seemed to be the only straight bar in the West Village, because it made for a quiet place to talk, and both of us got a kick out of not conforming to the rules of Pride Weekend. We moved in together two months later and have been together for the past eleven years, but neither of us ever had a burning desire to get married. The institution of marriage didn't seem to hold much for us, and we didn't need to measure our relationship according to that standard. We thought of it as maybe the means to kitchen gifts and a fun party, but it wasn't essential, and we certainly weren't going to go searching for marriage in a state other than New York. We just figured, "How much of a marriage is it if we're not legally married when we return home?"

In any case, my transition had made marriage absurd, at least from a legal point of view. If we had been married before my transition, we could remain a legally married same-sex couple—but only in some states. In other states we could get legally married *after* my gender changed, but only because those states didn't legally recognize my change. In other words, even though for (almost) all intents and purposes we were simply two women, in some states we'd still be considered "straight"—if that makes any sense. And in other states our marriage would be invalidated by my change of gender.

Trust me, I'm getting as confused by all of this as you, but suffice it to say that in most of the states that set out to prohibit same-sex marriage with the passage of DOMA-esque bills—declaring that marriage is a union only between a man and a woman—a trans-person really screws up the definition of marriage. And we haven't even started talking about intersex people, who scramble legal definitions even more.

In short, my gender change had, in one way or another and in one U.S. state or another, disqualified me from the game of marriage. Why would my life-partner, Claire, and I want to enter into such an institution, indeed a legal contract, where not only the status of our marriage but the status of my gender was dependent on what state we happened to be in?

But then it happened. Marriage equality became a reality in New York, and suddenly both Claire and I were overcome by how much we really wanted this bond we'd been denied. The day after the N.Y. equality bill passed was not only our eleventh anniversary but also the first day of Pride weekend in New York City again. Claire and I knew we wanted to finally tie the knot. We held hands in a West Village park, and I whispered in her ear, "How about on the count of three we both simultaneously say 'Will you marry me—yes!'" We both said, "One, two, three," but Claire was too excited to follow the script and just screamed, "We're getting married!" West Village revelers applauded us, and all of a sudden we were engaged. After not knowing how much we'd really wanted this, now we couldn't live without it.

A couple of months later, we attended the wedding of Lauren Blitzer and Chely Wright. Lauren is known for her civil rights activism, and Chely had become famous as the first mainstream country singer in Nashville to come out as a lesbian. As the wedding neared, Claire and I labored over what to wear, the best gifts to buy—all the trappings of a traditional wedding. Then we got lost driving to the ceremony in Connecticut and even bickered (rare for us) about the directions and how to best get there. It was all so stressful. Something beneath the surface was irritating us, but we didn't know what it was.

There were other same-sex couples at the wedding, most of whom we already knew, but the majority of guests seemed to be straight. A guest or two seemed to even be a bit unsure about the whole gay marriage thing. During the dinner following the ceremony, kids ran around a big lawn playing tag. Babies were bounced on the hips of proud new mothers. We genuinely loved meeting the other guests and getting to know old friends of the brides, but it was a bit awkward to decide when to come out to strangers. We chalked that up to being par for the course at a wedding, which, with the exception of just six U.S. states (plus D.C.), has always been the ceremony *par excellence* that heralds straightness. Even at a gay wedding, we felt like we didn't belong.

Claire and I became aware of the fact that, frankly, maybe we didn't really like weddings at all—even for this fantastic couple we adored. We were afraid to admit what was going on at a deeper level: We had been denied the opportunity of marriage for so long—our entire lives—that now we couldn't fully participate in *any* wedding. Even though we were engaged, we still felt "if marriage wouldn't have us, we wouldn't have it." Sure, we could enjoy a nice time and engage new friends in good conversation, but we dare not give ourselves over emotionally to this tradition that had excluded us for so long.

Then it was time for the brides' first dance. They were both stunning in their gorgeous strapless white gowns—quite similar, actually, to my first wedding costume oh so long ago. Everyone was anticipating, whether one likes weddings or not, an undeniably beautiful expression of love and commitment.

Lauren and Chely went to the front of the dance floor, stepped into the spotlight, and Chely took the microphone, with which she's so comfortable. She said, "Lauren and I have been so inspired by the family and friends who have come here today, and nothing will ever change that. We've also been deeply inspired by the same-sex couples we have known, many of whom have joined us. We would like to not only dedicate our first dance to all of you, but also invite all of the same-sex couples here tonight to the dance floor, to share our first dance with us."

I looked at Claire. We were both stunned. We'd never dared to share a slow dance at a straight wedding before, but could we do it at a gay wedding? The same hesitation was palpable through the rest of the room. *Really?* everyone seemed to think at the same time. *You want* us *to dance with each other for your first dance, and in front of all of these straight people?!*

All at once, almost half the crowd rose and joined the brides on the dance floor. We proudly stepped into the spotlights, hand in hand with our partners. Many of us were so touched that we'd been invited to share the first dance that tears started to flow. Claire and I were so inexperienced at slow dancing in public we didn't even know whose hands went where; we finally decided our hands would go around each other's waists. Straight couples ringed the dance floor, admiring us. Older people smiled at us. Babies continued to be bounced on the hips of beaming new mothers, and kids continued to play tag in the grass, bored with all that adult stuff. Unbeknownst to them, they were nonetheless learning the lesson that will make marriage equality an unquestioned right for future generations.

We were not only part of Lauren and Chely's wedding, but now part of every wedding. Every union, every mutual expression of love, every legal contract binding two people until-death-do-us-part. As with our own engagement, once we saw what it was like to be accepted as a couple, we suddenly wanted the recognition we'd thought we didn't need. Damn, do we like weddings now!

When *our* first dance was drawing to its triumphant, loving close, the DJ kicked the dance music into high gear—and you know we LGBT folks corner *that* market! Claire and I had never gone out dancing; in fact, we hardly ever dance at all, and certainly not at weddings. But that night we danced ourselves silly and sore. And we learned a tradition we will carry on at our own wedding: sharing our first dance with the couples who showed us the way, rising up and stepping into the spotlight.

Photo:
Country singer Chely Wright (left) and her bride, LGBT activist Lauren Blitzer. *Photo by Claire Jones.*

Lesbian Wedding Blessings and Curses

∴

Judy Scheer and Jen Sorensen

Lesbian Wedding
BLESSINGS
and CURSES
by JUDY SCHEER and JEN SORENSEN

CURSE: TWO MOTHERS-OF-THE-BRIDE
YOU ARE GOING TO WEAR YOUR GRANDMOTHER'S WEDDING DRESS, AREN'T YOU?

BLESSING: REGISTERING AT RESTORATION HARDWARE
SALE
THESE KNOBS ARE DIVINE!
WHICH ONES?

CURSE: BRIDESMAIDS WHO ARE EXES... OF BOTH BRIDES.
YOU SMASHED MY HEART INTO–HIC!–A MILLION TINY PIECES, BUT I NEVER STOPPED LOVING YOU.

BLESSING: "YOU MAY NOW KISS THE BRIDE" IS REDUNDANT... AND HOT!
SORENSEN

The Best Laid Plans

On the previous page, top to bottom:

"A powder-blue Vespa was my engagement gift to Amanda Oliver," explains Sara Graefe (riding on the back). This photo was taken just after their wedding in Vancouver in 2006; they've since expanded their family and have a four-year old son. "We continue to ride out the highs and lows of our relationship, as does any long-term couple," says Sara, "but we know we're both on board for the long haul."
Photo by Ross den Otter and Sarolta Dobi, Pink Monkey Studios, pinkmonkeystudios .com.

Kathryn (with goggles) and Jennifer Wenzel-Ziegler got engaged on a dog-sledding adventure in Michigan's Upper Peninsula. "Jennifer planned the proposal to be a surprise; the kennel staff were in on it," says Kathryn. "The guide stopped at a beautiful, peaceful place on the trail with snow-covered pine trees arching overhead. Jennifer went down on one knee, took off her oversized mitten, and held out a ring. "Stop crying, your face will freeze," I said. "Kathryn," she said, "will you marry me?" "Yes!"
Photo courtesy of the brides.

Erika Nakamura (left) and Amelia Posada (right) were married September 4, 2010 in Santa Barbara, Calif., with Erika's brother (center) officiating. "I wanted to impress Erika's East Coast family," says Amelia, "because there's nowhere more beautiful. We are so fortunate to have families who totally embrace and celebrate who we are." Erika, who grew up "Jewpanese" in Tokyo, and Amelia, who's half-Chicana/half-white, met at a drag show Erika was DJing. On their first date, Amelia ordered carnitas tacos although she'd gone meatless for the previous fourteen years. "God, it's so great to be on a date with a lesbian who's not a vegetarian!" said the unsuspecting Erika. It must have been an omen: The two women ended up becoming butchers, proprietors of Lindy & Grundy in Los Angeles, which sells "local, pastured, and organic meats." At their wedding reception, they butchered all the beef that they served, and named each table for a "cut" (New York Strip, Tenderloin, etc.). As for the future of these brides? "I picture us as old little grouchy butchers together," says Amelia.
Photo by Maro Hagopian, marohagopian .com.

Eschaton, or The Gay Divorcées

∴

Erika Dyson

The first time my ex-wife proposed, we were in a bus headed from Singapore to Malaysia. Actually, Lory did not really propose. She suggested she might some day and asked what my answer might be. My answer was no. Not a tentative no, a definite no. I was alarmed, and perhaps a little offended, which was confusing to us both. And she was deeply hurt.

I gave many justifications for my answer, if not the bluntness with which I delivered it. Marriage is the first step to divorce, I reasoned. Look at her family. Look at mine. Good people, doing their best in one untenable relationship after another. Thank goodness divorce exists, for everyone's sake.

Also, I thought I had made it clear to her that in the movie of my life, the one that runs in my head, marriage was not there. This absence was not some side effect of being queer. Things just don't occur to me sometimes.

Until I fell in love with the dreamy Andrea in my twenty-second year, it would never have occurred to me that I was a lesbian. Andrea was a "prop tart" at a summer theater where we both worked. The first time I saw her, she was building a picket fence around the prop shop garden. Her hands were strong and tanned, and when she looked up from hammering in a fence post, I was instantly smitten (I have a thing for women who work with their hands). But even after discovering true love, at least for that summer, marriage was still not in that movie of my life. I think this is why I was a little offended when Lory sort-of proposed. Didn't she know me?

This was not the last time we discussed marriage, but my opinion did not waver. I even waxed quasi-theological when the subject came up. Think about the conditions of your birth, I insisted. (I study religious history; recourse to creation stories is an occupational hazard.) Lory was conceived in marriage and born in divorce. She routinely dropped this factoid into conversation when trading childhood reminiscences. Her mother (now an out lesbian) and her father (a Mormon with a Father-Knows-Best complex) were married just three months. Her next stepfather lasted six months before her mother left him. Didn't she know, as any scholar of Christianity knows, that the Creation sets the terms of the Eschaton?

The Eschaton is the end of history, its ultimate destiny, the fulfillment of God's plans and promises for humanity. If Lory's parents' divorce was her creation story, what could we expect but divorce at the end of times?

Lory's and my relationship began one year before the awkward Malaysian bus ride. We were both working at the Boston production of Blue Man Group, where I was the wardrobe supervisor. Lory had a smile that could power a city, and she made me beautiful maple candlesticks on her wood lathe. I was smitten.

We had a clandestine affair—she was my boss—until I moved to New York for graduate school in 2000. After September 11, 2001, I moved into Lory's Greenpoint (Brooklyn) apartment, in part because I was in love, in part because I hated Columbia University housing, and in part because I was sure no one would intentionally drop a plane on Greenpoint (on this last point, so far, I have been correct).

The second time she proposed, it was on a dare. I wince as I write this because I know how it sounds. Lory and I were in a Boston hotel room, killing time before she had to go to a meeting with the Blue Man production team. The subject of marriage came up, and she informed me that she likely would never ask me again; my response in the bus had been too painful. If I did not ever want to be married, she added, she would have to decide whether she wanted to stay in the relationship. She loved me, but she wanted to be married.

At this point, I panicked a little. I was indescribably sad at the thought of her leaving me over something as irrelevant as marriage. So

I dared her to ask me to marry her. She hesitated, and then did. And I said yes.

I know this is not a romantic (or promising) proposal. I know how I felt in the pause before she responded. Dishonest. Perhaps resentful. Definitely desperate. I loved her. I was so proud that she was mine and that I was hers. Still, I did not want to get married. However, if she cared more about marriage than I cared about not being married, then marriage was a reasonable compromise.

When I saw her tears and beaming smile after the pause, my heart felt enormous because I had made her so happy. I then felt that I had done the right thing. Unfortunately, feeling good about doing the right thing is not the same as being happy about something for its own sake. But I was quite happy for a while.

Two years after the bus-ride proposal, Lory and I were married for the first time at my mother's and stepfather's farm in Maine. Because same-sex marriages were not recognized in Maine at the time, we would marry again in Canada, but that is getting ahead of the story.

Our lesbian clambake wedding (yes, we thought that was funny, too) coincided with the great Northeast blackout of 2003. Half of the Eastern seaboard had gone dark, but we did not take this as an evil omen. Instead, we rejoiced that it had not reached us in the middle of Maine, and that it stranded only a few of our guests. Several New York friends arrived at the rehearsal cookout with jubilant tales of outfoxing rental-car agents, braving intersections without traffic lights, and surviving seemingly interminable gridlock as they fled the city. It added to the excitement of the evening that so many had beaten this blackout of almost biblical (if one believes God would work through electrical grids) proportions.

As the sun went down, the evening Maine air turned velvet and gold. An excess of excellent food started coming out of the kitchen and off of the barbecue. My brother presided over the grill with *Cook's Illustrated* precision. A mutual appreciation society formed, composed of those who had escaped New York and those who admired them. Lory and I stood back and watched happily as the New Yorkers, our various parents, family, friends, and several members of the Spiritualist church camp next door melded into one exuberant, chatty mass.

On the day of the wedding, if I had ever had qualms about marrying, I could not remember them. We held our ceremony in the backfield, with a riot of wildflowers and the mountains behind us. My childhood friend Ian welcomed everyone to "the procedure," as my grandmother called it. His welcome somehow included a parable involving Liza Minnelli (not exactly a peerless example of marital success). My stepfather gave a beautiful benediction. Lory and I exchanged the vows we had written ourselves.

During the ceremony, we left space for the guests to say what they wished about love, marriage, Lory and me, their own marriages, or anything related. Several did. When my Aunt Judy stood and talked about how in love she was with my Uncle John after almost twenty-five years of marriage, almost everyone cried. When Lory's mother's girlfriend likewise declared her love, Lory's mother grumbled that she had been "outed," but even my grandmothers looked delighted.

I was so happy during the day that I bordered on incoherence. If getting married meant acknowledging the love, gratitude, and respect

Lory and I had for each other, for our families, and for our lives, then I was entirely convinced that it was for me. I was perfectly willing to entertain the idea that my prior views on marriage were, well, limited.

After the wedding, people told us that ours was one of the most beautiful they had been a part of, and we believed them. Our favorite assessment of the day, however, came from the grandmother who had dubbed the wedding "the procedure" (she could not bring herself to call it a wedding). Describing the day to my great-uncle, she said simply, "Well, it was lovely, but it was illegal." When he pressed her for more specifics, she drawled, "Well, I've never seen so many braless women in my life." Lory and I took this as proof-positive that our celebration was a resounding success.

The second time Lory and I married there were no omens for good or ill, but perhaps a few signs that I, at least, might have heeded. A week after our Maine ceremony, we eloped to Toronto. Our Maine wedding had been lovely, but we wanted to be married legally. We wanted to make a point that marriage between two women deserves the same recognition, protections, and benefits that heterosexual unions receive.

Also, the *New York Times* had recently started using the word *marriage* to describe legal unions between same-sex couples in Canada, and we wanted to encourage what we thought was progress toward equal treatment of non-heterosexuals. We had submitted an announcement to the *Times* after Maine, but the reporter who had called to fact-check it explained that we would have to make it legal before the newspaper would agree to publish the announcement as a "wedding" and not a "commitment ceremony." If we married in Canada, the reporter assured us, we were in.

Our elopement was rushed and a little disorienting, as I suppose many are. Although obtaining the license was a simple affair, we had not anticipated how hard it would be to find a judge to marry us at Toronto's City Hall. Michael, the concierge at our bed-and-breakfast, rescued us. When I called him to ask for suggestions, he cooed into the phone, "Come home, darlings, I'll take care of it."

By the time we got back to the B&B, he had arranged for a United Church of Christ minister to stop by after she finished with a funeral in another part of town. He also appointed himself maid of honor and enlisted Zeke (the self-described "houseboy") to be our best man. Reverend Ellen arrived soon after, bearing pink roses for us. After a few questions about formalities and payment, we followed her into the opulent parlor and were married again.

I don't remember much about the ceremony itself, except the shock of hearing the "dearly beloved" language of the standard Christian service. After the heartfelt and improvised speeches at our Maine wedding, it seemed wrong. I could feel the alarm rising in my chest as I parroted back the words Reverend Ellen read from the *UCC Book of Worship*. This wedding was not about us; it was a "procedure." Clearly we, or at least I, hadn't thought this out.

Again, Michael rode to the rescue. Congratulating us, he gushed about what a momentous occasion it was: two women legally marrying, with all of the bureaucratic and logistical bother of heterosexual weddings. It was important for us personally, but we also owed a debt to a lot of feisty Canadian homos who had made it at all possible, and we should not forget it. His enthusiasm dispelled my uneasiness somewhat, but I could not shake the procedure feeling. I never mentioned this to Lory because it embarrassed me.

We returned to New York the next day and dutifully-slash-defiantly sent wedding announcements to our hometown papers. *The New York Times* published our announcement as promised, and so did Lory's hometown paper, the *Monterey County Herald*. This caused a minor op-ed-page tussle when an irate *Herald* reader wrote in to accuse us of being two Brooklyn lesbians (true) with no connection to the area (not true) who were shamelessly using his local paper as a platform to promote an immoral political agenda (not entirely wrong, though not immoral). I fired back a two-thousand-word answer, was praised by the editor for my eloquence, and then edited it down to 350 words so she could print it.

On the day the announcement ran in Monterey County, we also made the five and eleven o'clock news on the local Salinas television station. It had sent a camera crew out to the city of Monterey's famous Canary Wharf to do a live on-location report about the first same-sex union reported in the *Herald*. What our wedding had to do with John Steinbeck or tourist traps I have no idea, but I did crave smoked salmon sandwiches for days after.

These two weddings became our creation stories. At least for a while. They told how and why we became wives: conventional titles, albeit in an unconventional configuration. They overwrote Lory's birth story and my metaphysical convictions about the inevitability of divorce. The gods of electrical grids had banished my doubts and smiled upon the community we made in Maine; in Canada, we became bound together by language and laws not of our own making. We had just as much chance to thrive in our relationship, or fail spectacularly, as any heterosexual couple.

Following our weddings, we found out how many of our friends were closet readers of the *Times'* Weddings/Celebrations page. We marched in marriage equality demonstrations. I learned the word *heteronormativity*. I debated with friends (but not with Lory) whether same-sex marriage was really good for "the gays."

We registered as domestic partners in New York City and had a good deal of fun with the sunny clerk at City Hall figuring out how to fill out the forms. Apparently, being married disqualifies you from becoming domestic partners—assuming, of course, that you would be married to one person and a domestic partner with another. The clerk let us register anyway, grinning and seeming to enjoy the conundrum. We bought a house. We hyphenated our last names.

After a while, though, our relationship turned into something else. Not good. It eroded. Micro-compromises and nano-resentments chipped away at what I had once experienced as expansive and solid. Fights multiplied over silly things, such as the putative supremacy of Frank Sinatra's vocal stylings. I became adept at evading conversations about important things, such as having children or our waning sex life. I was terrified of disappointing her and convinced that I was. I could never, it seemed, live up to what she kept telling me married life should be. I became guilty of slight acts of negligence. Culminating in obstinate denial.

At times I experienced her as committed and romantic, happy

even, but still I sensed her resentment. How she experienced me, I am sure, was no less paradoxical and no more liveable.

So, I regrouted the bathroom in our new house. Lory refinished the woodwork on the upstairs closets and learned plumbing. I swept the front walk and talked to the neighbors. We had friends over for brunch each weekend that Lory was not traveling (Lory traveled a lot for work). I hid from her in my research. And because Lory had no use for religion, I hid my research from her. I became someone I didn't like; she became someone I didn't recognize, someone I even hated for a while.

The process of separating was excruciating for me. "The nonsense" (my pet name for our separation and divorce) stretched from Thanksgiving to the next August. It was punctuated by the deaths of several people very close to us and with a random totaling of my car. Ironically, at the start of the nonsense, it was me fighting to stay married. She was done. She went to Europe and I packed my things and moved out. I began to feel unstable. Thank goodness for friends who will tell you the truth, even when that truth is that they can't handle your anger. Thank goodness for therapists.

This was our Eschaton. Two lesbians—rainbow-swathed marriage equality poster girls, wives, best friends—decided to divorce for entirely ordinary, human reasons. Good people, doing their best in an untenable relationship. Thank goodness divorce exists, for everyone's sake.

But divorce did not exist for us. Remember, we, or at least I, hadn't thought it out.

To get married in Canada, you show up, fill out some forms, show them your passports, and hope you have a Michael and a Reverend Ellen.

In less than twenty-four hours you are legally bound. To start the divorce process in Canada, you have to be a resident of the country for *a year*.

The residency requirement allegedly resulted from the U.S. government putting pressure on Canada to make it harder for Americans to divorce there—to keep Canada from becoming the "Reno of the North." This may not be true, but when I heard it, I found a new focus for my abundant, free-floating resentment.

As for same-sex divorce in the United States, state legislatures generally have not written divorce rules into same-sex marriage laws, and few LGBT legal organizations seem to be pushing for it. Judges have denied divorce petitions from gays and lesbians on the grounds that their marriages were not recognized as legitimate in their respective states. New York did not recognize same-sex marriages in 2005—the time the nonsense began—and you can't write a law to negate something that does not exist.

In the airless and electroshock aftermath of our decision to separate, the inability to divorce felt like madness. We had slipped out of the predictable, if baroque, legal structures and social fictions regulating marriage into something undefined and unmoored. It was entirely possible that Lory would remain in my life forever, becoming the conversation that I would have with any new lover in the name of full disclosure. I hated it. It was a bad dream: repetitious, helpless, frantic with frustration.

Friends tried to make me feel better by reminding me that since same-sex marriage was recognized hardly anywhere, it really wouldn't affect my life. *Thank goodness there is not equality under the law. Your marriage never did matter.*

Other friends offered schemes: Get a divorce in Holland. Get a job in Canada. Or Massachusetts. Sue the state of New York. Make Lory move to Canada (she wanted the divorce, after all).

Ignore it, some said. Please stop worrying about it. Please stop talking about it.

In the middle of the nonsense, Dan, a friend and mentor, wrote me a long email. Some years earlier, his wife had left him for a neighbor, leaving him with five children, the youngest around three years old. The advice Dan offered was something like this:

Reject any clichéd bravado. Reject the idea that what doesn't kill you makes you stronger. Sure, scar tissue is stronger than skin. But you don't want to be the emotional equivalent of *The English Patient* by the time you die.

Instead, think about divorce as a rearrangement of your body. The process tears you apart, or feels like it. Limbs, innards, brain peeled into wedges like an orange, heart stretched and torn like dough. Then you reassemble into a whole new kind of organism: looking just like you did before, but without any clue about how to operate this newly configured you.

The promise is, if you are willing and if grace is possible, you may find that you're capable of things you never thought you were before. Different. In considerable pain. Awkward. Somewhat clearer. Somehow hopeful.

This is what I wanted—not Lory, tethered to me by paperwork and notarized forms. I wanted grace and hope. I felt myself being reassembled. I wanted to see what I was capable of next. I wanted clarity.

So Lory and I hired very smart lesbian lawyers. We agreed on what each of us would take materially from the relationship. In April 2007, we filed our separation agreement with the New York clerk of courts office. The clerk stamped and approved the agreement and mailed it to our lawyers. Then we waited.

I was optimistic. In February 2008, a New York Supreme Court justice ruled that two women married in Canada could seek a divorce in New York courts. Three months later, we received notice that our separation would be converted into a divorce unless we informed the court we had changed our minds. A month later, Governor David Paterson directed all New York state agencies to treat same-sex marriages as they would any out-of-state marriage. All good signs.

On October 14, 2008, Stephen Rossini, senior court attorney for the Kings County Supreme Court, signed our divorce decree. I found out in an email from the Brooklyn courts' automatic notification system that the status of our case had changed from "pending" to "disposed." Not trusting this, I emailed my lawyer and she responded by congratulating me.

I was numb, but my monkey brain chattered frantically. What if senior court attorney Rossini did not realize Lory was a woman because of the unusual spelling of her name? What if he was just busy, signing our papers without looking closely at them? What if he discovered his mistake and took it away?

So far he hasn't. So far I have remained divorced.

With each realization that I was done with the nonsense, the creeping anxiety that had been my constant companion slowly receded. I began to feel right in ways I had not in many years. I became able to mourn, to feel some compassion for both Lory and myself. I like this newly configured me. I feel fearless and clear, at least most of the time.

I don't know why the legal dissolution of that which had already dissolved allowed me to do this, but it did. None of this is logical. If it was, I might have seen the difference between happiness over doing the right thing and happiness for its own sake. I might have paid attention to my misgivings, paid better attention to who I was becoming as a wife. I might have paid better attention to my wife. I am not sure I have forgiven either Lory or myself for how we ended. But I am grateful that I was able to disentangle from her and find myself again. Divorce is important, both emotionally and legally: Good people need the ability to get out of untenable relationships.

In June of 2011, reversing the usual order of things, New York made same-sex marriage legal—three years after the state courts began granting same-sex divorces. The next month, the Pentagon certified the repeal of "Don't Ask Don't Tell." My new partner, Marisa, who is a marine, and I marched with the first active-duty military float ever to be included in a gay pride parade. All good signs that things are changing.

There is another meaning of Eschaton worth considering, beyond the "end of times," or the culmination: The word in Greek means "on edge." We are "on edge" when we sense impending disaster and know our own limits, our capacity for irrationality and fear. And in biblical apocalyptic thinking, Eschaton is a time of radical violence and transformation before the "new heaven and new earth." I think, too, of the old hymn in which God troubles the waters that must be crossed by those who want change. When you get to the other side, if you do, you will be different. Maybe better, maybe worse.

Divorce is where I became a different organism. It could have happened otherwise but, like Lory, perhaps I, too, was born—or reborn—in divorce.

A few weeks ago, Marisa, her own divorce from her husband just finalized, told me that I didn't have any reason to fear: It was unlikely that she would ask me to marry her. She's not interested in that institution anymore. It made sense. But my response was not what either of us expected. This time I did not panic, but told her instead that I might ask her. Someday. Because I love her, and because the entirety of that feeling may need those words.

I am excited to see what happens next.

The Back Door to Marriage

∴

N'Jai-An Patters

Marriage was never my thing. I never wanted to be, or have, a wife. Don't get me wrong, I'm all for marriage equality; anyone who wants to get married should be able to do so. I even liked to imagine myself ending up in a committed, long-term relationship. So why not marriage?

Initially, there was the terminology problem: *Wife* was a non-starter for me. It called to mind *The Brady Bunch* and *Leave It to Beaver* reruns, sanitized white worlds of bygone eras. Too many women I knew seemed to lose themselves when they became wives, as if the title and its history were bigger than all their best intentions. I was also annoyed by the ways that a once-rich queer liberation movement was often boiled down to this single issue by mainstream lobbying groups. I worried that in trying to convince others that we were just like them, we were losing sight of the ways that being different could open everyone's eyes to new possibilities. Finally, I questioned the state's interest in regulating anyone's sexual life.

Little did I know that my trouble with the "wife" title would soon be eclipsed by my realization that I was tangled up in a marital drama—one that would lead to a personal investment in marriage equality that I never could have imagined.

I met Kelly on Mother's Day 2008, a couple of months after my twenty-ninth birthday. I emailed her after seeing her profile on an online dating site, and we quickly made plans to meet at a coffee shop in my south Minneapolis neighborhood. She was smart and funny, and I was taken by the way she lived in her body. Each stride, each gesture, was so fluid; I loved watching her move. We talked for hours that first day, and before long we were spending most of our free time with each other. A year later we were living together, and a few months after that, we began talking about starting our own family.

Before you cue the violins, you should know that our growing love for each other did not inspire us to want to get married. I still had my linguistic and political hang-ups, and Kelly had been deeply disillusioned by marriage. Several years before we met, she married her first girlfriend—in an unofficial religious ceremony in the upper Midwest, and later in a legal ceremony in Massachusetts. Raised to believe that marriage lasted until death, Kelly felt like the end of that relationship—and the seeming ease with which her ex walked away—took the meaning out of marriage for her. We were committed to each other and wanted to spend our lives together, but marriage didn't offer us a meaningful way of expressing our connection.

I was happy with the everydayness of our love. Every meal we shared, every comfort we offered, every time we came home to each other, we were affirming our commitment. By sidestepping the grand declarations of a wedding, our daily lives gave us repeated opportunities to choose each other and be chosen.

So there I was, happily coupled with someone who, like me, wasn't interested in rushing down the aisle. I figured we would continue to live our lives, maybe buy a house, and have a couple of kids. We'd obtain legal protections for ourselves, especially once we had children. Still, marriage held little interest for us, and since we lived in Minnesota, it wasn't an option anyway.

But as we got serious about baby-making and house-buying, marriage began to take up more and more of my attention, though not in a way that I could have anticipated. As things turned out, it was not my love for Kelly, our increasingly intertwined financial lives, or even the prospect of having children that pushed marriage closer to center stage. Instead, I became deeply and personally invested in lesbian marriage through the back door of divorce.

Kelly and her ex had made their marriage legal while they were living in Massachusetts, but they broke up after returning to the Twin Cities, where lesbian marriages aren't legally recognized. As a consequence, they were never legally divorced. A few test cases had gone through the local courts, but when Kelly and I began trying to conceive our first child in the winter of 2010, no gay couple in Hennepin County had been granted a divorce.

The rationale went something like this: Granting a divorce recognizes that a marriage took place, and since Minnesota defines marriage as being between one man and one woman, granting legal recognition to other states' marital unions—even for the purposes of dissolving them—is contrary to the law. At the same time, getting a divorce in Massachusetts or another gay-marriage state wasn't feasible because of the residency requirements tied to divorce. Either Kelly or her ex would have had to relocate to a state that recognized gay marriage and live there for a year—establishing residency by paying taxes, registering to vote, and obtaining a local driver's license—in order to be able to file for a divorce.

Our lives were in the Twin Cities; we couldn't just pick up and move, and we didn't have any right to ask or expect Kelly's ex to do so either. So divorce didn't seem to be an option. But even though I didn't feel a strong need to be married to Kelly, I certainly didn't want her to be still married to someone else.

I began to spin worst-case scenarios that made me a little crazy. I knew that when a woman in a hetero marriage gives birth, her husband becomes the legal father of the child regardless of genetic paternity. Could something like that happen to us? Would the legality of Kelly's marriage prevent me from obtaining a second-parent adoption for the child we hoped that she would have? Worse still, would her ex have a stronger legal claim to our child than I would?

What about the house we wanted to buy—would it be considered marital property? On the other hand, how could there be marital property if our state didn't recognize the marriage? What if we moved or the laws changed?

The thought that most upset me was simply that Kelly was still married to her ex. For all my beliefs about the separation of church and state and the broader possibilities of queer liberation—or even my vision of legal and familial connections beyond marriage—it really bothered me. Could there be space for *me*, for our life together, with this unsolved divorce problem hanging over us?

Clearly, marriage meant something to me. Otherwise, I wouldn't have been so troubled by the marital limbo in which Kelly found herself. Kelly hadn't even been in touch with the ex for years. She had dated other people, had rebuilt her life, and had started a new career; she was making a lifelong commitment to me, and she was trying to get pregnant with our child. The ex was really a non-issue; Kelly had healed from that relationship. Still, the marriage lingered, outlasting the relationship, the intimacy, even the feelings of loss and betrayal.

That marriage became a roadblock for me. I was wary of moving forward with our plans to have children and buy property for fear that I would be in an even more legally precarious position than the one in which same-sex partners already find themselves. I was also forced to admit my emotional insecurities and my need for resolution of Kelly's previous marriage. I decided that there was only one way to get my questions answered: We needed to talk to a lawyer.

Finding one should have been a simple prospect; we were practically swimming in a sea of them. We each had family and friends in law school, studying for the bar, or already practicing as attorneys. With all the lawyers in our sphere, I was sure that *someone* would be able to tell us *something*. But as we tapped friends and family with questions, I began to notice a pattern in the frustrating answers we received.

They fell into two categories: The first went something like, "Well, here where I am [in a state outside of Minnesota] . . . , so you'd probably need to . . . " The second went, "This would be so much simpler if it were a 'regular' [read: straight] divorce." Everyone agreed that we had a real legal quandary, and everyone was uncertain of how it might be resolved.

I can't fault them for the confusion. In the first three years that Kelly and I were together, the national gay-marriage terrain had undergone seismic shifts. First California shocked gay folks everywhere by adopting the anti-marriage Proposition 8; then Iowa, our neighbor to the south and the prototypical heartland state, surprised the country by legalizing gay marriage. To contend with the shifting sands of state-by-state marriage, it was clear we would need to find a specialist.

Acknowledging that freedom and peace of mind come neither easily nor cheaply, we sucked it up and hired someone who specialized in LGBT family law in Minnesota. Our lawyer calmed my fears about the threats that Kelly's marriage represented to our life together, but she wasn't terribly optimistic about Kelly's chances for divorce. She took the case, though—and more than a little money—and promised to keep us posted on her research and any developments in the courts. Soon after, she contacted Kelly's ex and had the former couple sign all the necessary dissolution papers. All that's left for us to do now is wait for friendlier prospects in the courts.

About a year after we first retained her, the lawyer informed us that a gay couple *had* been granted a divorce in Hennepin County. This was tremendously promising, and we're hoping that it's just a matter of time before Kelly's divorce becomes legal. As promising as some of the legal developments have been, though, we are also keenly aware that the 2012 ballot will allow Minnesotans to amend the state constitution to *ban* gay marriage. Such a ban would effectively squash Kelly's prospects of getting a divorce—but it would also eliminate any legal claims that her ex might have to our children or property.

The legal reassurances were nice, but I was equally calmed by the simple act of helping Kelly pursue the matter. No matter how it turns out in court, the fact that she retained counsel and signed papers stands as a symbolic divorce. In fact, the more I thought about it, the more I realized that divorce is a significant part of the gay marriage movement—and not just because of the obvious need to legally dissolve marriages that have reached their expiration dates. It's also crucial for subsequent relationships, because we do need formal recognition for those with whom we do—and *don't*—choose to spend our lives and build a family.

So have my views about marriage changed? Kelly and I have exchanged rings, though I wear mine on my right hand and she wears hers on her middle finger. We bought a car together. We're in the process of buying a house and trying to make a baby. We sometimes speak of having a big party, complete with a slideshow and embarrassing dancing. She even refers to me as her wife sometimes, and when I hear that word spoken in her voice, I don't mind it a bit.

Looking at our life together, it's hard to tell that we're *not* married. When I think about marrying her—after the laws change—I'm hard-pressed to marshal any real objections. My protests from years ago seem so pale in the face of what we've been through and the life we're building together. It's hard for me to imagine being any more committed to Kelly than I already am, but if such a thing is possible, I'm ready for it. Even if it means saying "I do."

Innocence Maintained

∴

By Melissa Sky

Kissed a girl, won't change the world
But I'm so glad I kissed a girl.
—"I Kissed a Girl," *cowritten and sung by Jill Sobule*

When I was first coming out as a lesbian, I vividly remember how I cried, secretly, in the privacy of a bathroom stall at my cousin's wedding. I cried for the losses I expected in accepting myself for who I knew myself to be. I fixated on the mundane ritual of wedding guests clinking their forks on their glasses to encourage the newlyweds to kiss: I would never know this, I mourned.

And yet, a decade later, I watched with wild joy as the guests at my very own lesbian wedding did just that. How had so much changed in such little time? Activism. And I was proud to be a part of it.

I was one of those people who came vibrantly alive in the university. I finally found a place where I belonged, and I met communities of like-minded people. I became bold and fought tirelessly on many issues, including gay rights. I met my wife at the height of this heady time. The details of our love story are irrelevant: I chose her, she chose me. We loved intensely. We got engaged. Gay marriage was not yet legal in Canada, but we planned a commitment ceremony anyway and kept working to change the law through an organization called Canadians for Equal Marriage.

Like any good feminist, I learned early on that the personal is political, so I consciously used my own love story to advance gay rights. When my manicurist or dentist saw my engagement ring and asked about my fiancée, I used the "she" pronoun. I considered marriage a privilege that queer people were excluded from, a right to work toward, and so on the glorious day that my home province, Ontario, legalized same-sex marriage, I raced to the city hall to get a marriage license application.

I was turned away. I argued that the law had just changed, but to no avail. By the time I got home, however, there was a message on my voice mail confirming that I could indeed get a license to marry. Access to that piece of paper was revolutionary, and we celebrated the triumph fully.

The next day, my fiancée and I were reading the paper and noticed an article about how the first same-sex marriage license in the county had been handed out, but the city could not release the names of the recipients. That was us! We had a long talk and decided to use our story to further the cause, consciously becoming posterdykes for queer marriage. A few days later, our smiling faces were plastered in full color on the front page of the *Brantford Expositor*, under the headline "Local Couple Makes History." The article spurred a very public wave of support and dissent, with our right to marry dissected at kitchen tables across the county.

After that, a stranger riding a bicycle might yell, "Congratulations!" as I took the garbage out, and waiters would ask in hushed tones if we were "that couple," then whisper, "Good for you." But we also had a dead skunk left on our doorstep. It was a strange time.

We accepted all the reactions, negative and positive, because we knew that while kissing a girl might not change the world, kissing her publicly and insisting on the right to fully love her could. I know we changed our own small corner of the world.

I've been waiting for so long
Now I've finally found someone to stand by me . . .
—"The Time of My Life," *sung by Bill Medley and Jennifer Warnes*

My favorite memory of my wedding day was when my wife and I slipped away from the guests to take a moment to breathe, connect, and look back at the community and celebration we had created. We held hands and kissed under the stars, which sparkled like the twinkle lights in the giant white tent where the people we treasured—straight, gay, old, young—were dancing and laughing together. I teared up to see such harmony. It remains a powerful image of hope for me, a reminder in tough moments why activism is a worthy pursuit.

We had already been together for six years, but somehow living as a married couple was different. At first I bridled under the term *wife*, although I was elated to be married. But that reflected my resistance to the traditional heterosexual wife role, and I was confident that I could redefine that. While I didn't know exactly what being a radical, queer, feminist wife would look like, I was inspired to try to be one.

I threw myself into domesticity with the same passion I had once devoted to political causes. We did everything young couples are supposed to do. We bought a dream home and lovingly crafted it to be a space of safety and beauty. We earned esteem and promotions in our professions. We decided to start a family. We lived a very conventional life, at least on the surface, and struggled with the conventional pressures that accompany those life choices.

In some critical ways we became the clichéd couple we never wanted to be: too much responsibility and work, too little spontaneity and playfulness. Intent on being the best we could be at everything we pursued, we wore ourselves thin. My mother often warned us that the idea that you can have it all is an illusion, but we bristled at the suggestion. We were hard-working, resourceful, smart women; of course we would make it.

When we were exhausted and overwhelmed, older women would remind us that we were in the midst of the hardest time of our lives as the parents of a young child. We clung to their promises that it would get easier, though. Our days seemed like a never-ending to-do list, with little space for dreaming. So, some dreams died.

I did get a dream job, working as a teacher at an elite private school, one of the best in the country. The downside was that it required me to commute two hours every day and work incredibly long hours, so most of the housework and childcare fell to my wife. The job came with exceptional demands and rewards, and I was thrilled and deeply fulfilled by it, but my wife was unimpressed. She was unhappy with the lifestyle it forced us to live, yet she refused to move in order to lessen the commute because that would mean leaving the home we had invested so much care into crafting. Eventually she gave me an ultimatum: the job or her. And I chose my family.

Sadly, she made a different choice. Almost a year later, on a mundane evening as we watched a *Survivor* finale on TV, she turned to me and said, "I don't think this is working." And later, "I'm in love with another woman." With those words I was brutally thrust into the darkest time of my life.

Why do the stars glow above?
Don't they know it's the end of the world?
It ended when I lost your love.
—"The End of the World," *sung by Brenda Lee*

I learned the meaning of the word *devastation* in the wake of her words, my whole sense of myself and the world becoming a clear-cut, ruptured landscape of shrieking, ugly pain. I found myself lying on the floor and sobbing for hours, trying to find reasons to get out of bed, brush my teeth, get on with things.

This loss was not clean. It would have been so much better, I often thought, if she'd just died, for then I could cherish our memories. She'd be gone, but there would be no betrayal, no shame. I wouldn't have to continue to see her, to lose half my time with my child to her, to argue endlessly over everything for years, to wail about how it just wasn't fair, it just wasn't fair. It *wasn't* fair. My wife's mistress stole my wife, my home, my child, my life, and I couldn't do anything about it but sink to the depths and acknowledge this as a dark night of the soul.

I had to radically transform myself: a phoenix in flames. Now I was burning alive, but one day I would soar again, I promised. I needed to rediscover myself and write a new story about what happened, about the world, and about love, because nothing made sense anymore. In the first year after the divorce, I often woke from a recurring nightmare in which my wife and I were leading opposing armies. I would catch her in a vulnerable position and stand poised with a sword, deciding whether to slit her throat or not. I could never do it; I'd put down my sword. And that's when she'd stab her sword through my chest and I'd wake screaming.

Having invested so much of my life's meaning in her and our family, I couldn't reconcile how she could destroy them so callously. What did they mean, then? What did anything mean? Especially marriage.

Hadn't I been careful in selecting a partner? How could I have misjudged her character so entirely? Hadn't we both denigrated how easily people seemed to choose divorce? Weren't both our sets of parents still happily married, having weathered the intense ups and downs of life together? Was my faith in the promise of marriage a joke?

Maybe I'd been foolish to buy into the hetero-patriarchal ideal. Like most women, I'd overinvested in it. The bitter irony that I'd fought for the right to this despair did not escape me. Although I knew logically that I did everything I could to save my marriage, the shame stuck. And it wasn't just a personal failure but a public one. A historic failure. All the pressure we had taken on as posterdykes of the cause weighed on me. I worried about the public humiliation of the newspaper finding out, because it had done several follow-up articles with us when I got pregnant and when it ran a feature about the local LGBT community. As a member of the sad first wave of gay divorce, I felt I'd let everyone down.

So I reconsidered marriage. I'd always known that, alongside all the beautiful things that it could be, it was also a fundamentally conservative institution. Historically, the state controlled the populace by defining legitimate families, the church controlled them by defining legitimate sexual relationships, and men controlled women by defining legitimate womanhood, which could only be secured by becoming a proper wife and mother.

Globally, marriage today is hardly a pretty picture for women. Outside of the Western world, marital rape is often still legal. It was only declared a crime in Canada in 1983 and a human rights violation by the UN in 1993.

Nonetheless, women continue to fantasize about "their big day." Despite my education, political beliefs, and sexuality, I entered into this conservative institution quite freely, fought to do so even, and sacrificed to try to make it work. Was I just another dupe?

When the most privileged people on the planet can't sustain a marital success rate over 50 percent, what value can marriage hold? And that's not even accounting for the unhappiness—or infidelity—among many who remain married. Maybe humans aren't naturally monogamous, and maybe it's unrealistic to expect that while everything else in life changes your connection to one particular person will not. The institution itself seems a failure when well-intentioned people can't make it work. I had thought I could take a liberal feminist approach and change the institution from the inside, but I guess I didn't. So was that my failing? My ex-wife's? The institution itself? I still don't know. And maybe I never will.

I don't know for certain how I'll live my life
now alone without my beloved wife.
—"Beloved Wife," *written and sung by Natalie Merchant*

After my divorce, I learned to live with searing, unanswerable questions, along with the ocean of pain. Then, because the universe has a bizarre sense of humor, my healing process involved becoming a gay wedding videographer. This continues to fill me with irrational laughter and an illogical sense of satisfaction.

After I sold our dream house in the country, I moved back to my old university city, hoping to remember the vibrant, idealistic me I had once been. I made new vows to myself—namely that I would never again give up my dreams for anyone else. I duly set about rediscovering the very things I'd let go of in my relationship: community, art, politics.

I began by exploring filmmaking. This new hobby was encouraged and nurtured by my new girlfriend, a woman I knew from the past who became a wonderfully gentle and strong "yes" for me. And what more can we ask of a lover? In a poem my ex-wife had given me that defined my notions of love, there is a pivotal line that reads, "I will hold open a place in the world for you to be whoever you choose to be." The woman I chose to trust with my heart post-divorce does just that. Through her events business, she provided opportunities for me to develop and showcase my experiments in film. Out of it came a documentary series called *3 Questions*, which focused on creating a community conversation between local queer women about their sexuality.

Watching theaters packed with women laughing uproariously at something I created on the big screen rivaled my wedding day in terms of joy and hope. I was invited to promote the series at the first ever Gay Wedding Show in our region, and that's how my gay wedding videography business began.

I knew it was emotionally risky to get involved in the wedding business, yet I felt pulled toward it. The first wedding I shot was both exhilarating and horrific. The wedding itself was gorgeous, reminding me of my own. And that's why I fell apart. Once my responsibilities were met, I drank far too much alcohol and, back at my hotel room, sobbed hysterically in front of my girlfriend. These were incoherent, loud cries that anyone would be embarrassed to have witnessed, but I was stripped bare of all pretense and control, all the wounds rubbed raw again. My girlfriend—bless her—just put me in my pj's, tucked me in, and held me.

I didn't expect my second wedding job to be as difficult. I figured

I'd had my meltdown, I'd processed things, and surely I was moving on. Then the minister used the word *covenant* during the wedding rehearsal, and I couldn't stop hearing the word in my head for days afterward. Covenant. Covenant. *A sacred relationship of commitment.* This is what I mourned, I realized: my loss of faith. I mourned for that girl who stood in a white sparkling dress on the most beautiful day of her life with an overflowing heart so trusting and pure. I'm so sad that I can never be her again. All I can do is aspire to be another woman: one no longer innocent, but wise and strong.

To this day I struggle with jadedness but don't let it win. I choose a story and life I can live with, and it must include love. I do choose to love again; who would I be if I didn't?

I was watching a movie with my five-year-old son, and my eyes teared up over a romantic moment. He scoffed at me, "Mommy, you just love love." And it's true, I do. But don't we all want to be "the one" for another person? To find worth in someone and have them feel the same for you? To share and witness another's life? You don't need to be married to do that, but weddings are the ritualized, legal recognition of that unique bond.

And maybe that's where the wedding videography comes in. Videography allows me to be part of the rituals of love again. I get to feel around the edges of this sacred thing without committing myself. I document and preserve it, affirming that yes, once upon a time, there was great love. I saw it. I'm the one who captured how it radiated from the very bodies of the couple being married. I stand as witness to the miracle of finding another who feels like home. I am present at the birth of a family. So mundane. Yet so miraculous.

Be careful with each other, these fragile flames
For innocence can't be lost
It just needs to be maintained.
—"Innocence Maintained," *cowritten and sung by Jewel*

Will I marry again? Will I take another vow? I can't know that. I vacillate between a shockingly deep yearning to do so and a ferocious, self-preserving resistance. For now, I am simply learning to love again, while honoring my wounds and their dark gifts. This phoenix does soar, but for now I make vows to myself alone.

Yet I have reconciled the value of marriage. As humanity's highest enactment of commitment and intimacy, it's a valiant striving toward what is most noble and beautiful in us. I can't *not* believe in that. So maybe part of that pure girl remains—the one in the sparkling white dress who believed. Maybe there's hope that innocence can't be lost after all.

Perhaps that girl is the one who compels me now to this calling: to witness for others. To make art and history of their unions. It could be she who makes me see, through my pain, *Hey, here it is happening again: this wondrous thing of two people choosing each other as true companions. Willing to take their chances, to struggle, to throw themselves into it despite everything. A triumph of hope. Of idealism. Of love.* And if that's foolish, I want never to be anything else.

The Wedding Tablecloth

∴

Joan Lipkin

I'm seven years old, watching my mother embroider a wedding tablecloth she says will one day be mine. She is very serious about this wedding tablecloth. It follows her different places, draping across her lap like a skirt over her capris when she sews on it in the summer, looking like a blanket warming her legs when she works on it in the winter. Sometimes it is in the living room, along with the clear acrylic shoe box full of colored threads, as she sits in her leather chair in the corner while my brother and I lie on the floor coloring or slide up and down the black linoleum hallway playing Superman, bath towels around our necks secured with giant safety pins from our baby sister's diapers.

Sometimes the tablecloth is in the bedroom she shares with my father that opens onto the fire escape overlooking the backyard of our large and drafty apartment on the south side of Chicago. My mother has her hands full with three young children and not much money as my father builds his therapy practice. When she retreats into the bedroom, I am compelled to follow her and climb up on the bed, where I watch her fingers pull the thread through the cloth and back again, and I catch sight of the thimble, its silver surface dimpled like a strawberry.

"How come you wear a thimble, Mom?"

"So I don't prick myself when I'm sewing," she says.

Sewing instantly becomes more exciting to me. There is danger at the door.

"How come you would prick yourself, Mom?" I ask.

"How come? How come?" Seeing my crestfallen face, she offers to let me thread the needle. A peace offering.

"Put the end of the thread in your mouth so it gets wet and pointy—it's easier to put through the eye of the needle that way."

I am excited; I get to use my spit for something. This is not easy, though. I squint, because even at seven I wear glasses, and they slide down my nose as I try to thread the needle.

"Here, I'll do it," she says.

"No, I can do it. Let me."

Inherent in this exchange is the power struggle that will dog us all our lives. I beg, she denies. I beg some more and then she allows me, with a puff of exasperation.

On the fourth or fifth try, I thread the needle.

My mother bought the tablecloth from a pushcart on Halsted Avenue. When my mother goes to Halsted, she sometimes picks up blintzes and borscht and herring that remind her of the tastes of her home in New York and of the tiny grocery store that my grandfather ran on the Lower East Side. Sometimes she misses her family, and I think those are the times she wants to eat funny food or speak Yiddish with my father.

The tablecloth came with a ready-made design, kind of like color-by-numbers. I wonder why she doesn't make up her own design. She is just cross-stitching flowers and little houses that are already there. And when she tells me this is my wedding tablecloth, I wonder if I'm supposed to live in a little house like the ones on the tablecloth, even though we live in an apartment, not a house, with the Fauchons above us and the Kellers above them and Mr. Stepanek, the janitor, and his family in the basement.

The tablecloth is big; my mother will spend more than a year embroidering it. She tells me that it's banquet-sized, and I ask her if all weddings are supposed to be big. She nods absentmindedly, thread in her mouth. I ask if she had a big wedding, but she doesn't answer.

I later find out that she didn't have a wedding at all. She made all kinds of plans for one and even rented a hall, but my father's mother objected so strongly to his marrying a greenhorn from such a poor family that my mother cancelled it. Instead, when my father got his commission from the army, they went down to City Hall for a civil ceremony. She thinks they may have gone out to lunch at the Edison Hotel afterward.

∴

One Sunday summer afternoon, we take a trip in our Oldsmobile to Evanston to see the Balcerzaks. Car trips are long when there are three kids, only two backseat windows, and no air-conditioning. My bare thighs stick to the plastic seats. Then I get carsick and throw up all over my green cotton dress. I feel humiliated and gross.

When we arrive, Mrs. Balcerzak sizes up the situation. She tells me I can change in Sue Ellen's room and wear some of her clothes. I've never met Sue Ellen, but I guess she must have dresses my size.

While my mother pulls my stained dress over my head in Sue Ellen's room, a boy walks in. "It's a boy!" I shout and try to hide behind my mother. "Go away," I scream.

"That's not a boy," says my mother, "that's Sue Ellen." But I am terrified by this skinny girl with dirty-blond short hair wearing a striped T-shirt and jeans. She is seeing me naked, except for my white underpants, ruffled socks, and Mary Janes. I start to cry.

I will remember this moment for a long time. It led to a series of questions that I had no one to talk to about. Why was her hair so short? Why was she dressed like a boy? Didn't she want to wear dresses that showed her legs like all the other girls I knew?

I was frightened of Sue Ellen, but I was also excited by her. At seven, she touched something in me that I could neither understand nor name.

I am sixteen. Feminism is in the air, and I have used my babysitting money to buy a paperback copy of *Sisterhood Is Powerful*. I see a poster for The Chicago Women's Liberation Rock Band thumbtacked to a wall at the university, and I want to go. I drag along my little sister, who is twelve, with me because I'm afraid to go by myself. Or maybe I am already afraid to be myself.

The band is playing in a cold, dirty basement. The women in the band and those in the audience don't look like any I am used to seeing. They have long hair that looks like they don't comb it, or at least they don't roll it around orange juice cans or iron it like my friends and I do. Or they have short hair. Really short. They wear jeans and T-shirts. I suddenly remember Sue Ellen. What frightened me about her, I realize, has faded. What excited me about her seems to be taking hold instead.

Most of the women in the band don't wear bras, even if they have big breasts. I can see their nipples. Some of them have bad skin. None of them wear makeup, not even lipstick. I think they might be lesbians, at least some of them. But I don't know much about lesbians yet, because even though I am curious enough to search under *lesbians* in the library card catalog, I don't find much there, and the few books I do find and furtively flip through in the stacks, I'm too afraid to check out. I don't want anyone to see my name among the signatures on the check-out card.

The women in the band look beautiful to me. I like the way they play the drums or guitar or lean easily against each other, talking and smoking. There are no men in the room; it feels secretive and safe.

I want to tell my mother about The Chicago Women's Liberation Rock Band when I get home, but I don't. I tell myself that it's because I don't want her to know that I sneaked over to the university and took my little sister, now sworn to secrecy, without her permission. But there's another reason: I know my mother would not approve of braless, defiant women who have formed some sort of clandestine society that excludes men. She would have thought it an unwholesome environment for a teenager, maybe even a dangerous one.

My mother likes it when boys call the house looking for me. By sixteen, I have already had many boyfriends. I am popular in the way she never was. She never had a boyfriend before my father—she was studious and helped take care of her younger sisters while her mother and father worked the store. When my father first asked her to go on a date, she turned him down, saying she had to iron. Then, perhaps in a moment of daring, she said he could come watch her iron if he wanted her company.

One day, during this time of boyfriends and popularity, I remember the wedding tablecloth. What has happened to it, I wonder. My mother tells me it is in my hope chest. My hope chest? Yes, buried in the hall closet, between the hanging plastic bags of dry cleaning and the shoe racks, my mother has stashed away a hope chest for me. "Where did it come from?" I ask her. "When did you get it?"

As she often does, my mother gently mocks me, repeating my questions without answering them, waving me away. Later, while she is in her bedroom reading and smoking her Kents, I sneak back to the closet and the chest. It smells like mothballs inside the chest, and the only thing in it is the tablecloth. It lays cool and folded and smooth, except for the embroidered bumps of little houses, like the one I assume she expects me one day to inhabit.

The wedding tablecloth stays in the closet for the next few years, but I do not. In college, I go to a lesbian bar. I buy a Diet Coke and sip on it all night while it goes flat. And I look at the women, many of whom look like boys. But I can see the outlines of their breasts and how their bodies are shaped, even in baggy jeans or painter's pants. They look very beautiful to me. They look like freedom, like they are living their lives without asking anyone's permission. When I look at them, I see possibility.

In time, I will go home with one of them. We will have an emotional, tempestuous, and very short affair. All I really want is her hands on me. I get dizzy from the feel of her hands on me, and the hands of the next woman and the next.

One night at the bar, I meet a woman who will become my first serious lover. I am twenty-one and just out of college. She moves into my apartment and comes home from her job as a surgical tech in a hospital with a ring, a thin gold band. She wordlessly slips it on my finger, and I understand that I have crossed over to some new, forbidden place.

I buy cube steaks at the meat counter of the grocery store because they're the cheapest cut, and I banter about my "husband" with the butcher. I occasionally like to say husband and flash my ring. And although I am a budding feminist, I like to think of myself as a wife. It makes me feel both petite and powerful—like the adult woman I have been waiting to become. I love it that someone loves me enough to call me her wife, to say she wants to be with me forever, the way my mother is with my father.

On weekends, we go to the bar and she sits with her arm around me, or slowly drinks bottled beer as she watches me dance. We do not tell people we are married. We have not even discussed whether we are married. It's the 1970s, and our friends are talking about collectives and three-ways and non-monogamy. I only wear my ring at home, or when I go to buy cube steaks from the butcher, a place where I can have a conversation that tests out what it feels like to be adult and married.

One day, an editor at a journal where I freelance asks me to lunch. He is twice my age, married with children, and has published a lot of books. I am thrilled that he may want to talk about my work. But he looks bored when I bring up ideas for articles. He wants to talk about my personal life.

"Don't you have a girlfriend?" he asks. "I thought you were a dyke."

I blanch and feel sick to my stomach—as if I'm stuck in the back of a hot car with no air-conditioning again. I don't want to be so easily defined by something that feels so personal, and with language I have not chosen. I don't answer, and he loses interest in me and my work.

My relationship ends and is followed by another and another. I'm not feeling as safe or as excited as I did in that basement listening to The Chicago Women's Liberation Rock Band—not when my straight friends are drifting away because they have boyfriends or husbands and I have . . . something else. I'm tired of being nervous when a girlfriend picks me up from work. I'm upset that my mother never wants to hear about who I'm seeing. The one time I bring a girlfriend home for Thanksgiving it is a disaster. My mother doesn't know how to introduce her to the other guests, and she doesn't look at either one of us the whole weekend.

I decide that being with women is too hard for me. I am too much of a coward to be a lesbian. I want to be married. I want to talk honestly to the butcher about what kind of meat my husband likes to eat. I want people to know that someone cares deeply about me, and I want to be able to talk about that person without feeling ashamed and compelled to change pronouns. I decide I will give up women.

I have a big twenty-fifth birthday party and invite all my lesbian friends. We have a great time, and I don't tell anyone that this is also my going-away party, because I intend to start dating men and want to get married. But at the party someone catches my eye. I decide to delay my plans.

Still, I try dating men again. One becomes a serious boyfriend, and then my fiancée. The sex is okay, sometimes even better than okay. I am vaguely happy to be able to bring him home to meet my family, but sometimes I feel flashes of anger or sadness. And while it feels good to hold his hand at the movies or walking down the street, I continue to think about women. I wonder if it is like my mother wanting to eat blintzes or borscht or herring. Those tastes and smells and textures were in her memory and imagination, and she kept returning to them.

Then I come to my senses. I'm not going to be able to give up women; I crave them too much. I break off my engagement and return to women, wondering if I will ever again find a woman who will call me her wife.

I recently moved from the Midwest to New York City, where my parents have returned to live out their final years. I sublet a studio around the corner from their apartment, and my days are scheduled partly around their needs. I share some meals with them, take them to afternoon concerts, help with their care. Questions continue to fill conversations with my mother, but these days they are more about the past than the future.

The other day, I asked her about the wedding tablecloth. Where was it, I wondered. Had it made its way from the closet in Chicago when my parents moved? Could I finally claim it as my own?

"I gave it away," my mother tells me.

"What? You gave it away?" I feel sickish, then blurry with tears. "When? Why, why did you give it away?"

"I don't know. I just did. Years ago."

"But who did you give it to, who?"

She can't remember. I am stunned. She spent more than a year embroidering that tablecloth, then just gave it away.

At dinner several nights later, my mother remembers. She gave it to the daughter of a friend who was getting married.

"What friend? What daughter?"

"What does it matter? It was just a tablecloth," she says. "I never even got a thank-you. They got divorced three months after the wedding."

Later, in the privacy of my studio, I think about her disappointments, about the wedding she never had and the one she must have imagined for me. How it must have confused her when, after having had so many boyfriends, I brought a girlfriend home. How humiliated she must have felt at that long-ago Thanksgiving.

Though she talks a lot, my mother has never really been good at talking seriously with me. She still retreats when it gets hard—making the suddenly urgent phone call, or trying to clear the dishes she can barely lift these days. So I am left to fill in the gaps. I don't know what went through her mind when my first woman lover moved in with me. I don't know if my brief engagement to a man made her feel relieved or skeptical. And with each new woman in my life, does she wonder, as I do, if this, at last, will be the one?

I am upset for days after learning she gave away the wedding tablecloth. I cry for her and for myself, for the wedding neither of us had. I cry for this remnant of my childhood and for the part of my mother that I will never have.

I wish she had asked me before she gave it away. I might have said, "Hold on to it. Maybe I'll have a big party to celebrate something else in my life: my work, my art, my friends."

How odd it is to live so intimately with someone and know them so well in some ways, and in others not at all. I look at my mother these days, tiny and wizened, her recollection of names and dates fading, and I try to understand what is in her heart that she cannot say. Maybe giving away the tablecloth was not an act of hopelessness or resignation. Maybe it was an act of love.

"What does it matter? It was just a tablecloth," she says. In calling it just a tablecloth, maybe my mother is saying that a wedding was not that important after all, that she understood I had chosen a different life, one that is still very full and very much mine. She didn't need to discuss it. She just privately and quietly released me from her expectations.

Don't Hide Your Bride Pride

∴

Monica Palacios

"I feel like we got married tonight," I said, smiling at Dyan as we lay naked on my bed.

She nodded her head yes, kissed me, and whispered, "Me, too." I didn't ask her to marry me; I simply verbalized what we both were experiencing. Oh sure, we had just exchanged incredibly powerful orgasms and had eaten a whole bag of peanut M&M's, but the sugar and the sex didn't feel as potent as this surreal moment of luscious in-loveness.

Prior to this bliss, we had never talked about the serious topic of marriage, because we both had recently exited relationships. We fought off the instant attraction as best we could, but four months later here we were, agreeing to spend the rest of our lives together. First, though, we were going to order Thai food.

Growing up, I understood marriage to be a *good thing* because every day I witnessed my parents' love and respect for each other. That sweet night with Dyan was definitely a *good thing*—the moment just felt right and true. So within a month, we had rings made and moved into our married apartment.

When we slipped rings on each other's fingers at Santa Monica Beach, six months after we had moved in together, no one told us to kiss the bride, and there were no weepy relatives—only squawking seagulls overhead, and sailboats floating on the pretty, blue-green Pacific. We didn't need an audience to witness our union or a certificate stamped "hitched." We didn't require spectators because we knew we were soul mates, and that was all that mattered. One of our deepest connections was that we both identified as Chicana lesbians, and the pride of our Mexican ancestry and Chicana/o culture was paramount to our desire to merge as one.

On the day we declared ourselves married, we began to refer to one another as "my wife." When I talked about us onstage in my solo performances, I spoke about being married, called her my wife, and playfully mentioned her as "the Mrs." or "the little woman." Because of this openness in my work, friends and even strangers always asked, "How's your wife?"

For us, being married was an emotional, spiritual, Chicanas-in-love commitment, and the word *wife* was part of the equation. We didn't feel we were adopting a heterosexual institution; we couldn't, the law wouldn't allow us to. And at the time—1989—it didn't matter to us. We just wanted to be together forever: married. And that's what we told our families.

For the most part, they respected our coupling. When I brought my wife home to San Jose to meet mi familia, they were more confused with us being vegetarians: "Ay, mi'ja, you girls don't eat carne asada tacos? That is a sin!"

The other aspect that my family had to deal with was the fact that my older sister is also a lesbian: Double Dyke Familia. I believe this Sapphic sisters phenomenon helped my family understand the importance of my marriage—or, confused the hell out of them. Either way, Dyan was welcomed into the Palacios' pack. Sure, there were those occasional insensitive remarks from both of our families over the years, but these were rare and reflected society's inescapable influence. What was important to us was that our mothers respected us as wife and wife. Their stamp of approval was priceless.

Outside of our families, our everyday life as a lesbian couple was treated decently. For the most part, people were kind. Every now and then, however, we'd get harassed by male punks wanting to take us down by shouting, "Lesbians!"

To which we would reply, "And proud ones!"

When I had to deal with a health issue that put me in the hospital, Dyan was by my side the whole time, and no one told us she had to leave because she wasn't a family member. To insure that we didn't have to deal with the hospital or doctors discriminating against us, we had made sure beforehand that we held each other's power of attorney for healthcare. The nurses and other staff did sometimes ask, during my four-day hospital stay, that curious and annoying hetero classic: "Are you sisters?" We would tell them, "No, we're married." To which they responded with polite smiles and by slowly walking out of the room—backward.

The day I was released from the hospital, the doctor instructed, "No intercourse for six weeks." As Dyan held my hand, I asked, "What about orgasms? Can I experience those?" A married woman has to know about post-op lesbian sex rules, right?

Dyan turned red and so did the doctor, but he managed to mumble, "Yes, you can have orgasms."

Even in this awkward moment, he didn't blurt out some homophobic remark. Being treated so fairly by the medical world felt empowering, especially since we had heard horror stories of queer couples experiencing hate and discrimination during medical emergencies. We felt very lucky.

As time went on, we were often looked at as a perfect couple, our outer shell of matrimony reflecting sweetness and love. But what people didn't know was that our chocolatey center needed attention, and we both were ignoring it. As beautiful as this union was, we started to slowly implode—which led to a separation and then divorce after seven years of being together.

I know, hard to believe. Didn't we sound like an adorable couple, wanting to be together forever? Well, sometimes life can suck. Big time.

There's no need to divulge the devastating details of this unraveling, but it was horribly sad. And what kept me from pulling my head off my shoulders was the fact that we were *not* legally married.

The emotional and mental strain was already fierce and debilitating enough; I couldn't imagine dealing with the cold reality of divorce lawyers and paperwork (I just ripped up the old power of attorney when I found it again years later). Thank the goddess we hadn't purchased a house together or created children.

My family, who had grown to truly love Dyan and to respect us as a couple, was saddened when I announced our disconnect. In a weird way, I was happy they were feeling down—it proved they genuinely cared about us. Our marriage also felt real because we used the word *divorce* interchangeably with *breakup*, unconcerned that it only applied legally to heterosexuals at the time.

The decision to divorce was mutual, and technically we survived it. But emotionally we both paid a steep price. Yes, I have loved other women since my partnership with Dyan, and there will be more in my future . . . at least one . . . okay, maybe seventeen . . . but marriage? I don't think so. Go ahead, call me bitter, but that's how I feel fifteen years later.

Even if I don't envision matrimony in my own future, though, I do believe same-sex marriage should become legal at the federal level. I didn't really understand the importance of this until the 2004 presidential election. That's when, as queer people and our allies were becoming more vocal and visible about legalizing same-sex marriage, George W. Bush promoted the so-called *protection* of marriage between a man and woman. His repetitive, obnoxious announcement—coupled with the fact that eleven states put anti-gay-marriage measures on their ballots that year, was a deliberate attack on LGBT Americans.

"Gay people have their domestic partnerships and civil unions—

and that's good enough," was the mantra right-wingers spewed. Well, you know what, folks? It *isn't* good enough, and that's why queer people are demanding marriage equality. Only marriage provides the certainty and security couples can count on in everyday life and emergencies.

I wasn't romantically involved with anyone at the time, but I could feel the hostility. Bush's plea to "save" the institution of marriage was hate-mongering covered in faith-based bullshit. And it was frightening how so many in the country believed his diseased discourse and repeated the ignorant comment, "If gays are allowed to marry, what's going to stop them from marrying their pets?!" Yeah, I couldn't wait to tie the knot with my little Cha-Cha and have our honeymoon at Petco.

Vomit. That was my reaction to Bush being reelected and all the anti-gay marriage initiatives passing. Three days after the horror, I fought back with a new show I premiered in Los Angeles, entitled *Get Your Feet Wet*. In it, I beat the crap out of a piñata that looked like George W. I know, real mature—but it was fun! I should have the right to marry whomever I want, even if I don't want to marry again.

Bush did an exceptional job at maintaining the country's homophobia toward same-sex marriage throughout his second term. But his followers were shocked and angered when, on May 15, 2008, the California Supreme Court ruled that lesbian and gay couples have the same constitutional right to marry as heterosexuals.

I had been following this case because my lesbian sister, Eleanor, works for the National Center for Lesbian Rights (NCLR), and her organization was the lead counsel in favor of marriage equality. When I first heard the mind-blowing proclamation, I shouted, "What a burn on Bush!"

Two weeks later, I was at the annual fundraiser dinner for NCLR with my sister in San Francisco with more than one thousand lesbians, and the energy in that room was beyond estrogen. It was Queer Love Pride Power to the max. Everyone understood that this triumph was about more than matrimony: The monumental ruling finally acknowledged lesbian, gay, bisexual, and transgender Americans as valued members of this country. As I sat there soaking up the loving spirit in the air, I couldn't help but feel that my work as a visible Chicana lesbian writer/performer had contributed in some small way to this groundbreaking moment of justice. Being an out queer artist for more than twenty-five years, promoting positive images of LGBT people, was paying off. I didn't have a wife with me that night, but it didn't matter because I was in the gayest city in the world with my lesbian sister and a huge crowd of proud women.

After this euphoric evening, I created a new show: *Amor y Revolución* (Love and Revolution). I wanted to declare same-sex marriage to be revolutionary, so of course I had to have my lesbian bride backup dancers. I also highlighted the ridiculousness of how the media made such a circus out of the gay marriages that took place that year by donning a ringmaster outfit and making the lesbian brides jump through hoops as they exchanged their vows.

The show was fun and a hit, but, as it came to an end in August, the sad reality was that California's Proposition 8—the gay marriage ban—was gaining momentum. I fought back by proudly putting up a NO ON PROP 8 sign in my apartment window, attending rallies throughout Los Angeles, and having a NO ON PROP 8 group come and speak at one of my shows in October, a month before the elections.

As in the 2004 presidential campaign, I felt personally attacked by all the gay-bashing. A homophobic army was donating millions and millions of dollars to paint same-sex marriage as a threat to America, especially to "the poor little children!" The only saving grace about the few weeks before the election was the thought that we were getting rid of Bush, and Barack Obama was coming in to save us.

Well, we all know the outcome of that 2008 election night. *Yay!* to the first black president. *Boo!* to the passage of Prop 8. The history-making right for same-sex couples to marry in California was now just history. I had thought my Golden State was hipper and more happening than ever, but Prop 8 stunned all of us.

Three years after that huge defeat, I'm still exhausted by it all. I surprised myself by going from divorcée to marriage activist. I couldn't help it: People really pissed me off with their ignorant and hurtful, vicious lies.

Recently, the great state of New York legalized same sex marriage, joining Vermont, Connecticut, Iowa, New Hampshire, and Massachusetts. That victory gives me hope, but my NO ON PROP 8 sign stays up in my window until *all* LGBT Americans can say "I do."

And who knows, maybe I might be a wife one more time. The other day, my sister, Eleanor, told me, "Never say never. You might fall in love again. Girl, don't hide your bride pride."

Happily Ever After

On the previous page, top to bottom:

Rebecca (left) and Priya marry on Martha's Vineyard.
Photo by Kelly Prizel, kellyprizel.com.

Shaneequa (right) and Jacquetta jump the broom.
Photo by Kelly Prizel, kellyprizel.com.

I Do (x 2)

∴

Lesléa Newman

When I was twelve years old, I watched *National Velvet* and fell to pieces at the sight of Elizabeth Taylor. Those eyes! That hair! If only I could be like her. But I resembled her as much as a frog resembles a unicorn.

Now, thirty-six years later, at last Liz and I had something in common: We married the same person twice. Though unlike Elizabeth Taylor and Richard Burton, my beloved and I did not divorce before we wed again.

Our first wedding was perfect in every way. September 10, 1989 was sunny but not too hot, humid enough to make my hair curl but not frizz. I felt like a movie star in my suit with its three-quarter-length cream-colored jacket and black miniskirt. My intended looked exceptionally handsome in a dashing off-white silk shirt and crisp black pants. As my love and I stood under a *chuppah,* Rabbi Rebecca watched us sign the *ketubah* and exchange rings. As soon as my betrothed broke a wineglass underfoot, our friends yelled "Mazel tov!", lifted us up on chairs, and paraded us about the room. The DJ was splendid, the food so delicious even the vegetarians ate the chopped liver, and the photographer outdid herself. There's nothing about my wedding day I would do differently. So why go through it again?

Because the person I pledged to have and to hold forever and I are both women, so our vows meant *nada* when it came to the law. But all that changed on November 18, 2003, when the Massachusetts Supreme Court decided that same-sex couples have the right to civil marriage. Of course not everyone danced a *hora* around the kitchen like we did when we heard the news, and there was a flurry of activity to try and strike the court's decision down.

Still, ever the optimist, I took our wedding outfits to the cleaners.

Even though Mary and I had decided to wait a few months to apply for a marriage license so we could keep our anniversary date intact, I made my way to Northampton's City Hall the morning of May 17, 2004, the first day marriage licenses were available to same-sex couples. As I strolled up Main Street, I remembered the first gay pride parade I had attended, nineteen years earlier. I had marched up this very same street next to a woman who wore a paper bag over her head so she wouldn't be recognized and lose her job. We'd passed a minister who had hauled a coffin out to the curb to remind us we were all going straight (so to speak) to hell. My, how times had changed.

The city clerk had announced that she'd be opening her office at eight thirty. By seven, about fifty couples were lined up on the sidewalk. An hour later, they were joined by hundreds of supporters who could barely contain their joy. One woman handed out plastic miniature-white-wedding-cake bubble-blowers. Someone else had baked an actual three-tier wedding cake for everyone to share. A child wearing a T-shirt that read I LOVE MY TWO MOMMIES gave out homemade muffins. The owner of Pride and Joy, our local LGBT book and *tchotchke* shop, served mimosas. I made coffee and water runs. A man waved a homemade banner that read, "And they lived equally ever after." A young woman from the University of Massachusetts held a sign that simply read, "It's about time."

At exactly eight thirty, the crowd parted like the Red Sea so that Gina Smith and Heidi Norton—along with their sons, Avery, age seven, and Quinn, age four—could make their way to the front of the line. As they advanced, the crowd broke into a spontaneous chant, "Thank you! Thank you! Thank you!" to acknowledge that Gina and Heidi were one of the seven plaintiff couples in the lawsuit responsible for the morning's festivities. When the two women emerged a little while later, after filling out their paperwork, they were greeted with loud cheers and applause, and pelted with birdseed (politically correct Northampton residents would never throw rice, which has been known to swell inside birds' stomachs and prove fatal). I stood on the sidelines, tears streaming down my face, as the couple and their children beamed.

The very air hummed with joy outside City Hall that day. It was like being on another planet—one where love, not hatred, is the rule of the day. Even some of the newspaper reporters cried as couple after couple walked out the door of the building hand in hand, or holding children in their arms. After applying for marriage licenses, many couples walked the two short blocks down to the courthouse to obtain a waiver of the usual three-day waiting period between applying for a license and actually getting married. Waivers in hand, the couples returned. Some had waited ten years, some twenty, some thirty, and they didn't want to wait a minute longer to enjoy the legal rights and privileges that marriage allows.

As the sun moved across the sky, more and more people joined the celebration. The Raging Grannies serenaded the group with their own renditions of "Going to the Chapel" and "Here Come the Brides." Someone handed out roses; someone else looped plastic rainbow-colored Hawaiian leis around everyone's neck. More food arrived. DJs, wedding planners, and caterers handed out business cards. A justice of the peace stood there sweating in her long robe—the temperature was now in the eighties—so that anyone who had applied for a marriage license and received a waiver could get married on the spot.

By the end of the day, 113 couples, 112 of them gay or lesbian, had applied for marriage licenses in my little town. Normally, 250 couples apply in a *year*. When the one token straight couple emerged from City Hall, the crowd froze in stunned silence before someone yelled, "They can get married, too!", which made everyone laugh before they clapped and cheered.

At about five o'clock, Mary got off work and met me behind City

Hall. Being good little lesbians, we started cleaning up the area where all the weddings had taken place. As I tossed a paper cup into an overflowing trash can, someone pointed to a vase of flowers and asked if I wanted to take them home.

"Whose are they?" I asked.

"I don't know," the woman said. "They were delivered earlier and no one claimed them."

"Look, there's a card," I said, and plucked it from among the pink roses. I read the words aloud, "In memory of Barbara and Valerie. Not in their lifetime, but in yours. For everyone." Though I didn't think I had any tears left in me, my cheeks grew wet as I absorbed the words. Next to September 10, 1989, the day Mary and I vowed to love and cherish each other until death do us part, May 17, 2004 was the most emotional day of my life.

Until September 10, 2004 arrived. My second wedding day.

Again, the afternoon was picture-postcard perfect. With no witnesses save the flowers in our backyard, I stood beside the woman I had loved for sixteen years. How had we arrived at this miraculous moment? My love hails from Bayamon, Puerto Rico. I am a nice Jewish girl from Brooklyn, New York. We were born twelve years apart. Yet, somehow, both of us managed to make our way to Northampton, Massachusetts, come out, find each other, embrace each other, and stay together long enough for the state we call home to sanctify our union and grant us the rights we deserved.

While this was a momentous moment, in some ways not much had changed. Except for her once jet-black hair, now streaked with silver, Mary looked the same as she had on our last wedding day. I like to believe that despite the crow's feet and laugh lines now decorating my face, I, too, looked much as I had a decade and a half earlier. What *had* changed was the way we felt about each other. At a wedding Mary and I attended years ago, the minister ended the ceremony by saying to the newly married couple, "May today be the day you love each other least." Those words had struck a chord in me then, and they came back to me now as I looked into Mary's eyes and felt how much our love for each other had deepened and grown.

And so, we turned to face the justice of the peace, and in the same outfits we'd worn on our first wedding day, we exchanged the same rings and said the same vows we had spoken fifteen years before. We'd planned on ending our ceremony with the Jewish tradition of breaking a glass underfoot, as we had done the first time we wed, but before Mary did so, I recited the poem I had written for that wedding—which meant so much more to us today:

BREAK THE GLASS

(for Mary Grace Newman Vazquez)

Break the glass
for even in our happiest moments
let us not forget
those who hate us
those who fear us
those who destroyed our temple

Break the glass
for that which was
is no longer
and can never be again:
our separate lives have ended
our life together has begun

Break the glass
and all that would stand
in the way of our joy:
those who hate women and lesbians
those who hate Jews and Puerto Ricans
those who hate themselves

Break the glass
and as the glass shatters
let the four winds scatter
the shards
up to the heavens
and let each become a star

so that every night
we can look up at the sky
and see how hatred can be transformed
into something beautiful
by our love
Break the glass

After Mary stomped on a wineglass wrapped in a cloth napkin, our justice of the peace, who is also a lesbian, said with a quiver in her voice the words we never dreamed we'd ever hear: "By the power vested in me by the state of Massachusetts, I hereby pronounce you legally married."

As Mary gathered me in her arms, there was no need to say, "You may now kiss the brides."

The Book of Love

∴

Audrey Bilger

When I first came out as a lesbian in my mid-thirties, I looked for books. It's what I do any time I make a change. A decade before that, I stopped eating meat, and I read every book I could find on being a vegetarian. If I was gay, I wanted to do my homework and make a plan. I was and am a literature professor, so reading is my job, and books help me make sense of the world.

From Wedded Wife to Lesbian Life, an anthology edited by Deborah Abbott and Ellen Farmer, came out the same year I did—1995. I had just ended my fourteen-year marriage to a man, and I was relieved to discover I wasn't alone. Here were stories of women who had started out adhering to the usual life script, the one I had followed: girl meets boy; girl marries boy. But for some girls, the traditional roles didn't fit. They wanted to meet other girls. As for the storybook happy ending, legal marriage between two women seemed like such an impossible dream that coming out meant turning one's back on the institution entirely. You could have a lesbian life, but few believed you could ever be a wedded lesbian wife.

As a thirty-something newbie lesbian in the '90s, I found myself between two worlds. Riot Grrrls were a few years younger than me, stirring up the Third Wave of feminism. Many of the women featured in *From Wedded Life* were children of the '40s and '50s, so none of their stories was exactly like mine. I had come of age to a personal soundtrack of Iggy Pop, Talking Heads, and REM. I spent my twenties as a DJ at a college radio station, spinning alternative music and feeling awkward about having married so young—not because I knew all along I was gay, but because who got married at twenty-one in the '80s? Not the people I knew in grad school, who seemed so hip and jaded. Maybe only a few friends from my past.

I grew up in the middle of the country in the middle of the twentieth century. In rural Oklahoma, USA. As an adolescent and young teen, I read everything I could get my hands on, but nothing I encountered in school or local stores did much to challenge the status quo. The majority of books by women I came across were popular romance novels. My girlfriends and I traded and devoured bodice-rippers with titles like *The Flame and the Flower* and *Sweet Savage Love*. Gender roles were crystal-clear in these paperbacks: The heroines might loathe

the male leads through much of the book, but that only made it sweeter—and more savage—when hate turned to love.

At sixteen, I got a boyfriend of my own. He was just abusive enough to resemble the men I had read about, but he was sensitive, too, a guitarist and wannabe songwriter who played Harry Chapin ballads and worshipped Neil Diamond. We were nerdy introverts together for a few years, and my next big relationship, which began right after I turned twenty, was with the man I ended up marrying.

In one of those retrospectively ironic twists of fate, I first hooked up with my future husband at a gay Halloween party. I hadn't known any out gay kids in high school, but in college I had one gay male friend who worked with me at the Student Union information desk, and he invited me. I got the impression it would be a small, underground sort of gathering, so I decided to check it out. Instead, I was surprised to see forty or fifty people, most of them gay—women dancing with women, men with men. I had no idea there were more than a handful of gay people in the state of Oklahoma, let alone at Oklahoma State. My straight friends and I stood out, but I felt accepted because I was cool with the whole gay thing (I was conscious of being an observer, not a judge, of not freaking out). I ended up drinking way too much and went home with this man who was in one of my philosophy classes. We became a couple after that, and for fourteen years we made a go of it.

If I were writing my life story as a work of fiction, aware of all I know now, I would have had the protagonist do something else at that party. Not drink so much. Ask a woman to dance. But we live our lives without knowing what's on the next page, sometimes without even understanding the subtext of the present moment.

I got married because that's what you did in that part of the world at that particular time. I wasn't a very good straight wife. I always wanted to be somewhere else, and I kept running away from the label. When my husband and I left Oklahoma to enter the graduate program in English together at the University of Virginia, I discovered feminism. Fueled by *The Second Sex* and *The Daughter's Seduction*, among other books and articles I read, I began to resist being defined solely by my relationship to men. I didn't want to be a "Mrs.," and "wife" sounded like the subordinate half of a necessarily restrictive conventional duo. My husband and I started dividing up the housework, and though we tried to play outside the gender system, it was hard to shake off the idea that he was "helping" me if he did dishes or mopped the floor. When I became the first to find a full-time professor job and started supporting us both financially, our marriage began to fray at the edges.

And Then I Met This Woman—that's the name of another book I bought when I came out, and the title pretty much sums up what happened next. Because I love music, I had taken up the drums in my early thirties—and got plenty of books to help me learn to play. When I embarked on my first tenure-track job, I started an all-female blues band. I met a guitarist—*this woman*—and I stopped being a straight wife. My husband and I had been friends, companions, and, increasingly as our lives got more complicated, antagonists. The woman was flirty, fun, and attractive to me in a way I'd never known. Even though she and I didn't work out, I had opened up a new chapter, and I wasn't going to turn back.

I had a lot to learn. Until I dated a woman, I never knew what heterosexual privilege meant. That's the way privilege works: When you have it, you're unaware of it. As a straight wife, you're in a particular box. You've reached a certain life goal that single women are supposed to want. You can hold your husband's hand or give him a peck on the cheek as you walk down the sidewalk, and you don't even notice you're doing it. Neither does anyone else. Your relationship is sanctioned, even blessed, by those around you.

Although Southern California, where I had moved shortly before I came out, was a long way from Oklahoma, two women could still get stared at and worse for holding hands in public places, or for being in the wrong place at the wrong time. At the conservative college where I taught, when I told some colleagues I was now gay, they discouraged me from being out until I had tenure. I learned to hide, to monitor my behavior and conversations. Sentences could be stumbling blocks. Watch the pronouns. Don't get too personal.

I began to understand that the mythic quality known as "gaydar"—a sixth sense that supposedly allows gay people to identify one another—is really just a reading skill. Once you realize that people around you might possibly *not* be straight, you can read people and situations that were previously hidden. I was doing this with literature: rereading Virginia Woolf, who was married to a man but loved women; checking out Gertrude Stein, who made a home with her lover Alice B. Toklas; learning from Henry James about "Boston marriages," where two women lived together and may or may not have been *together*.

For those who follow the basic script and never ad lib or ask questions, heterosexuality is all-encompassing. Marriage can only be between a man and a woman because that—or so they say—is the very definition of marriage. Forget Shakespeare's "Let me not to the marriage of true minds admit impediments," where marriage means a deep bond and connection: Marriage is exclusively for opposite-sex couples. The Defense of Marriage Act—a *defensive* document if ever there was one—enforced this straights-only view of the institution. DOMA made its way onto the books in 1996, the same year I fell in love with my wife-to-be.

It's fitting that I met Cheryl in a bookstore. Also fitting that our meeting revolved around music. We were both in bands of our own, she as a guitarist, me on drums. I saw her band play in the bookstore coffee shop near my college one Friday night, a year into my new lesbian life. I went up and introduced myself at the break. Girl meets girl. We talked about the venue. She made a joke about dictionaries (you had to be there). I told her my band would be playing that same place next week. Nothing out of the ordinary, but the subtext—which I could read quite clearly—was curiosity and interest. When she returned the following week, and I saw her across the room at the coffee counter as I laid down rhythms on the drums, I knew I was looking at my future. I could tell from the way she tilted her chin and looked the world in the face that she was strong, smart, fierce, and imaginative. I couldn't wait to turn the next page.

We count our first meeting at my bookstore gig—fifteen years ago now—as our anniversary. She asked me to marry her the year after we met, and I said yes, even though we knew that wasn't a legal option. We started wearing gold rings on the fourth fingers of our left hands, and we moved in together to begin the adventure that has been our shared life.

Around that time, we went to a lesbian commitment ceremony, a wedding in everything but legalities, and we both agreed that though it might be nice to make promises in front of friends and families, we didn't see the point if in the end you couldn't call it marriage. Like many lesbians and gay men we knew who were in serious relationships, we thought of ourselves as "married" (always with the scare quotes). We called each other "partner," and squirmed when acquaintances identified us as "girlfriends" or, worse still, simply "friends." Because I had been married once before, I felt frustrated when people downgraded and redefined our relationship. I missed the advantages of a relationship that gets affirmed by society in general; I missed my straight privilege, my acknowledged role as wife.

During the time we've been together, we've seen the world around us change, as lesbian and gay stories have achieved greater visibility. In 1997, we—along with the rest of the country—could read on the cover of *Time* magazine the headline from Ellen DeGeneres: "Yep, I'm Gay." Although she paid for that declaration in the short term, the tide of public opinion was moving in her—and our—favor. Ellen was just a couple of years older than me, and her public coming out helped me cope with the time I still had to spend closeted at work. I knew I would get there, too. The following year, not long after I received tenure and started to come out at my college, news of the tragic slaying of Matthew Shepard sparked a national discussion of how hostility to gays and lesbians could lead to brutality. As an out lesbian at school, I was able to speak up about LGBT issues and could work to create a better climate for my colleagues and students.

In my life so far, I've gone from living "by the book"—bound by convention—to writing new kinds of stories that evolve over time. In the early twenty-first century, I, along with many other LGBT people, have been revising the marriage plot. By working to change laws and regulations that are *on* the books, we aim to build a better future.

Four years into our relationship, in 2000, Cheryl and I watched in dismay as our neighbors put signs on their lawns in support of California's Proposition 22. The text of this initiative, which would make its way onto the books by majority vote, declared that "Only marriage between a man and a woman is valid or recognized" in the state. As our neighborhood filled with YES ON 22 declarations, we felt exposed and increasingly unwelcome; as similar marriage bans passed in states around the United States, we began to feel like outsiders in our own country.

We didn't go to San Francisco in 2004 when Gavin Newsom started issuing marriage licenses, mainly because we couldn't work out the logistics. The window was small, less than a month as it turned out, and we worried about getting our hopes up for nothing. The marriages were nullified later that year, but by that time, Massachusetts had legalized same-sex marriage, and the march toward equality was gaining force.

Those San Francisco same-sex weddings paved the way for Cheryl and me, along with 17,999 other couples, to wed legally in our home state in 2008. The sequence of events had gone like this: After the San Francisco marriages were dissolved, that city, along with gay and lesbian rights organizations, took Proposition 22 to court, claiming that it violated the California constitution's guarantee of equal rights to all its citizens. When the case made its way to the state Supreme Court, the justices upheld the constitutional principle of equality and struck down the proposition, removing the impediment to same-sex marriage. What resulted was a "summer of love" for lesbian and gay couples like us.

On first hearing about the court ruling in May of that year, we couldn't believe it was true. We went online and read the decision. We read the analyses. We looked for the catch. We recalled what happened to our lesbian and gay friends who had married in the San Francisco Bay Area, and we wondered if we could bring ourselves to take the plunge. We knew that our marriage would mean nothing to the federal government, thanks to DOMA, so we would have to continue to live in contradiction—citizens of this country, but not on par with straight citizens. Would we get to call this marriage? Could we take away the scare quotes? To add to our doubts and worries, Proposition 8—the initiative to amend the state constitution to prohibit same-sex marriage—had made it onto an upcoming ballot, and the summer of love became one of struggle, as polls showed that there was a chance it might pass. What could we do in the face of so much uncertainty?

Reader, I married her. Writing this adaptation of *Jane Eyre*'s famous line, I feel happy and proud. In my literature classes, we talk about how, in Victorian novels, women's lives end once they cross the matrimonial finish line. To be a wife in nineteenth-century England was to close the book on your own story. In the legal definition of marriage at that time, the husband and wife became one person—and that person was the husband. That's why at weddings they used to say, "I now pronounce you *man* and wife." Same-sex marriages, I now saw, could change that equation. Whether it's husband and husband or wife and wife, the old roles get a makeover when freed from traditional gender imbalances. After twelve years together, Cheryl and I knew what we were getting into. Neither of us had to kneel down and pop the question. Instead, we took a stand and claimed our right to be each other's wives.

We didn't dress up and walk down the aisle. Like all of those 2008 California weddings, ours was a shotgun affair—rushed planning with an undercurrent of fear. No one knew when the state might pull the plug. There was talk of suspending all same-sex marriages until the ballot decision came down. One courthouse closed because they refused to issue licenses to couples like us. And the hateful vitriol from some of the Prop 8 proponents was downright scary. Few people I know got the wedding they would have planned had they been given more time and security.

Cheryl and I talked about throwing a party, but because we have many close friends, we couldn't whittle down the guest list to anything that would be reasonable, given the time constraints we were under. If we asked fifty people, another fifty would be offended. We decided to elope in the most low-key fashion possible: We asked our Unitarian minister friend Ricky to marry us, and we set up a double date to see the movie *Mamma Mia!* at a Hollywood theater with him and his husband, Peleg, who would be our witness. At dinner before the film, we ordered pizza, signed the papers, and then—in an instant—we were legally wed.

Our marriage stands. After Prop 8 passed, the courts stood with us and declared that we and the other couples from the summer—and autumn—of love were still married in the eyes of the law.

Then, in 2010, the marriage ban was struck down as unconstitutional, with Judge Vaughn Walker ruling that people can't vote to strip fellow citizens of their constitutional rights. The right to marry, he said, does not revolve around gender roles, and the state has no interest in telling people how to run their personal lives and how to set up their homes. Even more, he declared that there's no such thing as gay marriage. There's just marriage, something everyone deserves.

That's how Cheryl and I feel. Although legal recognition of our union has nothing to do with our feelings for one another, it puts us on the same footing as our straight friends and neighbors. And though we've had to fight for our rights—and are still fighting on a national level—we believe that the tide of history is with us. Our story is part of a larger one, about freedom and justice, about the pursuit of happiness, and when all is said and done, about love.

Four (Same-Sex) Weddings and a Funeral

∴

Susan Goldberg

My girlfriend proposed—if you could call it a proposal—over the phone, long-distance, on a Sunday afternoon in October 2003. Cordless in hand, I was rooting through my fridge for something to eat when she said, "So, what do you think about getting married?"

I paused, the cold air from the refrigerator blowing in my face.

The previous summer, the Canadian province of Ontario had, finally, granted same-sex partners the right to wed, and all of a sudden "gay marriage" was the topic of every conversation, garnering its own special section of the editorial pages each day and forcing

Canadian queers to consider the question: Will you or won't you now that you can?

Not us, I had thought about me and Rachel. After all, we were good feminists. We both had master's degrees in women's studies, for God's sake. We had been well schooled in marriage's economic, not romantic, origins—in the idea that modern marriage is rooted in archaic notions of women as chattel. Not for us the need for state sanction, that piece of paper from City Hall. Not for us the capitulation to tradition.

And then she asked. And all of a sudden it *was* us. When I asked her why, Rachel simply said, "It felt like a good approximation of where our relationship was at the time."

She had a point. Eight and a half years in and counting, there we were. We'd just spent the previous year rescuing the relationship from near ashes, sitting across from a skilled therapist as we learned to talk to each other all over again, to wipe clear that pane of murky glass that seemed to have grown up between us and distorted our images of each other. She'd finished her doctorate, had gotten a tenure-track job teaching at a northern Ontario university. I'd built up my freelance career. We were looking at houses up north; I planned to move from the apartment we had shared in Toronto to be with her in the fall. And we had booked the first flight for our sperm donor to fly in from Vancouver so we could begin the process of trying to have a baby.

"Um," I said to Rachel, "okay."

And that was that. We were getting hitched.

We didn't tell anyone for a few weeks. At first Rachel didn't want to tell anyone, ever. She wanted to elope, have a secret ceremony at City

Hall and never mention it again. I think she was scared. If we said it out loud, if we told anyone, it would be real.

But we were also scared of my family's influence. I come from a family big on big Jewish weddings—weddings of the white-dress variety, with dozens of attendants. Weddings that cost tens, if not hundreds, of thousands of dollars. Weddings with DJs and klezmer bands, with first dances, with disposable cameras on the tables, with open bars and mashed-potato bars and (I swear) kosher hot dog carts wheeled in at midnight. Weddings preceded by a year's worth of Friday night dinners in honor of the engaged couple. Did I mention my aunt owns a bridal store? We had lots of reasons to be afraid.

Slowly, though, we both warmed to the idea of a public ceremony—on our own terms. We began to plan our ideal wedding: outside in the summer, maybe on one of Lake Ontario's islands. Fancy outfits. A big party with family and close friends. A string quartet. We'd find a way to afford it.

And then we told my parents. More precisely, on a Sunday evening in November, we invited ourselves over for dinner at their suburban Toronto home and told them about our baby plans.

"And there's one more thing," I said.

"There's more?" my mother said, weakly. My father just grinned as he sat next to her on the family room couch, where she spent most of her time these days.

"There's more," I confirmed. "We're getting married."

What I thought was an afterthought became the main event.

"You're getting *married*? When?" asked my mother. "Where? How?"

We began to outline our vision: summer, outside, family and close friends—

"Well," she interrupted, "you'll have to do it here. At our house."

Rachel and I looked at each other. I was about to explain why we couldn't possibly hold the wedding at my parents' house when Rachel said, "That would be lovely."

"What were you *thinking*?" I asked her in the car on the way home.

"Well," she said, "it's just that it's your *mom*."

My mom. Who had reached out in dozens of small ways to my girlfriend over the years. Who had helped pave the way toward my father's slow but eventually steadfast acceptance of both my relationship and my sexuality. Whose chicken soup Rachel—at the time a vegetarian—ate without hesitation. My mother, battling breast cancer, lying there on the couch.

And that was the end of our first wedding and the beginning of the second. By the next morning, my mother had notified all our relatives. I came home that evening to a half-dozen messages of *mazel tov* from scattered cousins, aunts, and uncles, all promising to be there for our "big day." By Tuesday morning, my mother was in full swing, brainstorming caterers and flower arrangements, guest lists and officiants.

"Um," I said, "I'm not sure we can afford all this."

She paused. "Oh Susan," she said, "we'd like to pay for it."

It was a vast gesture of acceptance that I should have anticipated and hadn't, and the fact that I hadn't suggests that I was more caught up in doubts about the legitimacy of my own marriage than were my parents. For them, this wasn't a "gay wedding." It was their daughter's wedding, and, damn it, they were going to do it up right.

So we set the date, June 13. We met with the caterer. We negotiated the guest list, capping the number of my parents' friends to, in my mother's opinion, an impossibly small amount that continually edged upward. (We had conversations like this: Her: "Gloria's coming." Me: "But she's not invited." Her: "I know. I told her that. And she's still coming.") We found a rabbi—possibly the only one in the city who would agree to perform both an interfaith (Rachel is a very-lapsed Catholic) and same-sex wedding. A secular humanist Jew, the rabbi's only conditions were that the ceremony contain no reference to God and no sexism. We could live with that.

We booked the string quartet, asked my sister-in-law to do the flowers. I applied for our marriage license: The forms hadn't yet been updated to reflect the new legislation, and so my name was entered under the heading "groom." I wondered which of the two men in line ahead of me at the registrar's office would be a bride. After much convincing on the part of family and friends, we even registered, spending a couple of giddy hours debating china patterns and testing the fine blades of luxurious German knives.

In the meantime, we bought a house up north. We flew our donor in for a second try, then I flew to Vancouver for the third—which "took." I was pregnant. My parents were over the moon. So was the rabbi.

Then my mother's chemo failed.

Through all the planning, we had tried to ignore the question that hovered, unspoken, in the backs of our minds: Would she make it to June 13? Back in October, we had been optimistic. Yes, my mom was weak, but for the past three years, each successive round of chemotherapy, each new drug, had held the disease at bay. Over the past twenty years, she had survived, against astonishing odds, two previous bouts with cancer, one ovarian, one breast.

The disease was the product of mutation 5382insC of a gene now known as BRCA-1 (BR for *breast,* CA for *cancer*). Women with this mutation—women like my mother and her mother, who died of ovarian cancer in her forties, and *her* mother, who died of breast cancer—have an up to 46 percent lifetime risk of developing ovarian cancer, and a 50 to 85 percent chance of developing breast cancer. One in forty-five Ashkenazi Jewish people—like my mother's family—carry a BRCA mutation, as opposed to one in eight hundred to one thousand individuals in the general population. Their daughters—women like me—have a 50 percent chance of inheriting that mutation.

Although my mother had tested positive for the genetic mutation, I had resisted testing. Never mind that I was pregnant—and potentially with a daughter to whom a family legacy of cancer could be bequeathed. Never mind that my mother's cells were coded to multiply beyond her body's capability to sustain them. I couldn't think about my *own* mortality, let alone my mother's. We thought she was invincible. We were counting on her track record of almost miraculous resilience. Why would this occurrence—breast cancer, now metastasized—be any different?

And yet it was. By April, she was vomiting up most of what she ate and had started spending nights as well as days on the couch, because the walk up the stairs was too hard. She found it increasingly difficult to breathe.

We all saw a third wedding coming, but we hesitated. Finally, my mother said out loud the words no one else had been able to say. She'd spent the night at the hospital in respiratory distress; the doctors had drained two liters of fluid from around her right lung, the one that didn't have a catheter in it already. We had an appointment with the palliative care doctor the next morning.

"Susan," she said, "I don't think I'm going to make it to June 13."

"We'll change the date," I said. "We'll do it sooner." She nodded. My father just looked into his lap as he sat next to her on the couch. I didn't cry until I phoned the rabbi to reschedule.

We settled on Mother's Day, May 9, three weeks away. It was the closest we could fathom pulling everything together. It would be a truncated affair, just family and a few close friends at my parents' house. No quartet. Our families changed their flights. We flew up north, signed the lawyers' papers on the house, flew home, found rings and outfits at a local shopping mall, met with our midwife. We printed our *ketubah* (no God, no sexism) off the Internet; no time to commission anything custom. I had a pre-wedding pedicure, and then burst into tears when the polish smudged.

"All I want is for my toenails to look nice," I wailed in the car on the way home. Rachel looked at me sideways. "Is it really your toes you're upset about?"

Meanwhile, my mother deteriorated rapidly. She had moved from the couch to a hospital bed we'd set up in the family room, but she could no longer get comfortable. Even small efforts, such as going to the washroom, became overwhelming. My father spent hours trying to convince her to eat something, anything, but she wasn't hungry, so her body wasted, wisps of chemo-thin hair framing her gaunt face. She had coughing fits that left her exhausted. Some combination of drugs and disease left her unfocused and anxious, confused or annoyed.

"I know I'm not making sense," she told me.

"It's okay," I said. "You don't have to make sense."

The night before the ceremony, we ordered in Thai for the immediate family members who had congregated. My mom napped in the family room while we ate quietly in the kitchen, unsure how to work her decline into the celebration, how to acknowledge such sorrow in the midst of what was supposed to be joy.

"I'm not sure I can go through with this," I told Rachel at the door as she left to meet her mother at our downtown apartment. I was going to sleep at my parents' home, on night duty.

The next morning, the tips of my mother's fingers had turned dusky and I wasn't able to rouse her. But her chest rose and fell, and so I called up denial, found the now-much-too-big clothes she wanted to wear and laid them out, to help her into later on. She died while I left the room to eat breakfast, while my father was at his computer, printing out his toast to the brides.

"Excuse me?" said the home-care worker. "Miss? I think that your mother is not breathing."

I closed her eyes, rested my forehead against hers for a moment. We held the funeral the following day. My cousins, already assembled for the wedding, were pallbearers. The wedding caterer fed the hundreds of people who showed up at the house following the burial. Rachel and I exchanged rings privately, then sat *shiva.*

The fourth wedding was on June 13, in my parents' backyard—a much smaller affair than we'd originally planned, just family and a few close friends. We served hors d'oeuvres and lunch. In the photos of the ceremony, we all look so sad under the *chuppah.* My father and brother are holding back tears, my sister-in-law wears dark glasses, and Rachel and I clutch each other's hands while staring into each other's eyes, biting our lips. At three months pregnant (with, as it turned out, a boy, who would be named for his Bubbe), I am barely showing.

When the time came to break the glass at the wedding—because, according to Jewish tradition, in each *simcha* we are always reminded of our sorrows—we couldn't do it. We tried, but maybe there had been too much sorrow already. Our high heels simply pushed the glass deeper into the soft ground, where it stayed resolutely whole, unbroken, unbreakable.

Seven years and two children later, it's still difficult for me to talk about my wedding. When I tell the story I get weepy. When I hear other people, queer or straight, talk about their own nuptials, I get jealous. On the outside I nod and smile, but on the inside I am consumed with longing for what could have been: the party, funny toasts, the quartet, the champagne, the joy. I fantasize about my mother standing up with us, reveling in family and food and friends.

And then I remind myself that there is no such thing as a perfect wedding, despite what the marketers would have us think. And I remind myself that my wedding(s), as vastly imperfect as they were, brought together family and friends from around the world. That, because of my queer, shotgun wedding, my mother's siblings and nieces and nephews, as well as Rachel's mother, got a chance to see and talk to her and say good-bye. I think about the day of her death and how we were already gathered at my parents' house, and how we cried and talked and ultimately laughed about my mom. Her big talent had been bringing people together, and she had managed to do it one more time. All because her daughter was getting married. To another woman.

And that's the thing about weddings: Done right, they bring together more than two people. They knit families and friends together, make us collectively stronger. And that's why, for me at least, the issue of gay marriage resonates: The human rights it protects and enshrines extend beyond the two brides or two grooms to their parents, their siblings, their communities.

Not that I'm an advocate for marriage. I'm still ambivalent about the institution as a whole, reluctant to assign it a significance beyond the political, the administrative. I'm still kind of sheepish about the whole decision. And yet, I do know this: that when our rabbi sat down with us to do the paperwork and asked me, "Do you come here willingly?" and I answered, "Yes, I do," something shifted inside me, and I began to weep. And for the first time in a very long time, they were not tears of sorrow.

Has getting married changed anything for me and for Rachel? Hard to say. Our wedding was just one of a half-dozen major life events that took place within a six-month span: my mom's death, obviously, but also the move to a new city, the transition from urban student renters to suburban professional homeowners, the baby. The combined stress of all of these (compounded by severe sleep deprivation) nearly drove us apart within the first year of our first son's life; by the time our second son arrived, we'd mostly recovered. In between the two babies, I summoned up the courage to get tested for the BRCA mutations. I'm negative. I'd love to tell my mother that.

And I do. I tell her things most days. On the ring finger of my left hand, under the gold wedding band that I picked out so hastily, I wear my mother's diamond engagement ring. My sons like it when it catches the light and throws rainbows onto the walls. I twist the ring and tell my mother about her grandchildren, about how six-year-old Rowan reads and reads, about how his little brother, Isaac, finally consented to his first "big boy" haircut, about our kitchen renovations, what we're having for dinner. Both kids are fascinated by death at the moment; Rowan in particular asks us to tell him the story of my mother's last day at regular intervals.

"And then what happened?" he asks. "And then what did you do? And you were very sad? And where did she go?"

I explain about burial, about bodies returning to the earth, but my stubborn romantic streak whispers: *She's right here, inside us.* He likes that I wear my mother's ring—"To remember her. Because she died. Right, Mom?"

And Rowan likes, he tells us, that we are married.

"Why?" we ask him. "Why do you like it?"

"I don't know," he says. "It's just good."

'Til Death Do Us Part

∴

Patricia Cronin

In 2000, I was given the opportunity to create a dream sculpture with a grant from the Grand Arts foundation. And I already had the idea for a three-ton marble work.

Living in New York City had made me acutely aware of the historical public sculptures that adorn the major parks and prominent squares of the city. I loved these sculptures—nationalist, virile, victorious—but found them lacking because they overwhelmingly depicted men. There were almost none in which to see *my* reflection publicly commemorated.

I tried to locate real women—not women as allegory—honored in public spaces. Hidden in obscure, less prestigious spots in Manhattan, the only sculptures of individual women I could find were a statue of Eleanor Roosevelt, a bust of Golda Meir, Joan of Arc on a horse, Gertrude Stein, and then Alice in Wonderland and Mother Goose. That was it. In all of Manhattan, two children's storybook characters and just four real women. I was dumbfounded.

So I did what Aristotle said an artist does: looks out and sees the world as incomplete and tries to complete it in his [her] studio. This is singularly the best part about being an artist: solving a problem by *creating* something.

In addition to correcting the glaring omission of women represented in public as heroes, I also wanted to address one of the closest issues to my heart: the failure to give gay Americans the basic human right of legal marriage. By not being able to have a legal wedding, we're robbed of the seamless acceptance heterosexual couples experience. And since the federal government won't accept same-sex marriages or civil unions, my partner, the artist Deborah Kass, and I had to pay lawyers to draw up legal documents (wills, powers-of-attorney, and such) to provide us just a few of the 1,200-some legal protections of heterosexual marriage.

These documents are terribly depressing; they're only useful if one of us becomes ill, incapacitated, or dies. They're not about celebrating our life together, but about the end of it.

Just because my nation won't acknowledge us doesn't mean I can't. If all I am legally afforded is death, I could make as elegant a statement about it as I could muster. So I decided to carve those three tons of Carrara marble into "Memorial to a Marriage"—a dignified double funerary portrait of Deborah and me, lying naked and entwined in each other's arms.

I chose a nationalist form for the work—nineteenth-century American neoclassical sculpture—but I was building on the entire history of sculpture, which is one of death and the memorial. My sculpture would carry on a tradition thousands of years old—from anonymous ancients, to Canova and Gericault at the turn of the nineteenth century, to the twentieth-century feminist artist Hannah Wilke, all of whom designed and created their own burial markers, gravestones, sepulchers, and tombs.

In this and previous works, I've come up with an aesthetic strategy that involves using familiar subjects and materials but sneaks in political content. I've gone back in art history and inserted my own contemporary viewpoint within traditional forms—whether by painting erotic watercolors of two women that are so close up and cropped that many (straight) viewers can't tell what's going on; elevating the objects of desire for many young girls (plastic toy horses) by casting them in bronze; or, in the case of my memorial, subverting neoclassical sculpture in order to talk about gay marriage.

Once I had the concept and initial watercolor sketches for *Memorial*, it took three years to complete the transformation into marble. First, using live models with body types and hair textures similar to mine and Deborah's, I created a rough clay maquette one-third the size of the completed work. Then I did a slightly more refined clay version two-thirds the size, and finally an over-lifesize clay sculpture to the actual dimension. That was used to make a rubber mold, into which plaster was poured.

Because plaster is more resistant to touch than clay, I could carve it more finely, perfecting every inch, fold, finger, hip, toe, and curl of hair. Now I was ready for the marble. The plaster sculpture was digitally scanned, and from that scan, an amazing machine cut the block of marble into the rough shape of the piece, leaving about two inches extra for me to finish. My assistant and I spent three months of eight-to-twelve-hour days, six days a week, carving away with pneumatic chisels, rasps, files, stones, and, lastly, sandpaper.

The finished marble portrait closely resembles Deborah and me, but we're idealized: Even though we "weigh" three tons, we have no cellulite, thank goodness.

And then I needed somewhere to place the memorial. From conception, I designed this piece to be outside in the grass, hugging the ground. Since it was a sepulcher (a burial vault), it only made sense that it be in a cemetery, and specifically an American cemetery from the nineteenth century. I looked at Greenwood Cemetery in Brooklyn, but they had stopped allowing marble mortuary sculpture at the turn of the twentieth century because of the cemetery's proximity to New York Harbor and its industrialized pollution. So I kept searching.

My birthday in May 2002 was very sad. My father had died suddenly that month, and eight months earlier the terrorist attacks of September 11 had taken place just five blocks from my home in lower Manhattan. When Deborah asked me what I wanted to do for my birthday, I didn't feel like celebrating. But I had noticed that Woodlawn Cemetery in the Bronx had a historic walking tour.

Designed in 1863, Woodlawn is one of the best examples of the nineteenth-century "garden cemetery" movement: It's America's answer to the Père Lachaise Cemetery in Paris. While Parisian cemeteries are famous for their beautiful statuary in marble and bronze, they are also known for visitors' participatory experiences with the statues. Specifically, there are several bronze statues in Père Lachaise where the different body parts are rubbed for good luck—thus burnishing penises, buttocks, and the like to a golden yellow.

Woodlawn is also similar to Père Lachaise in that it's the final resting place for many historic figures. You can find artists, writers, civic leaders, entrepreneurs, entertainers, and jazz musicians there, from Elizabeth Cady Stanton to Joseph Pulitzer to Herman Melville to Madame C. J. Walker. Woodlawn is solemn and peaceful, with specimen trees, gorgeous architecture, and lovely statues from the robber-baron years of American history.

At the end of the tour I took with Deborah, I asked the guide if the cemetery allowed sculpture on graves. She said yes, so I began the process of picking the site for my sculpture and *our* final resting place. With the help of my gallery, Deitch Projects, Deborah and I bought a plot—the first piece of real estate I had ever owned. And it was fitting that we would choose to end up in the Bronx: My father was raised there, as was Deb's mother, while Deb's grandmother owned two children's clothing stores in the borough.

When you buy a funeral plot, it's like any other kind of real estate: You're looking for location, location, location. And you worry about who your neighbors will be. I chose our particular spot because its topography is that of a sunken garden. I knew that once the statue was in place, it wouldn't be easily visible from the road; I worried about vandalism. Since Grand Arts had invested a large sum in my project and it took me three years to make the piece, I certainly didn't want a homophobe coming along with a sledgehammer.

I took solace knowing that near our plot was buried Ralph Bunche, the first African American to win the Nobel Peace Prize. Also, an amazing sculpture by Attilio Piccirilli—one of the Piccirilli brothers who carved the Lincoln Memorial in Washington, D.C.—is around the corner. I must admit, though, that it felt a little daunting to join the illustrious company of acclaimed artists, musicians, writers, businesspeople, and politicians: Could our lives, our work as artists, and this sculpture measure up?

Having already exhibited my series of erotic watercolors all over the country in the 1990s, I was not terribly stressed about installing half-naked marble versions of Deborah and me on a very public burial plot. What I didn't anticipate was the vulnerability of putting the sculpture outside, atop our joint graves. As the only public expression of our lives together, *Memorial to a Marriage* would be open to the elements, politics, and jerks—and thus be the perfect metaphor for an artist. It's a very public life, being an artist, in which all of your successes and failures are well known.

On November 3, 2002, we once again took a walking tour at Woodlawn—this time focused on "The Beautiful Women of Woodlawn." The leaves on many of the three-hundred-year-old specimen trees were at their peak, gorgeous yellow and orange, and those that had fallen looked like petals on the ground. We strolled past magnificent McKim Mead & White mausoleums, Daniel Chester French angels, freestanding bronzes, Tiffany stained-glass windows, and Elizabeth Cady Stanton's tomb. And at the end of the hour-and-a-half tour, in front of two hundred friends, artists, and strangers, my sculpture was unveiled.

The tour guide, an art historian from the Cooper-Hewitt Museum, spoke about the sculpture and the grave in the same way she discussed the other sculptures we saw—as if the artist wasn't there. (The other artists had long been dead; mine was the first new sculpture in Woodlawn in many years.) Her talk was respectful and solemn, and when it concluded, the crowd broke into applause. Almost everyone felt the need to not just come over and talk to me, but touch me as well. In an art world and culture full of titillation, superficiality, and sensationalism, my sculpture obviously reached people at a deep emotional level. It brought up feelings of love, but also of death and loss.

Everyone was invited to a reception in the Woolworth Chapel at the cemetery, and then our close friends came back to our loft in Tribeca for pizza, red wine, and to watch *The Sopranos*. I had structured the events of that day like a funeral: a procession through the cemetery, a graveside service, a public reception, and finally a more intimate gathering at the family house. This was both an art gesture and a personal one.

The "opening" for my sculpture was, in a way, a preview of my personal closing. But the unveiling at the burial plot was not only a type of funeral: It was like a wedding as well. It was the only time our friends had come together to focus on the two of us as a couple—seriously, romantically, and in celebration. That they were celebrating a replica of us—the simulacrum rather than the living, breathing version—was still out of our legal control.

The response to the sculpture over the past decade has been amazing. We're the third most visited plot in the cemetery: There's Duke Ellington, Miles Davis, then Deb and me. The cemetery organizes historic-themed walking tours—jazz, art and architecture, Victorian, veterans—and somehow our statue is included on every one of them.

In addition to critical acclaim in the press (including an article in the *New York Times*, being chosen as one of the top ten shows of the year in *Artforum*, and even its own cartoon in the *New Yorker*), professors bring their classes to see *Memorial,* and students write research papers about it. There's a master's thesis on it, two recently defended PhD dissertations, and it's been discussed on many personal blogs. I've been introduced to people who, when they figure out I'm the one who made the sculpture, burst into tears while telling me how much it means to them.

At the cemetery, it's formally known as the *Cronin Kass Memorial*, but people sometimes ask to see "the two girls," or "the marble ladies." Unsuspecting viewers may come upon the statue and say, "Oh look at those two angels." But as they walk around it, the content of the piece slowly reveals itself. *Wait a minute—that's not two angels.* By then, viewers will have invested some time in, at the very least, a pleasant visual experience, but perhaps also considered a subject in a way that might surprise them and make them think about same-sex couples differently.

I used to drive up to the cemetery every six to eight weeks to "clean the girls." There would be pollen, bird droppings, and occasionally animal paw marks to wipe off. Around Thanksgiving, before the first snowfall, I would buy a car cover for the memorial and secure it with a bungee cord. A couple of winters ago, clever raccoons got in under the bungee cord and nested among our tangled legs for the winter.

But I recently decided to move the marble version off the plot. Pollution, pollen, acid rain, birds, and those raccoons made me reconsider leaving it outside for eternity. If I had the money, I would make a second one in marble and let this one slowly melt away. Instead, a bronze version has taken its place. Degas called bronze the medium for eternity, and it can weather, well, *weather*—both literally and politically. Now I can look forward to seeing what parts of us, as at Père Lachaise, will be people's favorites to rub against and burnish.

Currently, the marble sculpture is on tour at U.S. museums and university art galleries. I hope that eventually it will sell to a collector who will, in turn, donate it to a museum with a strong American or ancient sculpture collection; I would love to see it in New York's Metropolitan Museum. It would be fitting and instructive to place a political artwork of two women, created from a feminist perspective by a woman artist, in juxtaposition with ancient sculptures of warriors or single nude women created by men.

When I started making *Memorial*, gay marriage wasn't legal in any state, and was being used as a political football. When it became legal in 2004 in nearby Massachusetts, where I was born, Deborah and I could have married then, but we would have had to sign an affidavit that we eventually planned to move there. We don't, and it seemed counterproductive to lie in order to get officially recognized as a couple.

Then, on June 24, 2011, everything changed. The New York State Senate passed Bill #5416, allowing gay people to legally marry. Not civil unionize, *marry*. We were at our little beach shack in Long Beach, New York, without a television, so we streamed the senate vote online. What State Senator Thomas Duane said made me cry: "The only word that legally says family is: marriage."

Days and weeks of confusion followed while City Clerk offices around the state scrambled to prepare for the new law to take effect. We uploaded our marriage application and sent a wedding announcement to the *New York Times*. People asked what we would wear to the ceremony and I said "summer whites," knowing we had no dresses but that we would figure something out.

The *Times* called to fact-check our announcement—hooray, we were in! Then New York City said too many couples had applied for licenses to be married on that first legal Sunday, so there would be a lottery. Two good friends, a straight couple, agreed to be our witnesses, so they were on call. Having already been together eighteen years without the possibility of marriage, Deborah and I had to wait a little longer.

We finally got the call that we could marry on Sunday, so we held an impromptu "rehearsal dinner" with another couple the night before. The morning of the wedding, an older gay male couple (who had married in Massachusetts years ago) telephoned to congratulate us—but also to point out that there would be no estate savings under the New York marriage law. In fact, our income taxes will now be more complicated (read expensive), and if one of us becomes widowed the other will have to pay taxes for inheriting half of what we already consider ours. I took joy in our political (and romantic) victory, but it's just a very small step in the right direction: We still need the Defense of Marriage Act repealed.

We went to City Hall on the morning of July 24, 2011, with nearly nine hundred other New York City couples, waiting in the heat for three hours before getting into the building. Yes, there were protestors, but they were so unprofessional I'll call them hecklers. They held up pathetic signs that read BAD IDEA. Various gay organizations showed up, too, with rainbow-colored umbrellas to shield the brides, grooms, children, parents, and friends from the protestors' ridiculousness.

The first lesbian couple to marry had been together forty-seven years. I couldn't imagine what they had been through. Another couple was just eighteen and twenty, and had already been together five years. One reason I found compelling to marry Deb was so that younger people who are in love and inclined to wed can do so at the *beginning* of their adult lives, and have friends and family root for their relationship's longevity. The second reason was more personal: We were able to profess our love of, care for, and commitment to each other before the state. The ceremony was emotional, heavy. Even the judge cried.

Women's history gets erased all the time. Lesbian history is often not written at all.

But for as long as there is a Woodlawn Cemetery, guides will lead walking tours and have to say out loud the names of two lesbian women artists: Patricia Cronin and Deborah Kass.

I don't know how or when I'm going to die, but I find great comfort in knowing where I'm going to end up. What kind of person do I want to be until then? What kind of art do I want to make?

I wonder which one of us will be first to visit the plot when the other dies. If I outlive Deborah and the federal marriage law is only changed *after* she's gone, I think this sculpture is the only thing that will even come close to comforting me.

Will full marriage equality arrive in the United States in my lifetime? Or will I depart this world never having experienced all the rights of citizenship? I'm dying to know.

Photo from opener:
Patricia Cronin's over-lifesize Carrara marble sculpture "Memorial To A Marriage" (2000-02), Cronin Kass plot, Woodlawn Cemetery, Bronx, N.Y.
Photo by Patricia Cronin.

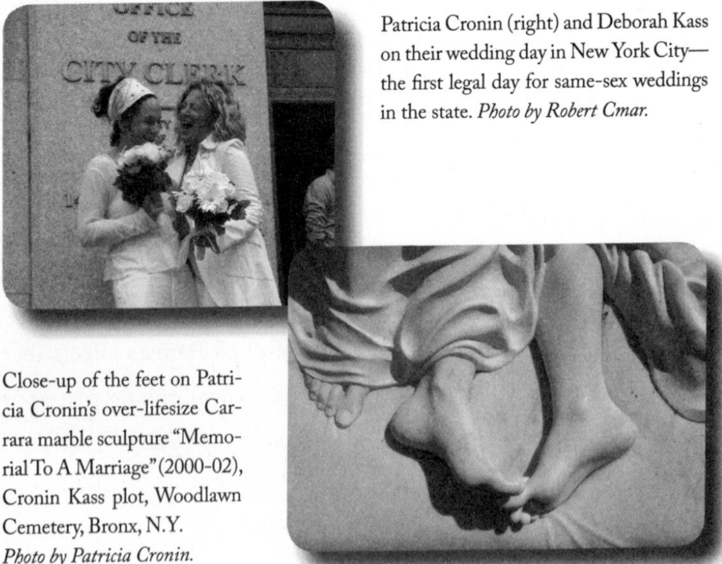

Patricia Cronin (right) and Deborah Kass on their wedding day in New York City—the first legal day for same-sex weddings in the state. *Photo by Robert Cmar.*

Close-up of the feet on Patricia Cronin's over-lifesize Carrara marble sculpture "Memorial To A Marriage" (2000-02), Cronin Kass plot, Woodlawn Cemetery, Bronx, N.Y.
Photo by Patricia Cronin.

A Girl Can Dream

∴

Caroline Gambell

We are in the attic of my best friend's house, arguing over who is going to hold the flowers. Lauren is worried that someone will find out that we touched the bowl of dried African violets that her mother keeps on her dresser. Or, worse, that we will drop it. Your parents won't mind, I insist, because it is *such* a special occasion. And besides, what is a wedding without flowers?

Anna, another friend from the neighborhood, is two years older and always the voice of reason: Why don't we put the bowl on the floor between us for the ceremony, so that we can't drop it? We agree.

Lauren and I drape pillowcases elegantly over our faces, and wrestle our grins firmly into masks of solemnity. Anna, our officiant, begins: Dearly beloved, do you? We do. The yellow afternoon sun streams in through an open window. The African violets look beautiful. I am six years old, and it is my first lesbian wedding.

Civil unions for gay and lesbian couples were made legal in Vermont in July of 2000, just one month after I came out as a lesbian to my friends and family. Not that I paid much attention to politics: I was too busy being fourteen and pining over my first real teenage crush. Holed up in my bedroom, I listened to Ani DiFranco and wrote (terrible) poetry about the exquisite pain of being in love. I was certain that my crush and I were destined to be together—she just needed to get rid of that boyfriend of hers. It soon became clear that she was not quite as convinced of this. It was the greatest tragedy of my barely teenage life.

I now know that I was tremendously lucky: My unattainable crush may have been the great "tragedy" of that time, but my coming-out experience wasn't tragic at all. My parents were instantly supportive, and my friends claimed that they already knew; Lauren, my one-time bride and lifelong friend, claimed that my fierce middle school obsession with Winona Ryder made it "so obvious." My school had an active Gay-Straight Alliance (run by an out lesbian couple who, adorably enough, taught in adjoining classrooms), and my liberal Connecticut college town had an LGBT community center and an annual pride festival. I complained bitterly about the lack of datable girls in town, but what lesbian doesn't? All things considered, I led a fairly charmed queer adolescence.

As my ill-fated high school crush faded with time, so, too, did much of my youthful political indifference. I felt a responsibility to educate myself on all things gay: I attended conferences for queer youth, participated in the first annual National Day of Silence, worked on a Gay-Straight Alliance supplement to my high school paper, and tried to stay on top of news related to gay rights, or, really, gay-anything. Although I experienced little overt homophobia in my daily life, I understood that I benefited from the tenuous privilege of circumstance that few queer teenagers—or even many queer adults—shared.

When the *New York Times* started running gay and lesbian "celebration" announcements in the summer of 2002, I anxiously awaited each newspaper delivery: Would there or wouldn't there be one this weekend? I worried each week that the *Times* might succumb to pressure and erase any mention of gay unions from their pages.

I would toss aside the front sections and go directly to the back pages of "Style," then start my systematic search through the smiling faces and pairs of names. Gay male announcements were somewhat exciting; lesbian announcements were a thrill. I read them aloud to my parents, who, to their credit, always looked up from the book review section and listened attentively. In addition to the simple pleasure of reading about two lesbians in love, I felt a tug of responsibility: to witness, in some small way, their union. For all the crazy bigots out there who would never read a lesbian wedding announcement, I would read 'em extra good.

But there was something impossibly sad for me about those first same-sex announcements. In a sea of twenty-something straight couples, the gay and lesbian couples simply did not belong. They were always older, and their announcements indicated that they had been together at least a decade, so some joked about indecision and wanting to be "sure" before they took the plunge. More than age, though, these first couples' announcements did not belong because their civil unions—the only option available in 2002, 2003, and beyond—did not mark a beginning, but rather affirmed what they had already built together. The straight couples' weddings had the privilege of being purely about romance; the lesbian and gay couples' were about political persistence and survival in the face of all odds.

I was driving south from Maine on May 17, 2004, the day that gay marriage became legal in Massachusetts. I was eighteen, enjoying my last summer at home before heading off to college in California. My (also queer-identified) friend and I cheered as we crossed New Hampshire's southern border and spotted the sign: MASSACHUSETTS WELCOMES YOU. Indeed!

"We should totally get married," Holly joked, half-serious. The suggestion caught me off guard: Sure, we had kissed a few times, but we were hardly dating. Was this what straight people felt every time they entered the city limits of Las Vegas? That heady mixture of possibility, recklessness, and youth? It made me feel terribly grown-up.

We turned on NPR and listened to the laughter and happy sobbing at town hall weddings across the state. I grinned at passing drivers. Even at seventy miles per hour, I could tell that the blur of trees had reached their green-gold peak of late spring; I remember it as the loveliest day of the year.

I had never been a member of a wedding party before—had really only attended a handful of weddings in my life, mostly for relatives—

and so I was excited to be a bridesmaid when two of my friends got straight-married in the summer of 2007. It was an unbearably humid day in central Ohio, and I was squirming in the first pair of high heels I had ever owned, but the ceremony was beautiful and the couple deliriously happy. There was plenty of dancing (barefoot, in my case) at the party afterward, and more than a few half-yelled renditions of our favorite Irish drinking songs.

If romantic comedies are any indication, it's always a little bit depressing to be single at a wedding. The day before I had flown out to Ohio, my ex-who-I-was-still-totally-in-love-with told me that she was getting back together with her ex before me and that we couldn't be in touch for a while (what is it with lesbians?). But more than being single, I was the gay one at a straight wedding in a state that defined (and continues to define) marriage as exclusively between a man and a woman. I was thrilled to celebrate my friends' commitment to one another, but couldn't get past a niggling sense of hurt that they had gotten married in a place where I was unable to.

I tried to explain this to another close (straight) friend as we drove together to a bar for the after-after party. I searched for an appropriate metaphor for why I suddenly felt so sad in the middle of my friends' "happiest day."

"Would you eat in a restaurant that had a NO GAYS ALLOWED sign out front?" I asked her. "Even if it was the only restaurant in town?"

She wasn't buying it.

"I don't think that's equivalent," she said. "And really, what does this have to do with our friends getting married?"

∴

Not long after the wedding, I signed a petition to put Proposition 8 on the ballot in California. Or, more specifically, I was tricked into signing a petition to put Prop 8 on the ballot.

It was September of 2007, a blindingly bright day in Southern California, and I was shopping for last-minute school supplies for my senior year at Pomona College. I was outside some big-box store in some anonymous strip mall when a friendly guy approached me with a clipboard. He gave his spiel about needing a certain number of signatures to get propositions on the ballot. Pegging me as a liberal, he pitched the propositions as: This one is to end factory farming, this one is to protect the lives of the young and vulnerable, this one is to get a gay marriage decision into the state constitution.

"We had a ballot vote a few years ago that banned gay marriage, but public opinion has changed so much in the past few years," he said. He gestured to a young, hip-looking woman holding another clipboard a few yards away. "She's really passionate about this issue." Then he leaned in closer, conspiratorially. "I'm not worried about this one at all. California is such a liberal state, once this is on the ballot, we can finally get marriage legalized."

To give myself *some* credit, I did at least see through his "young and vulnerable" rhetoric that masked a mandatory parental notification law for teenage girls seeking abortions. But naive and vulnerable outside my liberal arts college bubble, I fell for the cheerful man's sham liberalism about gay marriage. I wanted it to be legal in California, so I signed the damn petition.

A few weeks later, I realized what had happened. Feeling mortified, I kept my California voter registration even after I graduated from college in May of 2008 and moved to New York—just so I could vote No on 8. When the proposition passed, I still felt like I had committed some small treason.

I met Claire in the summer of 2010, after I had had enough of New York and moved back to Connecticut. I swear we didn't mean to fall in love: She was moving to D.C. in a few weeks, and besides, I was more than ten years her junior and therefore "*way* too young." We really did try to be friends, but we failed miserably.

I had a number of semi-serious girlfriends during college and in my first years in New York. I even thought I might have been in love with a few of them, though when the relationships ended (always with bitter tears and endless processing), I felt certain that my feelings had been either an illusion or an affliction. With Claire it was different: I fell for her fast and hard. There was no question: My heart beat in my throat, my stomach jumped every time I thought about her. *This was it.*

She introduced me to the writings of M. F. K. Fisher, and I read aloud to her from Joan Didion's *Slouching Towards Bethlehem*. She made elaborate dinners on the weekends we spent together, beef bourguignon or coq au vin, and I brought red wines from obscure vineyards in South Africa, which reminded her of her youth. The daughter of foreign service officers, she had led the international childhood I always dreamed of. She marveled at the fact that my parents still lived in my childhood home—"You mean you never moved as a kid? Not even once?" She came to Thanksgiving with my family and met my grandmother, who pulled me aside after dinner and gestured toward Claire, "I have a very good feeling about this one."

It didn't bother me that Claire was divorced—I referred to her affectionately as "my gay divorcée." By the bizarre ins and outs of state laws governing same-sex unions, Claire was legally divorced from a woman she hadn't actually married: She had been civil unioned in Vermont, but divorced in Massachusetts. Claire and her ex were still good friends—they had achieved the holy grail of functional, amicable lesbian breakups. It made me like her even more.

Like most children of happily married parents, I grew up wanting what my parents had. I imagined an egalitarian partnership with a hilarious and brilliant woman, two well-adjusted kids, a subscription to the *New Yorker* that would pile up on my nightstand, and a complete set of Le Creuset cookware. I didn't fantasize about joint-tax returns and health care benefits, but in my grown-up life, I began to understand the significance of those things. And as Claire and I did the crossword puzzle in bed on Saturday mornings, I started to picture having those things, both romantic and practical, with her. A wedding, a marriage, a life together.

In the end, this is what broke us up. It's true that the distance was too much, and the age difference too great, but the deeper truth was that she could not imagine a marriage with me. I wanted her to share my fantasy of a future, even if it was too early to tell, but she didn't. She had spent her youthful idealism imagining a marriage to someone else, and it hadn't worked out. "You deserve someone who wants that fantasy," she told me. And I think she might be right.

∴

Don't worry, I haven't given up on lesbian love or marriage. Just this month, I was invited to my first real lesbian wedding, just twenty years after my private ceremony with Lauren and Anna in the sunlit attic. The couple haven't yet decided when it will be or even where—both California natives, they are waiting to see how the continuing Prop 8 saga plays out in the courts. Then again, they might get married in New York, where they now live. Or in Washington, D.C., where they used to live. Or maybe even Iowa, because why the hell not?

The same-sex wedding announcements in the *New York Times* have changed substantially over the last nine years, though I haven't: I still approach the paper with eager anticipation each Sunday to read the Styles section. These days, there are almost always gay and lesbian couples featured, often two or three. And while there are still older couples, they're now announcing their long-awaited *weddings*, at which they'll renew the vows they took at commitment ceremonies years ago.

And there are also many young couples, people of my generation, who have come of age as queer in the last decade. Same-sex unions have been legally possible in some form for the majority—if not the entirety—of our "out" gay lives. We owe much to the queer activists that came before us, who have given us the gifts of hope and idealism.

But in a sense, I owe equal gratitude to that attic wedding with the African violets and pillowcase veils. There have been romantic setbacks since then, both political and personal, and I have flirted more than my fair share with jadedness. Yet I can always reach back to six-year-old me, who looked at her radiant bride in the yellowing afternoon sun and imagined the world as it should—and would—be.

The End of Civilization As We Know It

∴

Lydia Stryk

The characters: Edith, Bea

The time is the present.

Author's Note:

The End of Civilization As We Know It *is about two women who have led long, secret lives. This should be reflected in the style of the piece—the contained, secretive, controlled nature of their being with one another in the public world—and reflected in the dialogue, which is undemonstrative, never effusive. Looking over their shoulders to see if anyone is around or observing is second nature to them. The play is a recounting of what was forbidden and remains so. The past lives on in their present lives. The things these women are saying are highly charged, passionate, and erotic, but their expression is hushed, hinted, simply stated—an economy of expression, gesture, touch, that hidden gay people have lived with and refined to a high art. It might well be that they do not touch each other at all until the stage direction calls for it at the end of the play. Or, there may be a flicker of a hand over the other's cheek, so quick and light that it could be missed by the audience.*

(Two women in their seventies, dressed for a celebration, sit together in a waiting area.)

EDITH

Do you remember *your* wedding day?

BEA

Of course I do.

EDITH

Just checking.

BEA

And I remember my beautiful maid of honor, too.

EDITH

I was beautiful.

BEA

Are beautiful.

EDITH

Am beautiful.

BEA

My beauty.

EDITH

You made your mother leave the room.

BEA

That's right. So you could help me dress.

EDITH

Well, *undress*, first . . .

BEA

And then and there. I confessed my love.

EDITH

You were naked in my arms.

BEA

And then I started to sob.

EDITH

You couldn't stop. You choked on your tears. And you wouldn't let go. Remember that? You clung and clung.

BEA

You pulled away. And then you said—

EDITH

I said.

One day. You'll be *my* wife. One day you'll be *my* wife. You're *mine.* You're *mine.* You're *my* wife.

You're *my* life. Not his.

BEA

You kicked a chair across the room.

EDITH

I banged the wall with my head.

BEA

It bled and bled.

EDITH

Blood everywhere.

BEA

Blood on my dress.

(a pause)

Poor Pete.

EDITH

Poor Petey. Poor you and me.

BEA

It was not a happy day.

(a pause)

EDITH

Remember Larry's birth?

BEA

You held my hands.

EDITH

I was screaming.

BEA

Like it was *you* giving birth.

EDITH

My son.

BEA

And then you fainted clean away.

(a pause)

EDITH

Twenty years.

BEA

In and out of each other's kitchens.

EDITH

In and out of each other's arms.

BEA

(hurt) *Your* marriage.

EDITH

Served you right. I gave in. We became two wives.

BEA

You broke my heart.

EDITH

Another marriage. Doomed from the start.

BEA

You had the twins.

EDITH

Well, there was that.

BEA

Two young mothers with secret lives.

EDITH

All those years. And we never got caught.

BEA

(appalled at EDITH's memory lapse) That time in the playground.

EDITH

Oh Lord.

BEA

You forgot.

The sunlight was dancing in your eyes. I'd never seen such a beautiful face.

EDITH

All sound stopped. No playground, kids.

BEA

I scooped you up with my tongue.

EDITH

And then . . .

BEA

Mrs. Larson appeared. Out of nowhere!

EDITH

The Treasurer of the Ladies Church Bazaar. And you said . . .

BEA

"Mrs. Larson! Won't you join us?"

EDITH

She stood like a stone.

BEA

I was quaking inside.

EDITH

She shut her eyes. She turned on her heels. Her back like a blade.

BEA

I was shaking all over.

EDITH

You wouldn't let us leave together.

BEA

One stroller one way, one stroller the other.

EDITH

(impressed, taking BEA in) You'd never dared kiss me in public before.

BEA

I never dared kiss you in public again.

(A long pause)

(still in the memory) That night, I couldn't sleep for fear she'd tell the world on us. And they'd . . .

EDITH

They'd what?

BEA

Tear us limb from limb. Set the dogs on us. Well, take away our kids.

EDITH

Oh Bea . . .

BEA

I was quite sure, Edith, they were going to kill us. I had this dream. I never told you. A mob with torches. Mrs. Larson at the head. Lighting a ring of fire around us. Chanting we should die . . .

(a pause)

But it gets worse.

EDITH

Bea—

BEA

When I woke up, I wanted to run. And then . . .
(she struggles)

EDITH

Go on.

BEA

I decided to stop.

EDITH

Stop what?

BEA

Stop *us*. I couldn't live like that anymore.

EDITH

You never told me this before.

BEA

How could I?

EDITH

If you had left me . . .

(a pause)

I'd have jumped off the bridge.

BEA

And so would I. I'd have jumped in right after you.

EDITH

You kept away. I remember now. We were apart.

BEA

How long did that last?

EDITH

Oh, all the next day.

BEA

The whole day?

EDITH

Well, I might have stopped by near dinnertime.

To borrow an egg.

BEA

I think it was cream.

EDITH

Some of your sugar.

(a pause, BEA smiles)

Next-door neighbor.

BEA

That very last day, remember?

EDITH

I couldn't let go!

BEA

I looked up at you and in that moment—

EDITH

—I knew I wasn't leaving anymore.

BEA

No more good-byes.

EDITH

No more next door.

BEA

We waited for Pete.

EDITH

You sat him down.

BEA

"Sit down, Pete. We've got something to tell you."

EDITH

After twenty years. The lying was through.

(a pause)

Poor Petey.

BEA

Poor all of us.

(There is a pause of regret.)

EDITH

Twenty-five years together since then.

BEA

Makes . . . fifty years since the day we met . . . ?

(They stop. They study each other, questioningly, in wonder, disbelief.)

EDITH

Have you got the camera?

BEA

I do. Of course.

(fishing it out to show her)

Here it is. In my purse.

EDITH

The reception address?

BEA

Got it, *yes*. Have *you* got your glasses?

EDITH

(patting her pocket) Oh Lord.

BEA

You forgot.

(presenting them triumphantly from her purse)

I found them lying on your desk.

(EDITH takes the glasses. There is a long pause.)

BEA

Are you ready?

EDITH

(adjusting her collar, sitting up) Larry's boy found himself a beautiful bride.

(She looks at BEA.)

A beautiful bride.

(She turns away.)

BEA

What is it? . . . What's wrong?

(a pause)

EDITH

I'm not going in.

BEA

Oh Edith, come on.

EDITH

I never want to go to a wedding again.

BEA

But he's our grandson!

EDITH

I can't . . . anymore . . . I can't . . .

(a long pause)

BEA

I'll never make you go to a wedding again.

EDITH

(with quiet rage and despair) One day. You'll be *my* wife. You'll be *my* wife. One day.

(A pause. She gets up slowly, she takes a deep breath, steeling herself. Bea gets up. They take hold of each other's hands and begin to walk off stage together. Suddenly, BEA stops EDITH, takes her in her arms, holding her for some time, and then kisses her deeply. In public, for the first time in all these years. Then they walk off stage together.)

End of play

Wedding Song for Two Women

∴

Mary Meriam

Didn't I always know this leaf
in some cathedral in my mind
impossibly high with green relief
was with me intertwined?

Wasn't it her inside my book,
the queen of chance and understanding,
and wasn't she why I undertook
my painted look at landing?

Oh, falling this way, the light, the air,
this feeling through the atmosphere,
this holding her hand and kissing her there,
without her being near

the saddest edge of the spinning world,
this knowing and never knowing before
the stems and vines of longing curled
around her open door.

Contributors

Katherine Arnup is a historian, interdisciplinary scholar, and associate professor in the School of Canadian Studies at Carleton University in Ottawa, Canada. She is author of the award-winning book *Education for Motherhood: Advice for Mothers in Twentieth-Century Canada* and of more than two dozen articles on motherhood and on lesbian and gay families. She served as an expert witness in the Ontario and British Columbia marriage cases. She is writing a book on death and dying about her experiences caring for her sister and her parents and working as a hospice volunteer.

M. V. Lee Badgett is professor of economics and director of the Center for Public Policy and Administration at the University of Massachusetts Amherst. She is also the research director of the Williams Institute for Sexual Orientation and Gender Identity Law and Public Policy at UCLA. In 2008, *Curve* magazine named her one of the twenty most powerful lesbians in academia. In 2010, she was an expert witness in the *Perry v. Schwarzenegger* trial on the constitutionality of Proposition 8. Badgett lives in Northampton, Massachusetts, with her wife, Elizabeth Silver, and their two dogs.

Gloria Bigelow has appeared in three comedy specials for television, her most recent being *Fierce Funny Women*, currently airing on Showtime. She was also featured in the film *Laughing Matters . . . Next Gen*, which documented the lives and performances of five up-and-coming comics. She has performed at numerous festivals, including the New York Underground Comedy Festival, Michigan Gay and Lesbian Comedy Fest, the Outlaugh Comedy Festival, and Womenfest in Key West. Glo, as she is called, is currently chronicling her life as a black kid in the white suburbs.

Jennifer Camper is a cartoonist whose books include *Rude Girls and Dangerous Women* and *subGURLZ*, and she is the editor of two *Juicy Mother* comix anthologies. Her cartoons and illustrations have appeared in magazines, newspapers, comic books, and anthologies, and have been exhibited internationally. Visit her website at www.jennifercamper.com.

Mary Beth Caschetta is the author of a book of short stories and a recipient of the Sherwood Anderson Foundation Fiction Award. She lives in Massachusetts with her wife and their standard poodle, Violette Leduc. She is working on a novel.

Patricia Cronin is a visual artist and a professor of art at Brooklyn College, CUNY. She is a recipient of the Rome Prize in Visual Art from the American Academy in Rome, Italy. Her paintings and sculptures have been exhibited extensively in the United States and internationally, and are in numerous collections, including the Corcoran Gallery of Art in Washington, D.C. and the Gallery of Modern Art in Glasgow, Scotland. Visit her website at www.patriciacronin.net.

Rachel Darling works as an advertising copywriter by day and a jazz singer/songwriter by night, performing at clubs in the Twin Cities. She lives in Minneapolis with her author wife, Kimberly J. Brown, and probably too many pets.

Emily Douglas is the web editor at *The Nation* and formerly an editor at RH Reality Check. She has written on LGBT issues, reproductive health, women's rights, and the law for those publications as well as for *The Women's Review of Books*, *The American Prospect*, and others; she blogs at TheNation.com. From 2004 to 2006, she worked in legal advocacy at Gay & Lesbian Advocates & Defenders. She lives in Brooklyn, New York.

Erika W. Dyson is a poet, former theatrical costumer, and current assistant professor of American religious history at Harvey Mudd College in Claremont, California. Her research centers on church/state separation, science and religion, stage magic history, and people who talk to dead people. Her current book project examines the prosecution of spiritualist mediums and ministers arrested under fortune-telling laws at the turn of the twentieth century.

Sara Felder is a solo theater artist, playwright, humorist, activist, and juggler, based in Oakland, California. Her solo plays, all comedies, have included the themes of Jewish same-sex marriage (*June Bride*), the Israeli-Palestinian conflict (*Out of Sight*), mental illness (*Melancholy, A Comedy*), and grief (*A Queer Divine*). Felder ran away with San Francisco's Pickle Family Circus, was a featured act in Joel Grey's *Borscht Capades*, toured Cuba with Jugglers for Peace, opened for Joan Rivers, taught juggling in California prisons, and continues to perform and teach all over the world. Visit her website at www.sarafelder.com.

Caroline Gambell graduated from Pomona College in 2008 with a degree in gender and women's studies. Since graduation she has been an intern in public radio, a freelance writer and copyeditor, a nanny, a legal assistant, a clerk in a wine store, and a researcher in child development. She's pretty sure she wants to be a high school English teacher when she grows up. Caroline is currently a master's student at the Bread Loaf School of English, and lives in New Haven, Connecticut.

Cate Glass is a bike-commuting queer girl who has lived on both coasts. She is passionate about gender justice and equality in education, and she hates scented candles. She married Annie on July 2, 2011, in a long white dress. Visit her blog at www.categlass.wordpress.com.

Susan Goldberg is a freelance writer, and co-editor of the anthology *And Baby Makes More: Known Donors, Queer Parents, and Our Unexpected Families* (Insomniac Press, 2009). She lives in Thunder Bay, Ontario, with her partner and their two sons, where she blogs about cancer, sleep deprivation, small-town queer life, writing, and more at www.mamanongrata.com.

Stephanie Hallett is a writer from Toronto, Canada. She was the director of a hip-hop dance company for girls in Vancouver before moving to Los Angeles, where she now lives with her husband and is associate editor of Weddings for the Huffington Post.

Holly Hughes is a writer/performer who was either Jesse Helms's favorite or least favorite lesbian, or possibly both. Her books include *Clit Notes*, *O Solo Homo: The New Queer Performance* (co-edited with David Roman), and the forthcoming *Memories of the Revolution* (co-edited with Carmelita Tropicana). A 2010–11 Guggenheim Fellow, Hughes is currently touring a monologue, *The Dog and Pony Show*. She and her coconspirator, Esther Newton, are professors at the University of Michigan. When not promoting homosexuality in the classroom, they compete in dog agility with their three poodles and two terriers.

Kate Kendell has been executive director of the National Center for Lesbian Rights since 1996. Previously, she was the first staff attorney for the ACLU of Utah. She lives in San Francisco with her spouse, Sandy Holmes, and their two children. (Kate also has an older daughter.)

Davina Kotulski, PhD, is a psychologist, life coach, and the author of *Why You Should Give a Damn About Gay Marriage* (2004) and *Love Warriors: The Rise of the Marriage Equality Movement and Why It Will Prevail* (2010). She has appeared in several documentaries, including *Freedom to Marry* and *Pursuit of Equality*. Davina currently leads self-empowerment, creativity, and coming-out workshops. Visit her website at www.davinakotulski.com.

J. Keiko Lane is a poet, essayist, and psychotherapist. In addition to her literary writing, which has been published in journals and anthologies, she also writes essays about the intersections of queer culture, oppression resistance, and liberation psychology. She lives with her family in Berkeley, California, where she maintains a private psychotherapy practice and teaches undergraduate writing and graduate psychology and cultural studies. Visit her website at www.keikolanemft.com.

Leslie Lange lives in Yucca Valley, California, and is the author of the lesbian self-help manifesto *Dyke Drama: Your Guide to Getting Out Alive*. She also co-wrote (and had two cameos in) the award-winning short film *Tools 4 Fools*.

Kari Lerum is an associate professor of interdisciplinary arts and sciences and cultural studies at the University of Washington, Bothell, and an adjunct professor in gender, women, and sexuality studies at the University of Washington, Seattle. Her research, teaching, and everyday life musings often dwell at the intersections of sexuality, institutions, and culture.

Joan Lipkin is a writer, director, social activist, and cultural critic who divides her time between St. Louis, New York City, and other parts of the country. Her work is widely anthologized, most recently in *Women's Comedic Art as Social Revolution*, *Out & Allied*, *Feminist Disability Studies*, and *The Best American Short Plays 2005–2006*, and has been performed throughout the United States, Canada, and the U.K. She would be happy to shop for a wedding dress, as long as it's her own.

Phyllis Lyon is one of the pioneering lesbian activists of the twentieth century. She and her late wife, Del Martin, were among the cofounders of the Daughters of Bilitis, the first U.S. social and political organization for lesbians, and they edited the lesbian journal *The Ladder*. Phyllis and Del were also the first lesbian couple to join NOW and were active in San Francisco's first gay political club, the Alice B. Toklas Democratic Club. Trained as a journalist, Phyllis also wrote two books with Del: *Lesbian/Woman* and *Lesbian Love and Liberation*. Phyllis and Del were the first same-sex couple to be legally wed in California—twice.

Wendy MacLeod's plays have been produced around the country, including at The Goodman Theater, Steppenwolf, Second Stage, Playwrights Horizons, Seattle Rep, and the Magic Theater. Her play *The House of Yes* was made into an award-winning feature film. She is published by Dramatists Play Service and Playscripts, Inc.

Mary Meriam's poems have appeared recently in the *New York Times*, *Poetry Foundation*, *American Life in Poetry*, *The Gay & Lesbian Review*, *Bridges*, *Journal of Lesbian Studies*, and the anthologies *Two Weeks*, *Hot Sonnets*, and *Gay and Gray*. She is the author of *The Countess of Flatbroke* and *The Poet's Zodiac*, and the editor of *Filled with Breath: 30 Sonnets by 30 Poets* and *Lavender Review*.

Colleen Michaels is director of the Writing Center at Montserrat College of Art, where she hosts *The Improbable Places Poetry Tour*. Her work has appeared, or is forthcoming, in *The Patterson Literary Review*, *Blue Collar Review*, *The Mom Egg*, and *Literary Mama*, and her poem "Align" appears in an art installation at Crane Beach in Ipswich, Massachusetts. She lives in Beverly, Massachusetts, with her family and is a member of the Salem Writers Group.

Caridad Moro is a first-generation Cuban American who was born in Los Angeles and grew up in Miami. Her chapbook, *Visionware*, was published by Finishing Line Press in 2009 as part of their celebrated New Women's Voices Series. She is the recipient of an artist fellowship for poetry from the state of Florida and has been thrice nominated for a Pushcart Prize. Moro is an English professor at Miami Dade College and an English instructor for Dade County Public Schools in Miami, where she resides with her nine-year-old son and her partner, fellow poet Stacie M. Kiner. Visit her website at www.southernartistry.org/Caridad_McCormick.

Lesléa Newman is the author of sixty-four books for readers of all ages, including the children's book *Heather Has Two Mommies*, the short-story collection *A Letter to Harvey Milk*, and the novel *The Reluctant Daughter*. Her newest children's book, *Donovan's Big Day*, takes place on the day Donovan's two moms get married. Her newest poetry collection, *October Mourning: A Song for Matthew Shepard*, is forthcoming from Candlewick Press. Lesléa is a faculty member of Spalding University's brief-residency MFA in Writing Program. Visit her website at www.lesleanewman.com.

Monica Palacios is widely recognized at the forefront of Chicana/Latina, lesbian, queer, feminist performance. She has written and performed several one-woman shows and plays, including *Latin Lezbo Comic*, *Sweet Peace*, *Greetings from a Queer Señorita*, *Amor y Revolución*, *Clock*, *Miercoles Loves Luna*, and *Prom*. Her work has been published in numerous anthologies. Monica is an adjunct professor at UCLA and UC Santa Barbara. Visit her website at www.monicapalacios.com.

N'Jai-An Patters has a PhD in history from the University of Minnesota. She writes about gender and sexuality in modern America and works as a social studies teacher in Minneapolis, where she lives with her partner, Kelly.

Heather Purser, one of only two female commercial divers for the Suquamish Indian Nation of Washington State, writes and speaks fearlessly about her life and experiences growing up a multicultural lesbian member of her small tribe. In 2011, she successfully completed her efforts to bring about the legalization of same-sex marriage within

Suquamish tribal law. She lives on Capitol Hill in Seattle with her "roommate" Becca.

Chella Quint is a comedy writer and performer living in Sheffield, England, but she's originally from New York. She's behind the *Adventures in Menstruating* zine series, as well as a number of other comedy writing and performance projects that reflect her inner (and, okay, outer) geek. She still loves weddings. Visit her website at www.chellaquint.com.

Kimberly Reed is a Montana-born filmmaker now living in New York City. Her very personal documentary *Prodigal Sons* has won more than a dozen awards and has been shown around the world in theaters and on television. She was named one of *OUT* magazine's "Out 100" in 2010 and has been featured on such media outlets as *The Oprah Winfrey Show*, CNN, NPR, *Details* magazine, and "The Moth." She is also the recipient of a 2008 Yaddo residency. In Kim's next film, *50 States of Wedlock,* she and her fiancée Claire will request a marriage license in each state. Visit her website at www.kimberlyreed.com.

Amelia Sauter is a writer, cartoonist, martini lounge owner, and musician from Ithaca, New York. She pens a humor column for *The Ithaca Post* and shares cocktail and culinary adventures in *Edible Finger Lakes* magazine and the *Finger Lakes Wine Gazette*. She describes meeting her soon-to-be-wifey in *Dear John, I Love Jane* (Seal Press, 2010). Though their wedding date has not been set, Amelia has already bought a fabulous dress. Visit her website at www.drinkmywords.com.

Judy Scheer is a writer, actor, comedy improviser, and creative strategist. With careers intersecting advertising, broadcasting, and entertainment, she has numerous radio, theater, television, film, commercial, voice-over, and creative campaign credits. This is her first cartoon collaboration. She is married and lives in Los Angeles. Visit her websites, judyscheer.com and yesdesigngroup.com.

Stephanie Schroeder is an anti-assimilationist queer feminist dyke writer and activist. Her work has been anthologized in *That's Revolting: Queer Strategies for Resisting Assimilation*, *Up All Night: Adventures in Lesbian Sex*, and *Hot & Bothered: Short, Short Fiction on Lesbian Desire* (volumes three and four). She is a contributing editor at *Curve* magazine and also writes for Shewired.com, *GO Magazine,* and at Lesbian Life at About.com. She lives in Brooklyn, New York. Visit her website at www.stephanieschroeder.com.

Bette Skandalis lives in Cambridge, Massachusetts, with her lover, Jo, and her dog, Jimmy. She has read her story "Frosting on the Cake" on NPR, and is currently working on a memoir about growing up in a Greek family obsessed with grape leaves. You can find her stories at http://betteskandalis.wordpress.com.

Melissa Sky is a proud femme lesbian, feminist writer, and filmmaker. She has a PhD in English literature from McMaster University. You can read more of her work in *Persistence: All Ways Butch and Femme*, *Twilight Tales*, and *Judging a Book by Its Cover*. Her award-winning LGBT films are featured at www.femmefilms.ca.

Jen Sorensen is a cartoonist and writer best known for her political cartoon, *Slowpoke*, which has appeared in the *Village Voice*, *Ms.* magazine, the *Los Angeles Times*, and on Daily Kos and NPR.org. Visit her website at www.slowpokecomics.com.

Lydia Stryk's plays, including *Monte Carlo, The House of Lily, The Glamour House, American Tet, An Accident,* and *Lady Lay,* have been produced at, among other venues, Denver Center Theatre, Steppenwolf Theatre Company, Victory Gardens, The Contemporary American Theatre Festival, the Magic Theatre, and in Germany at Schauspiel Essen, Theaterhaus Stuttgart, and the English Theater Berlin. Visit her website at www.lydiastryk.com.

Linda Villarosa is a writer and editor who runs the journalism program at the City College of New York in Harlem. She lives in Brooklyn with her partner, their two kids, a dog, and a cat.

Candace Walsh is the author of *Licking the Spoon* (Seal Press, Spring 2012), a food memoir. She is also the editor of the Seal Press anthologies *Dear John, I Love Jane: Women Write About Leaving Men for Women* and *Ask Me About My Divorce: Women Open Up About Moving On.* She lives in Santa Fe, New Mexico, with her wife, Laura André, their two children, and two dogs.

Helen Zia, former executive editor of *Ms.* magazine, is the author of *Asian American Dreams: The Emergence of an American People* (FSG, 2000) and coauthor with Wen Ho Lee of *My Country versus Me* (Hyperion, 2002).

About the Editors

Audrey Bilger is the faculty director of the Center for Writing and Public Discourse and associate professor of literature at Claremont McKenna College. She is the author of *Laughing Feminism: Subversive Comedy in Frances Burney, Maria Edgeworth, and Jane Austen* and editor of Jane Collier's 1753 *Essay on the Art of Ingeniously Tormenting* for Broadview Literary Texts. She writes for *Ms.* magazine and the Ms. Blog and is a frequent contributor to *Bitch: Feminist Response to Pop Culture*. She is living happily ever after in Los Angeles with her wife, Cheryl Pawelski.

Michele Kort is a longtime journalist, senior editor of *Ms.* magazine, and co-editor of the Ms. Blog. She is the author of three books: *Soul Picnic: The Music and Passion of Laura Nyro*; *The End of Innocence* (with Chastity Bono); and *Dinah! Three Decades of Sex, Golf, & Rock 'n' Roll.* She loves basketball, '60s soul music, and chocolate-chip cookies. She lives in Los Angeles with her partner and their two corgis.

ACKNOWLEDGMENTS

WE COULD NOT HAVE USHERED THIS BOOK INTO THE WORLD WITHOUT the support of many generous associates, friends, and well-wishers. We are grateful to everyone who helped bring this project to fruition.

Thanks to the wonderful team at Seal Press, especially to our editor, Krista Lyons, for being enthusiastic about this book from its earliest stages, and to Brooke Warner.

Many thanks to Eva Talmadge, who generously advised us on our contract. Shree Pandya did outstanding research work and provided us with nearly flawless interview transcriptions. Research assistant Jeremy Merrill helped with our website and social networking and Greg Allen made us look good in our authors' photos.

We are most grateful to the talented photographers and blissful brides who allowed us to use their images. We'd also like to thank the editors at the online community of Offbeat Bride for hosting such a lesbian-friendly wedding site, where we discovered a number of these fine pictures.

Boundless gratitude to our contributors and to all of those who shared their stories with us, whether or not they made it into these pages. Your brilliant words (or images) will stand as a testimony to this great time of change.

To all those who work to make full LGBT equality the law of all lands, we also send our thanks. This book—this *movement*—doesn't exist without you.

Audrey also wishes to acknowledge . . .

I'm grateful, first and foremost, to Michele for being such an inspirational co-editor; you're an amazing writer, a whiz with the editing scissors, and an inspirational collaborator. Thanks for taking the plunge with me! I also want to thank Heather Antecol of Claremont McKenna College's Berger Institute for Work, Family, and Children, and Gregory Hess, along with the CMC Dean of the Faculty Office for their support of this project.

Thanks to my dear friends Ricky Hoyt and Peleg Top for the impromptu wedding ceremony; to Emily Chao and Zayn Kassam for cheering me on when I was wrestling with the book proposal; to Wendy Goldman, Emily Ryan Lerner, and Lisa Jane Persky for the magic of WELA; to Lisa Cody, Christine Crockett, James Morrison, and Keri Walsh for being such good friends and colleagues. To Cheryl, my own bride, I can only say that my world became richer when I met you. I'm so very proud to be your legally wedded wife.

Michele also wishes to acknowledge . . .

When my dad was particularly grateful to someone, he used the expression, "You're a scholar." Audrey, you're a scholar, in every sense of the word. Thank you so much for inviting me to join this project with you; I'm so glad that I just said "yes" without even thinking about it. You've been a dream collaborator, better than I ever could have imagined. And we still haven't had a fight!

Thanks also to my cheerleading squad of family and friends, foremost among them my partner, Miriam; my sister, Melissa; my dad, Norman; my dear girlfriends Paula, Babsy, Peach, Janie, and Margy; and my wonderful *Ms.* mates Michel, Jessica, and Annie. Thanks, too, to the three Lindas who keep me sane and to my agent, Ellen Geiger.

And thanks once more to our contributors: You took emotional risks to bring your writing to this collection. Audrey and I are honored you entrusted your fine work and your open hearts to us.

Selected Titles from Seal Press

For more than thirty years, Seal Press has published groundbreaking books. By women. For women.

Riding Fury Home: A Memoir, by Chana Wilson. $17.00, 978-1-58005-432-4. A shattering, exquisitely written account of one family's struggle against homophobia and mental illness in a changing world—and a powerful story of healing, forgiveness, and redemption.

Dear John, I Love Jane: Women Write About Leaving Men for Women, edited by Candance Walsh and Laura André. $16.95, 978-1-58005-339-6. A timely collection of stories that are sometimes funny and sometimes painful—but always achingly honest—accounts of leaving a man for a woman, and the consequences of making such a choice.

Offbeat Bride: Creative Alternatives for Independent Brides, by Ariel Meadow Stallings. $16.95, 978-1-58005-315-0. Part memoir and part anecdotal how-to, *Offbeat Bride* is filled with sanity-saving tips, advice, and stories for the non-traditional bride.

Sexual Intimacy for Women: A Guide for Same-Sex Couples, by Glenda Corwin, Ph.D. $16.95, 978-1-58005-303-7. In this prescriptive and poignant book, Glenda Corwin, PhD, helps female couples overcome obstacles to sexual intimacy through her examination of the emotional, physical, and psychological aspects of same-sex relationships.

Lesbian Couples: A Guide to Creating Healthy Relationships, by D. Merilee Clunis and G. Dorsey Green. $ 16.95, 978-1-58005-131-6. Drawing from a decade of research, this helpful and readable resource covers topics from conflict-resolution to commitment ceremonies, using a variety of examples and problem-solving techniques.

Mind-Blowing Sex: A Woman's Guide, by Diana Cage. $17.00, 978-1-58005-389-1. An instructive, accessible sexual guide that will help women and their partners make their sex life more empowering, exciting, and enjoyable.